Current Concepts of Suicide

Current Concepts of Suicide

Edited by

David Lester, PhD

The Charles Press, Publishers
Philadelphia

Library of Congress Cataloging-in-Publication Data

Current concepts of suicide / David Lester, editor.
     p. cm.
   Includes bibliographical references.
   ISBN 0-914783-45-9
   1. Suicide. 2. Lester, David. 1942–
   [DNLM: 1. Suicide. HV 6545 C976]
   HV6545.C84 1990
   362.2′8—dc20

DNLM/DLC
for Library of Congress   90-1600
                                                              CIP

ISBN:0-914783-45-9 (paper)

Contents

iii

Contributors

Alan Apter, MD, Department of Psychiatry, Albert Einstein College of Medicine, NYC.

Serena-Lynn Brown, MD, PhD, Department of Psychiatry, Albert Einstein College of Medicine/Montefiore Medical Center, NYC.

Lawrence G. Calhoun, PhD, Department of Psychology, University of North Carolina, Charlotte, NC.

George A. Clum, PhD, Department of Psychology, Virginia Polytechnic Institute and State University

Dorothy Ayers Counts, PhD, Department of Anthropology, University of Waterloo, Canada.

Dr. René F.W. Diekstra, Department of Clinical and Health Psychology, Rijksuniversiteit te Leiden, the Netherlands.

James R. Eyman, PhD, C. F. Menninger Memorial Hospital.

Paul C. Holinger, MD MPH, Rush-Presbyterian-St. Luke's Medical Center.

Steven L. Hughes, MA, Department of Psychology, Memphis State University, TN.

Martin Korn, MD, Department of Psychiatry, Albert Einstein College of Medicine/Montefiore Medical Center, NYC.

Antoon A. Leenaars, PhD, C.Psych, Windsor, Canada.

Miriam Lerner, MS, Department of Psychology, Virginia Polytechnic Institute and State University.

David Lester, PhD, Psychology Program, Richard Stockton State College, NJ.

Professor H. J. Möller, Psychiatrische Klinik und Poliklinik, Technischen Universitat Munchen, West Germany.

Dr. Ferenc Moksony, Department of Sociology, Karl Marx University of Economics, Budapest, Hungary.

Robert A. Neimeyer, PhD, Department of Psychology, Memphis State University, TN.

Herman, M. van Praag, MD, PhD, Department of Psychiatry, Albert Einstein College of Medicine/ Montefiore Medical Center, NYC.

Joseph Richman, PhD, Albert Einstein College of Medicine, NYC.

Alec Roy, MB, National Institute on Alcohol Abuse and Alcoholism, Bethesda, MD.

Kjell E. Rudestam, PhD, Program Director, The Fielding Institute/Santa Barbara, CA.

James W. Selby, PhD, Professor of Psychology, University of North Carolina/ Charlotte, NC.

Steven Stack, PhD, Department of Sociology, Auburn University, AL.

Steve Taylor, M.Phil, PhD, Department of Sociology, London School of Economics and Political Science, England.

Preface

Each January the president of the United States of America gives a speech to Congress in which he outlines his view of the State of the Union. He sums up what has been achieved in the recent past and what hopes and plans he has for the future. The present book is intended, in a similar fashion, to present a State of the Art account of where we stand today in our understanding of suicide and how to prevent it. Such a book could be written by one person, but that book, though it might have coherence and consistency, would in all probability reflect the biases of the individual author. There is an advantage to soliciting a number of experts on the topic to each contribute a chapter to a volume. This volume was put together in such a manner and, I hope, benefits from having a variety of perspectives and opinions. I selected the contributors with two aims. First, I wanted to include experts from outside of the United States, in order to avoid the narrow view often reflected by experts within one country. I was fortunate to obtain contributions from authors in Canada, England, Hungary, and West Germany. Second, I wanted to ensure that the different disciplines were included. I therefore invited anthropologists, psychiatrists, psychologists, and sociologists, all experts on suicide, to write from the point of view of their discipline. The major portion of this book is oriented toward discipline rather than topic. Of course, each author has chosen to focus on a particular topic within the broad field of Suicide, but this volume does illustrate how the different academic disciplines approach the study of suicide. Some may fault me for omitting particular specialities (such as public health, nursing, and social work). However, I feel that the major contributions to our understanding of suicide come from the formal research paradigms and theories grounded in the major academic disciplines. This belief guided my selection of what to include in this volume. I hope that this volume serves to introduce the reader to the study of suicide, to the knowledge accumulated in the past, and to areas where further research is needed.

1

A Cognitive Model of Suicidal Behavior

Steven L. Hughes and Robert A. Neimeyer

Suicidal thoughts and behaviors occur with an alarming frequency. While the official rate of "completed" (i.e., successful) suicide in the general population is quite low, on the order 10 per 100,000 (U.S. Statistical Abstract 1986), suicidal ideation and nonfatal, suicide-like behaviors are much more common. For example, in a survey of 313 high school students nearly 63 percent reported some degree of suicidal ideation and over 8 percent reported engaging in self-injurious behavior (Smith and Crawford 1986). The corresponding figures for college students appear to be in the same range, with studies reporting that between 4 percent (Westefeld and Furr 1987) and 15 percent (Mishara, Baker and Mishara 1976) of their sample had engaged in self-injurious behavior.

The primary method of suicide intervention in use today, a sort of atheoretical "crisis management" (Clum, Patsiokas and Luscomb 1979), has proven relatively ineffective. Primary preventive techniques, such as suicide intervention centers, attract individuals who are at high risk for suicide, (Dew et al. 1987) but have no effect on community suicide rates (Clum et al. 1979; Dew et al. 1987). Secondary prevention, including providing treatment (Pokorny 1966; Clum et al. 1979; Roy 1982) or aftercare (Ettlinger 1975; Kreitman 1977) to high-risk groups, also appears to have rather meager effects: as many as 50 percent of individuals hospitalized for self-injurious behavior engage in another self-injurious act within a year (Clum et al. 1979) and between 1 percent and 2 percent kill themselves within the same time period (Pokorny 1966; Greer and Bagley 1971; Pallis, Gibbons and Pierce 1984; Beck, Steer, Kovacs and Garrison 1985). The period immediately following hospitalization appears to be the time of highest risk: Roy (1982) reported that 65 percent of his sample of 90 suicide completers killed themselves within three months of discharge.

Attempts to predict the potential for future suicides have also met with limited success. Studies have identified a number of demographic variables, such as age and sex, which are related to self-injury but these variables are most useful in identifying groups, as opposed to individuals, that are at high-risk and, therefore, contribute little to a theoretical understanding of suicide. Similarly, a host of psychological variables are related to self-injury but none has the degree of

1

specificity necessary to be a useful long-term predictor of suicide (Lester 1970; Pokorny 1983; Beck et al. 1985). One researcher, who had conducted a long-term prospective study of 4800 psychiatric inpatients, concluded his report by stating: "We do not possess any item of information or any combination of items that permits us to identify to a useful degree the particular persons who will commit suicide, in spite of the fact that we do have scores of items available, each of which is significantly related to suicide" (Pokorny 1983, p. 257).

Because efforts to predict and control suicide have been only marginally successful, suicide represents a thorn in the side of the science of psychology. The present chapter will argue that a better understanding of *who* will commit suicide can be gained by considering *why* someone would chose suicide over any number of other possible alternatives. This position will be advanced by examining the cognitive activity of suicidal individuals. Three lines of research on suicidal individuals will be reviewed: research relating to their cognitive structure; research relating to their problem solving deficits; and research on their anticipation of the future. The review will focus on research with adult subjects because past research with children has rarely focused on cognitive characteristics, and in addition, important developmental distinctions exist between the groups, such as children's difficulty conceptualizing the future (Bemporad and Wilson 1978). This review will give rise to a model of suicidal choice, which will be based substantially on Kelly's (1955) psychology of personal constructs (c.f. Neimeyer, 1984). Before beginning a review of the relevant literature, however, four issues in suicide research will be addressed so that the literature reviewed may utilize the conclusions that are drawn. These issues are (a) the definition of types of suicidal behavior, (b) the temporal direction of the study, (c) the role of the various levels of suicidal intent, and (d) sample characteristics and comparison groups.

DEFINITIONS OF SUICIDAL BEHAVIORS

The first issue to be discussed is the need for clearly defined types of suicidal behavior. An NIMH task force on research in suicide (Beck, Davis, Fredrick, Perlin, Pokorny, Schulman, Seiden, and Wittlin 1972) proposed a tripartite classification consisting of (a) suicide ideators who are considering suicide but have not translated their thoughts into behavior, (b) suicide attempters who have engaged in self-injurious behavior which was not fatal, and (c) completed suicides, who have engaged in fatal self-injurious behavior. This system, while useful, tends to obscure important differences between the latter two groups. For example, many suicide attempters report that their self-injurious behavior was not intended to be fatal, (Bancroft, Skrimshire and Simkin 1976) suggesting that "suicide" was not "attempted" at all. In addition, gender differences are one of the most stable findings in suicide research: approximately three times as many women engage in nonfatal self-injurious acts while three times as many men actually complete suicide (Shneidman 1976; Pokorny 1983). In order to underscore the differences between the two groups while still acknowledging their similarities, the present chapter will adopt Kreitman's (1977) term ''parasuicide'' to refer to nonfatal self-injurious behavior.

The relationship between suicide ideators, parasuicides, and completed suicides is somewhat complex. Recent studies suggest that somewhere between 32 percent and 63 percent of the general population have experienced suicidal ideation at some point in their lives (Linehan and Nielsen 1981; Smith and Crawford 1986; Westefeld and Furr 1987). It seems reasonable to argue that suicidal ideation precedes any act of self-injury; therefore, both parasuicides and completed suicides represent subsets of suicide ideators. The studies cited above report that between 13 percent and 20 percent of the ideators in their samples have at some point engaged in parasuicidal behavior. Other studies suggest that both hospitalized ideator and parasuicidal groups have suicide rates of 1 to 2 percent per year (Pokorny 1966; Greer and Bagley 1971; Lester, Beck and Mitchell 1979; Pallis, Gibbons and Pierce 1984; Beck et al. 1985). Viewed from the other angle, between 32 percent (Fawcett et al. 1987) and 59 percent (Roy 1982) of the completed suicides do not have a history of parasuicide. These findings demonstrate that there is not a simple progression from suicide ideation to parasuicide to completed suicide.

TEMPORAL DIRECTION

The second issue in suicide research to be addressed is the temporal direction assumed by the study. An investigator of completed suicide is limited, obviously, to prospective or retrospective views of the individual who committed the act. Retrospective studies look backward in time in an attempt to identify differences between individuals who have committed suicide and those who have not. These ''psychological autopsies'' (Shneidman 1976) suffer from the lack of a true control group and the potential distortion of data collected after the fact (Fawcett et al. 1987). Prospective studies overcome these problems by obtaining a large sample, measuring the variables of interest, identifying individuals who subsequently commit suicide, and comparing suicide completers with the remainder of the sample. These designs are plagued by the low base rate of the behavior: completed suicide is relatively infrequent even in high-risk groups. As a result, a large number of individuals who do not commit suicide are classified, on the basis of psychometric data, as probable suicide completers (MacKinnon and Farberow 1976).

The problems inherent in studying completed suicide have led many researchers to study parasuicide and suicide ideation. The advantages of this tactic are clear: these behaviors occur at a much higher frequency than do completed suicides, the individual is available to report antecedents and consequences of the act or ideation, and studies may utilize cross-sectional or longitudinal designs. Cross-sectional studies of parasuicidal subjects obviously assess the individual after the behavioral fact of self-injury; inquiry into the antecedents of the act may be biased to an unknown degree. Longitudinal studies would provide important information about changes across time but are quite rare in suicide research.

ROLE OF SUICIDAL INTENT

The third issue to be addressed is the importance of assessing the seriousness of suicidal ideation and parasuicidal behavior. For ideators, seriousness is determined by assessing such factors as the persistence of and ability to control suicidal thoughts, the degree of planning that has occurred, the lethality of the contemplated act and deterrents to carrying out the act (Beck, Kovacs and Weissman 1979). Similar criteria are used to assess suicide intent in parasuicide: individuals who had well-formulated plans, chose highly lethal methods, took precautions against discovery, etc., are considered to have had a more serious intent than those who acted impulsively, chose a lower lethality method, and had a high probability of being rescued (Beck, Schuyler and Herman 1974; Freeman et al. 1974). Because there is considerable within-group variation along this dimension (Freeman et al. 1974; Bancroft et al. 1976), the level of intent in the sample being studied must be assessed so that the information may be used in interpreting results. For example, high-intent parasuicides are likely to be more similar to completed suicides than low-intent parasuicides, and high-intent ideators are likely to be at greater risk for self-injury than low intent ideators.

SAMPLE CHARACTERISTICS AND COMPARISON GROUPS

The fourth issue is the need to control confounding variables by employing heterogeneous samples and appropriate comparison groups. Some studies utilize all male or all female subjects, which limits the generalizability of the results. Because gender differences are among the most robust findings in suicide research, (Freeman et al. 1974) studies should include both males and females and incorporate this variable into statistical analyses. The majority of studies to be reviewed in the present chapter compare suicides or parasuicides with nonsuicidal psychiatric patients, a design that introduces the potential confound of suicidal ideation in the latter group. A stronger design would be obtained by including an additional group of explicit suicide ideators.

THEORETICAL POSITION

With these research issues in mind we can now describe our theoretical position. This essay will use Kelly's (1955) psychology of personal constructs as a framework on which to build a model of suicidal choice. In the Kellian view, people are much like scientists: "Like the prototype of the scientist that he is, man seeks prediction. His structured network of pathways leads toward the future so that he may anticipate it . . . Anticipation is both the push and the pull of the psychology of personal constructs" (Kelly 1955, p. 49). Human experience is seen as a creative endeavor in which hypotheses are constructed from past experience; confirming or disconfirming evidence is gathered as events are encountered and hypotheses are retained, revised, or discarded as the evidence warrants.

Suicidal behavior becomes more likely if this cycle is disrupted in one of two ways: when the future appears totally predictable, and one's hypotheses prove redundant; or when the future appears totally unpredictable, and one's hypotheses are no longer effective. Kelly (1961, p. 260) described the first of these "limiting conditions" to life as "when the course of events seems so obvious that there is no point in waiting around for the outcome." In this situation, the individual views the future as entirely negative and totally intractable, and the resulting "depressive fatalism" is likely to be ended by a well-planned, highly lethal suicidal behavior. The second limiting condition to life is "when everything seems so utterly unpredictable that the only definite thing one can do is abandon the scene altogether. It has ceased to be a game with perceptible rules" (Kelly 1961, p. 260). In this situation the individual experiences total anxiety and desperately grasps for some kind of certainty, even if certainty comes at the expense of endangering their own life. Suicidal behavior under this second condition is more likely to be impulsive and of lower lethality than behavior under the first condition.

A key feature of the personal scientist metaphor is that people give meaning to events rather than discover meaning in events. Consequently, a multitude of alternative meanings are possible in any situation. Kelly (1961) writes that "if there seems to be a genuine singularity in life's meanings, it stems primarily from the singularity of our own thinking" (p. 255). Depressed suicidal individuals, therefore, are victims of their own singularity. They are trapped in one invariant anticipation and blind to other alternatives. The anxious suicidal individual, on the other hand, has too many alternatives and is unable to select a single course of action from among the swirl of possibilities. Both of these conditions represent "anticipatory failure" (Neimeyer 1984, p. 55) because the individual's anticipatory system is not providing a meaningful framework for anticipating and responding to life's challenges.

The personal construct view of suicide attempts to strip the act of its pathological implications by viewing the act through the eyes of the individual. From this perspective, suicidal behavior serves to validate some important aspect of the individual's life. For example, a man who prides himself on being a good provider but has recently lost his livelihood may view his own death as one possible way of relieving his family's burden. As he exhausts other perceived alternatives, or if he is unable to conceptualize other alternatives, suicide becomes a reasonable choice to him. Committing suicide thereby represents an attempt to validate life's "essential meaning" (Kelly 1961, p. 260) even though physical life may be ended. The validational aspect of suicide is especially evident in "dedicated acts" (Kelly 1961, p. 259) in which an individual such as Socrates chooses death as the only means to affirm the meaning of the life he has lived.

The present chapter will utilize this personal construct conceptualization of suicide as a framework on which to construct a model of suicidal choice. The model will integrate three main lines of research on suicidal cognition: (a) studies investigating cognitive structure, (b) studies investigating problem-solving abilities, and (c) studies investigating anticipations of the future.

COGNITIVE STRUCTURE

Research relating to cognitive structure in suicidal individuals is the earliest cognitive research to appear in the suicide literature. Westcott (1885; cited in Levenson 1974) probably provided the earliest account of suicidal cognitive structure when he described the polarized way in which suicidal individuals view the world. Polarization—the tendency to construe situations in extreme terms with no intermediate "shades of grey"—can be viewed as a structural feature of the individual's construct system that extends across a number of content domains. Polarization in suicidal individuals was described through the years (Cavan 1928; Farrar 1951) but was not investigated empirically until the 1960s when Neuringer (1961, 1967, 1968, 1974) published a series of reports. Neuringer's sample consisted of hospitalized parasuicides, who had made a "bona fide suicide attempt" (suggesting, perhaps, a moderate to high intent), nonsuicidal psychosomatic inpatients, and normal hospitalized patients. All subjects were white males, and all were examined prior to treatment. Each subject completed a Semantic Differential measure (Osgood, Suci, and Tannenbaum 1957) that required them to rate eighteen concepts on eighteen 7-point scales. The rating scales consisted of three factors: evaluation (nine scales, e.g., good-bad); activity (four scales, e.g. passive-active); and potency (five scales, e.g. strong-weak). The concepts consisted of important people (e.g. myself, mother), theological entities (God, devil), political systems (communism, democracy), emotional states (e.g. love, shame, hate), and behavioral acts (e.g. suicide). Twelve of the concepts formed six semantically opposite pairs (e.g. life-death, love-hate). Degree of polarization was operationalized as the mean extremity of the concept ratings and as the mean difference in ratings between semantically opposite concepts.

The first report (Neuringer 1961) focused on the way in which subjects evaluated the concepts. On the nine evaluative scales, parasuicidal and psychosomatic subjects rated the eighteen concepts and six semantically opposite concept pairs in a more extreme fashion than the control subjects. The two psychiatric groups did not differ from each other, suggesting that evaluative extremity of these concepts is not exclusively associated with parasuicide. The second report (Neuringer 1967) focused on how the subjects rated the activity and potency of the concepts. For these nine scales, parasuicidal subjects rated the concepts and semantically opposite concept pairs in a more extreme fashion than the psychosomatic and control subjects, suggesting that this tendency is more distinctly associated with parasuicide.

In the third report, Neuringer (1968) elaborated his previous findings by focusing on how subjects perceived the two specific concepts of life and death. The data were analyzed by computing the difference between ratings of life and ratings of death on each of the three factors (evaluation, activity and potency). An analysis of the variance on these different scores revealed that on all three factors the parasuicidal group perceived a greater distance between life and death than did the psychosomatic and normal groups, whose feelings did not differ from each other. The finding of greater evaluative extremity in the parasuicidal group stands in contrast to Neuringer's earlier report (1961), in which parasuicidal subjects could not be discriminated from psychosomatic subjects on evaluative extremity. Parasuicidal subjects apparently evaluate some concepts, but not all, in an extreme fashion.

Aside from the parasuicide's extremity in rating, the three groups' ratings were qualitatively similar. On the evaluative factor, all groups rated life positively and death negatively. Mean potency ratings of life were between zero and one and potency ratings of death hovered near zero for all groups. Interestingly, the parasuicidal group rated death in a slightly negative direction on the activity factor, suggesting a rather passive view of death. In contrast, the two nonsuicidal groups rated death in a slightly positive direction on this factor.

In the fourth report, Neuringer (1974) focused on subjects' ratings of themselves and other people. Ratings of two concepts ("myself" and "other people") on three rating scales (one from each of the evaluative, potency, and activity factors) were analyzed by computing self-other difference scores for each of the three factors. Results indicated that the parasuicidal subjects perceived a greater difference between themselves and other people than did either of the other two groups, but only on the evaluative and potency scales. The parasuicidal group also differed from the psychosomatic and normal groups by providing negative ratings to themselves and positive ratings to other people, while the two comparison groups provided positive ratings to both. This finding contrasts with Neuringer's (1968) finding of qualitatively similar ratings among the groups, and it suggests that parasuicidal individuals experience interpersonal isolation because they view themselves as distinctly different from others (Neimeyer 1984; 1985).

Because Neuringer's original data were collected from parasuicides, his results reflect the individual's cognitive organization after the self-injurious act. A study by Neuringer and Lettieri (1971) addressed this issue by exploring how a sample of suicide ideators evaluated life and death. Subjects were thirty consecutive visitors to a suicide crisis center, who were classified into high, moderate, or low lethality groups. Ten individuals who were "in crisis" but not suicidal served as an additional comparison group. The subjects, all white females, completed a Semantic Differential measure (Osgood et al. 1957) similar to the measure used by Neuringer (1968), although only the evaluative ratings of life and death were reported in the paper.

In one of the few longitudinal designs seen in suicide research, subjects completed the Semantic Differential measure for 21 consecutive days. When ratings were collapsed across days, the high-lethality group was found to have evaluated life in significantly more extreme terms than the other groups, which did not differ from each other. Ratings of death did not discriminate among the groups. Calculating the mean difference between ratings of life and death indicated that high-lethality subjects perceived the greatest distance between the two concepts. The similarity in extremity shown by the high-lethality group and by Neuringer's (1968) group of parasuicidal subjects suggests that polarized construing of life and death may be an indicator of serious suicidal ideation, as well as self-injurious behavior.

The ratings were also analyzed longitudinally across the 21 day period. The high-lethality group clearly differed from the other groups by evaluating life negatively on all 21 days of the study. This finding is in contrast to Neuringer's (1968) sample of general parasuicidal subjects, who provided positive evaluations of life. The high-lethality group provided the most consistent ratings of all the groups, suggesting that polarized attitudes are quite resistant to change.

A visual inspection of the ratings across time provided a more detailed analysis that suggested additional group differences. For example, in contrast to the consistency shown by the high-lethality group, the moderate-lethality group vacillated between positive and negative evaluations: they rated life negatively on days 1–4, changed to a positive rating on day 5, reverted to negative ratings on days 6–13, became positive again through day 16, returned to negative ratings for days 17–19, rated day 20 positively, and rated day 21 negatively. The low-lethality group rated life negatively for the first 6 days of the study but switched to positive ratings for the rest of the 21–day period. The zero-lethality group rated life positively every day except for one, and was the second most consistent group.

On ratings of death, group differences failed to reach statistical significance. However, a visual inspection of the ratings over time again suggested group differences: the high-lethality group consistently evaluated death positively (19 of 21 days), the zero- and moderate-lethality groups evaluated death negatively on all 21 days, and the low-lethality group evaluated death negatively except for the first 3 days of the study. The high-lethality group's positive evaluation of death again contrasts with Neuringer's (1968) general parasuicidal group, who provided negative evaluations of death.

The distinct patterns of responding over time reported by Neuringer and Lettieri (1971) suggest that the failure of many group differences to reach statistical significance may be due to a small sample size (n = 10 for each of the four lethality groups) rather than a true lack of group differences. While there are intriguing differences between Neuringer's (1968) group of parasuicides and Neuringer and Lettieri's (1971) group of ideators, the confound in subject gender produces more tentative hypotheses than firm conclusions. A longitudinal study that compares larger samples of both parasuicides and ideators of both sexes would clearly be a worthwhile undertaking.

Wetzel (1976a) made an important step in this direction by including both males and females in a cross-sectional study of parasuicides, ideators, and non-suicidal psychiatric patients. His use of a Semantic Differential measure (fifteen 7-point rating scales and ten concepts) similar to Neuringer's (1968; Neuringer & Lettieri, 1971) facilitates comparisons among the studies. Wetzel (1976a) reported that the groups did not differ significantly in the rating extremity on any of the three factors, and that extremity did not discriminate between levels of suicidal intent in either suicidal group. These results suggest that suicidal individuals do not show a general tendency toward extreme ratings.

Turning his attention to specific concepts of life and death, Wetzel (1975a) found that the ideator group differed significantly from the psychiatric control group on total ratings of life and on a life-death difference score. The parasuicide group was intermediate on both measures. A visual inspection of the cell means revealed that the statistical significance was not due to rating extremity: ideators viewed life as slightly negative while the psychiatric controls viewed life as moderately positive.

When the parasuicide and ideation groups were ranked by current level of suicidal intent, total ratings of life were significantly related to degree of suicide intent in both groups. However, the differences in these total ratings were again influenced more by a difference in rating valence than a difference in extremity: the high-intent subsamples of both suicidal groups rated life as moderately negative, the psychiatric controls rated life as moderately positive, and the low- and moderate-intent groups provided intermediate ratings. Life-minus-death difference scores were distributed similarly to the ratings of life, and no group differences emerged on total ratings of death. These findings suggest that rating extremity alone is not adequate to discriminate between suicidal and nonsuicidal groups or within suicidal samples of differing lethality. The direction of the group's rating must also be considered.

Wetzel (1975b) also reported how the subjects rated the concept "myself." In comparison to the psychiatric control group, the suicidal groups again used ratings that were an equivalent distance from the midpoint and in the opposite direction, with the suicidal groups providing slightly negative ratings. When the parasuicide and ideation groups were ranked by current suicide intent, the total self-ratings were significantly related to degree of suicide intent in the ideator group and tended toward significance in the parasuicide group. Both groups showed a pattern of results similar to their ratings of life: the high- and moderate-intent groups had ratings of similar magnitude but opposite direction to the ratings of the control group while the low-intent group had intermediate ratings.

A case study reported by Rigdon (1983) elaborates on the view of self in parasuicide. As part of a study of death attitudes, a sample of college students provided ratings of themselves and their own death on thirty bipolar rating dimensions. This measure, the Threat Index or TI (Neimeyer et. al 1984; Rigdon et al. 1979), was also completed seven weeks later, at which time one of the subjects (a freshman named Cary) remarked that he had taken an overdose of sleeping pills three days earlier in an attempt to take his life. An examination of Cary's TI revealed that his system of construing death did not differ appreciably from the other subjects and was quite stable over the seven week period. He rated his own death negatively at both times. However, his ratings of himself reversed completely across the seven week period; at pre-test he provided 27 positive and 3 negative ratings, while at post-test he provided 3 positive and 27 negative ratings of himself. Rigdon interpreted these results as indicating that suicide becomes more likely when an individual's self-image becomes compatible with death. This pre/post design does not allow a closer investigation of the change in Cary's view of himself, although we might speculate that his self-view vacillated in the same way as did the view of life in Neuringer and Lettieri's (1971) group moderate-lethality ideators. In both cases death was consistently evaluated as negative.

Landfield (1976) attempted a broader investigation of suicidal cognitive structure by focusing on features of the entire construct system rather than specific concepts. His sample included high-intent parasuicidal subjects, low-intent parasuicidal subjects, suicide ideators, current long-term psychotherapy clients (who were subdivided into high- and low-maladjustment groups), long-term psychotherapy clients who had terminated therapy prematurely, and normal controls. His measure was a modified version of Kelly's (1955) role construct repertory test (Rep Test) in which subjects are required to compare and contrast pairs of role figures (such as family members, a person they consider happy, etc.) in order to generate fifteen bipolar dimensions. The fifteen role figures are rated on the bipolar dimensions to generate a matrix of responses. Landfield focused on three features of the group's construct systems: (a) constriction in construct application, which was operationalized as the number of times neither construct pole could be applied to a role figure; (b) constriction in content, which was measured by a qualitative rating of construct concreteness; and (c) degree of disorganization of the construct system, which was operationalized as lack of construct interrelatedness. Landfield hypothesized that the high-intent parasuicidal sample would score highest on each of the three measures.

His results provided initial support for his hypotheses: the high-intent group had the highest scores on the constriction and disorganization measures. However, some specific comparisons failed to reach statistical significance, perhaps due to the small number (five) of high-intent parasuicidal subjects. For example, the high-intent parasuicide group had a significantly higher disorganization score than the low-intent parasuicide group, the less maladjusted psychiatric control group, or the normal control group, but did not significantly differ from the more maladjusted psychiatric control group or the group of therapy terminators. This leaves open the possibility that system disorganization is associated with severe pathology in general rather than suicidal behavior in particular.

When a combination score was computed from the three measures the high-intent parasuicidal group had significantly higher scores in comparison with each of the other groups. This is clearly suggestive of a distinctive cognitive structure in high-intent parasuicides, one that is constricted and loosely organized. Additional support for this hypothesis was provided by Landfield, who had the rare opportunity of examining the Rep Test of a young woman who had completed the measure less than twenty-four hours before taking an overdose of tranquilizers. All three features of her construct system were in the direction Landfield had hypothesized. In comparing and contrasting the role figures, the woman generated a number of concrete construct dimensions, such as "drinks" and "likes long-hair music." On nearly 47 percent of the ratings she could apply neither construct pole to a role figure, suggesting a great deal of uncertainty in her construct system. Her Rep Test had an elevated FIC score, suggesting that her construct system was loosely organized. Landfield concluded that constriction of the construct system and system disorganization provide an instigating context for suicidal behavior.

ANALYSIS OF STUDIES OF COGNITIVE STRUCTURE

Suicidal individuals do not appear to have a general tendency toward viewing concepts in extreme terms (Wetzel 1976; Neuringer 1961). Certain concepts, such as one's view of life and death, may be rated more extremely by suicidal groups (Neuringer and Lettieri 1971; Neuringer 1968) although there is mixed evidence (Wetzel 1975a) on this issue. It is plausible to suggest that ratings of more personally meaningful topics, such as family members or various aspects of the self, may be characterized by greater polarization.

Although suicidal groups do not necessarily view concepts more extremely than nonsuicidal groups, they clearly invert the normative perceptions of nonsuicidal groups (Neuringer and Lettieri 1971; Neuringer 1974; Wetzel 1975a, 1975b; Rigdon 1983). The progression from a positive view to a negative one is not simply a gradual transition. Rather, it is characterized by instability, which may be a consequence of the more fundamental disorganization of the construct system (Landfield 1976; Neimeyer 1984; Neuringer and Lettieri 1971).

In terms of our model of suicidal choice, the following conclusions are advanced:

(a) Individuals who are not suicidal have a stable, predominantly positive view of themselves and their life. Death is consistently evaluated as negative;

(b) With low levels of suicidal ideation, the individual incorporates negative elements into the previously positive evaluative system, while death continues to be evaluated as negative. These negative evaluations tend to be time-limited and of relatively short duration;

(c) Suicidal ideation increases as more negative elements are incorporated into the previously positive system, but the individual's view of death remains negative. The construct system becomes more loosely organized as evaluations of self and life vacillate between positive and negative, leading to ambivalent anticipations of future events. Parasuicidal behavior at this point is likely to be impulsive and of low-lethality;

(d) At high levels of suicidal ideation, the individual has a stable view of himself and his life but now views these in predominantly negative terms. Death is given new meaning, and is evaluated positively for the first time. These polarized views of self, life, and death are quite stable over time, suggesting that the construct system is more tightly organized. Suicidal behavior occurring at this point is more likely to be well-planned and highly lethal.

Choosing to engage in suicidal behavior clearly indicates that more viable alternatives are not available. Indeed, Kelly (1961) writes that "one's personal constructions at the time of decision seem so completely dictated by the obvious that there are no practical alternatives left to explore" (p. 261). This lack of practical alternatives has received clear support through studies of problem solving in suicidal individuals.

PROBLEM SOLVING

This second line of research to be reviewed also begins with Neuringer's work. In a 1964 report based on the same sample described earlier, Neuringer hypothesized that polarization is a rigid, inflexible cognitive style that results in poor problem-solving abilities. Neuringer (1964) tested this hypothesis by having subjects complete two measures: the California F Scale (Adorno et al. 1950) and a modification of the Rokeach Map Test (Rokeach 1948). The California F Scale, which consists of 29 statements responded to on a 7-point Likert Scale, was designed to identify individuals who think in rigid categories. The Rokeach Map Test is a problem solving task that consists of a series of identical street maps on which subjects are required to draw the shortest route from one point on the map to another point. The procedure involves presenting two maps as examples to familiarize subjects with the task, and then presenting five more maps in order to establish a set pattern of responding. These first seven maps are identical except for street names being changed between trials. The test trials consist of presenting an additional five maps in which a change in the direction of an alleyway provides a shorter route and therefore requires the subject to alter his solution. A rather stringent definition of ridigity was used: a subject was considered rigid if he did not solve the problem by changing to the shorter solution on any of the last five maps.

Results supported both parts of the hypothesis. The parasuicidal group scored significantly higher on the California F Scale and were less likely to shift to the shorter route than both the psychosomatic and normal groups, who did not differ from each other on either measure. A later study (Levenson and Neuringer 1971), which investigated performance on the Rokeach in adolescents, obtained an identical pattern of results: significantly fewer parasuicidal subjects (4 out of 13) shifted to the shorter route than did the psychosomatic or normal subjects (11 and 12 out of 13 respectively). Levenson and Neuringer (1971) also reported that the parasuicidal group performed more poorly than the nonsuicidal psychiatric and normal groups on another problem solving task (the WISC Arithmetic subtest) even though the groups did not differ on level of intelligence.

Two other studies investigated inflexibility in problem solving using other measures. Levenson (1974) compared parasuicides with a nonsuicidal psychiatric group and a group of normal controls on two measures devised by Getzels and Jackson (1962): the Word Association Test, which requires the subject to generate multiple meanings of words; and the Unusual Uses Test, in which the subject is required to generate alternative uses for common items. On both measures the parasuicidal group performed significantly more poorly than the psychiatric group, who in turn performed more poorly than the normal controls.

Patsiokas, Clum, and Luscomb (1979) compared a sample of males admitted for parasuicide with a randomly selected sample of male psychiatric patients, none of whom had a history of parasuicide (although current suicide ideation apparently was not assessed). These researchers utilized the Alternative Uses Test (AUT; Wilson et al. 1975), which is a revised version of the measure utilized by Levenson (1974). Results indicate that the parasuicidal group performed significantly more poorly than the psychiatric controls. Since the two groups differed significantly in age and diagnosis, additional analyses controlling for these variables were conducted. Diagnostically, psychotic subjects performed more poorly than nonpsychotics but parasuicidal subjects performed more poorly than the controls in both groups. No significant effect for age was found. A stepwise discriminant analysis utilizing the AUT, two other cognitive measures (the Embedded Figures Test and the Matching Familiar Figures Test, neither of which discriminated between the groups), diagnosis, and age was also conducted. Of these variables, the AUT best discriminated between the groups.

These studies consistently report that parasuicidal groups perform more poorly than other groups on abstract problem solving tasks, although the role of mediating factors (such as level of depression) has not been explored. Recent research has extended these findings by focusing on the interpersonal problem-solving skills of suicidal individuals. This shift in focus made good sense. Interpersonal difficulty is the most frequently reported reason for parasuicidal behavior in adolescents (Withers and Kaplan 1987), college students (Bernard and Bernard 1982; Westefeld and Furr 1987), and other adults (Linehan, Chiles, Egan, Devine and Laffaw 1986). That interpersonal problems are reported twice as frequently by parasuicidal individuals as by suicide ideators or nonsuicidal psychiatric patients (Linehan et al. 1986) suggests that interpersonal difficulties are distinctly associated with parasuicide.

Schotte and Clum (1982) compared 96 college students who reported suicidal ideation within the past month with 79 students who had not experienced recent suicidal ideation. Dependent measures included the Scale for Suicide Ideators (SSI; Beck et al. 1979), a life-stress scale (Life Events Schedule [LES]; Saranson, Johnson and Siegel 1978), the AUT measure of impersonal problem solving used by Patsiokas (et al. 1979), and the Means–End Problem Solving Procedure (MEPS; Platt, Spivack and Bloom, 1971), which requires subjects to consider ten interpersonal stimulus situations and outcomes and to provide a means for achieving the stated outcome. The groups did not differ on the SIS—suggesting a low level of current ideation in the ideator group—or on either of the problem-solving measures. Only the LES discriminated between the two groups. To determine whether there was a relationship between life stress, interpersonal problem-solving skills, and suicidal ideation, median splits on the LES and MEPS were used to form four groups that were compared on level of suicidal ideation. Orthogonal contrasts of these groups revealed that poor problem solvers (below the mean on the MEPS) who were experiencing high stress (above the mean on the LES) had significantly higher ideation scores than the other groups combined. This finding suggests that a high level of stress by itself is not sufficient to produce suicidal ideation. Instead, a high level of stress in combination with interpersonal problem solving deficits is needed.

McLeavey et al. (1987) extended the investigation of interpersonal problem-solving by comparing parasuicides (self-poisoners of low to medium lethality), nonsuicidal psychiatric patients, and a normal control group on three measures of interpersonal problem solving: an eight story version of the MEPS (Platt et al. 1971); the Optional Thinking Test (OTT; Platt and Spivack 1977), which consists of four stories in which the subject must generate alternative possibilities for overcoming hypothetical interpersonal problems; and the Awareness of Consequences Test (ACT; Platt and Spivack 1977), which is a storytelling procedure in which the subject adopts the role of a protagonist who is exposed to a transgression, is asked to tell what happens in the protagonist's mind, and tells how the situation ends. Responses to the ACT were scored according to whether the subject's response included a reference to the possibility of transgressing, and whether the subject weighed the pros and cons of transgressing or not transgressing before providing an ending. An additional measure developed by the authors of the study (the Self-Rating Problem Solving Scale; SRPS) provided a measure of attitudes toward, and responses to, interpersonal problems.

Results indicated that the parasuicide group scored significantly lower on the MEPS and the OTT than the nonsuicidal psychiatric group, who scored significantly lower than the normal controls. This finding converges with results of studies of impersonal problem-solving tasks and suggests that deficits in both types of problem solving exist in parasuicidal individuals. On the ACT, the parasuicidal group included references to transgression less often than the normal controls but did not differ from the nonsuicidal psychiatric group. However, the parasuicide group was significantly less likely than the other groups to weigh the pros and cons of each conflicting choice, perhaps suggesting a somewhat impulsive manner of responding to this type of situation. The parasuicide group also showed the worst performance on the SRPS, suggesting that they respond poorly to their own interpersonal problems.

A study by Linehan, Camper, Chiles, Strosahl and Shearin (1987) provided a direct comparison of parasuicides and suicidal ideators on a three story version of the MEPS (Platt et al. 1971), an assertiveness measure, and an expectency measure of how much suicide would solve current problems. Relevant responses on the MEPS were subdivided into passive and active categories. The inclusion of two additional comparison groups (nonsuicidal psychiatric patients and surgery patients) and the assessment of intent in both parasuicides (moderate) and ideators (serious) made the study a particularly good example of suicide research.

Results indicated that the three groups of psychiatric patients were less assertive and provided more passive solutions on the MEPS than the normal group but that no differences existed among the parasuicidal, ideation, and nonsuicidal groups on these variables. However, on active solutions to the MEPS stories, the suicide ideation group showed the best performance, the parasuicidal group showed the worst performance, and the other groups were intermediate. This again points to poor problem solving in parasuicidal individuals but, surprisingly, suicide ideators showed good, active problem solving. The suicidal groups had a higher expectation than the psychiatric control group that suicide would solve their problems. Of the four dependant variables, suicide expectancy was the single significant predictor of suicide intent, and accounted for 16 percent of the variance.

Further analyses were conducted after subdividing the psychiatric groups according to the presence or absence of parasuicide history. No group differences emerged on assertiveness in either history group and the suicidal subjects in both history groups had higher expectancies than the nonsuicidal subjects. A different pattern of results was found on the MEPS. For subjects without a history of parasuicide, ideators provided significantly more active solutions and fewer passive solutions than parasuicides. For subjects with a parasuicide history no differences among the groups were found. This finding suggests that, regardless of current suicidal status, all subjects with a history of parasuicide are poor problem solvers. In contrast, current ideators who have never resorted to parasuicidal behavior are quite good interpersonal problem solvers. Linehan et al. interpreted this finding as suggesting that the ideators may have pursued hospitalization as an active solution to their current problems.

A study by Parker (1981) increases our understanding of how suicidal behavior is chosen over other seemingly more viable alternatives. His study focused on the personal meaning of various problem-solving behaviors within the context of a suicidal crisis. Parker had an initial group of 20 self-poisoning patients compare and contrast eleven conflict-resolution behaviors in order to elicit similarities and differences among the behaviors. The behaviors included the suicidal behaviors of "taking an overdose" and "choosing a sure means of killing myself," passive behaviors such as "doing nothing" or "getting drunk," and active behaviors such as "talking to the key person" and "seeking professional help." A total of 104 contrasting statements (e.g. useless and likely to fail—

effective in solving my problems; sensible and thought out—impulsive and desperate) were elicited from the subjects. These constructs were then examined by four judges, and nine constructs were chosen as representative of the sample. The final measure consisted of the nine bipolar constructs, which were presented as 7-point rating scales, and the eleven conflict-resolution behaviors.

A new sample of 29 patients admitted for self-poisoning was asked to consider their earlier crisis situations and rate each of the eleven behaviors on the nine bipolar scales. A mean split by score on the Suicide Intent Scale (Beck et al. 1974) produced two groups of subjects: those whose parasuicidal behavior was of low intent and those whose behavior was of moderate to high intent. The average ratings of the two groups on the repertory grid task were computed and these scores were subjected to an INGRID factor analysis (Slater 1972), with the objective of determining how patients of differing levels of suicidal intent viewed suicidal behavior in the context of their own personal strategies for resolving conflicts.

Results clearly reflected the group's difference in suicidal intent: the low-intent group viewed taking an overdose as quite distinct from actually killing oneself while the high-intent group viewed taking an overdose as very similar to killing oneself. The low-intent group construed overdosing primarily as a desperate escape from tension, while suicide was viewed as harmful and attacking of the key person. In contrast, the high-intent group viewed suicide as helpful and an effective method of expressing feelings. The high-intent group viewed talking to the key person as difficult, frustrating, and a form of denial of the real problem. The low-intent group viewed talking with the key person as sensible, helpful, but personally difficult. For both groups, talking to the key person implied an admission of blame, pointing perhaps to a potential invalidation that could be avoided through suicidal behavior. In both groups, suicidal behavior more evenly distributed blame between self and others.

Analysis of Problem Solving Studies

The studies cited above are consistent in linking poor problem solving with parasuicide. Current parasuicidal subjects perform more poorly than others on impersonal and interpersonal problem solving tasks, and subjects with a history of parasuicide are poor interpersonal problem solvers regardless of their current suicidal status. The two studies of suicide ideators suggest that poor problem solvers who experience high stress are more likely than others to consider suicide but that ideators who have never resorted to parasuicide perform quite well on hypothetical interpersonal problem solving tasks. Parker's (1981) study highlighted the personal meaning of various problem solving behaviors, and suggests that parasuicide is not simply a result of problem solving deficits. In parasuicidal subjects of low suicidal intent, talking to the key person implies accepting blame for the situation while taking an overdose tends to distribute blame more equally among the self and others. Taking an overdose is a desperate, impulsive act that is designed to escape tension. In high-intent parasuicides, talking to the key person also implies accepting responsibility for the situation, while suicide more equally distributes the blame. For such individuals, suicide is seen as a planned, sensible, and helpful act.

In terms of the present model of suicidal choice, failure to effectively solve life's problems results in painful invalidation. As these invalidations accumulate, the individual begins to view himself and his life negatively. Low levels of suicidal ideation appear when death is viewed as a possible solution to life's problems. If failure persists, the individual incorporates more negative elements into his view of himself and his life and instability of the construct system results. Anxiety increases and impulsive parasuicidal behavior may occur as an escape from tension. As the individual runs out of alternatives other than death, the construct system stabilizes again, this time with death being viewed in a positive direction, and life and self are viewed negatively. Well planned, highly lethal suicidal behavior becomes likely at this point.

This scenario describes a cumulative invalidation that occurs gradually, as the number of failures slowly rises. An alternative path to suicide would be followed if an individual were suddenly faced with potentially overwhelming invalidation. Regardless of the time element involved, suicidal behavior becomes most likely if seemingly promising solutions, such as talking to the key person or seeking professional help, invalidate important features of one's construct system. These findings lead us to speculate that just prior to the moment of self-injurious behavior the individual is clearly convinced that all viable alternatives have been exhausted and that the future holds nothing. This speculation leads us to the third line of research to be reviewed, studies relating to the suicidal individual's anticipations of the future.

STUDIES OF ANTICIPATIONS OF THE FUTURE

A study by Melges and Weiss (1971) addresses this speculation. They used a soliloquy technique to reevoke the state just prior to engaging in self-injurious behavior in fifteen individuals who had engaged in parasuicidal behavior in the previous month. Their measures included a suicide ideation scale, a Semantic Differential measure (Osgood et al. 1957) to assess view of future, and a measure of temporal extension. They first had subjects complete the test battery and then introduced the soliloquy technique, in which subjects were given a sheet of instructions that encouraged them to recall their experiences just prior to the parasuicidal behavior. Each subject attempted to recreate the experience in private and verbalized his or her feelings by speaking into a tape recorder. Following completion of this task, subjects completed a post-test battery. Subjects rated the soliloquy as moderately successful (6 on a 10-point scale) in helping them to recapture their mood; the soliloquy induced a significant increase in suicidal ideation and negative affect, suggesting that it was an effective technique. Results indicate that change in suicide ideation correlated the highest with change in view of the future, so that as ideation increased, the future appeared more negative and uncertain. Change in suicide ideation also correlated significantly with change toward shorter future extension, suggesting that the suicidal individual is so absorbed in the present that the future is literally beyond his comprehension.

Yufit, Benzies, Fonte and Fawcett (1970) pursued this issue cross-sectionally by comparing a highly suicidal group—consisting of inpatients on a Depression and Suicide Prevention Unit—a group of less suicidal outpatients, and a normal control group on a measure called the Time Questionnaire (TQ). The TQ was administered in a semi-structured interview format in which the subject was asked to select a year in the future and then answer a series of questions as if it were that future year. Responses were scored for extent of projection, amount of change fantasied, degree of detail, and consistency. Results indicated that the inpatient group had the lowest score on the TQ, and differed significantly from the outpatient and normal groups. In addition, when the inpatient group was subdivided into high- and low-risk categories, the high-risk group had lower scores than the low-risk group. A similar division by diagnostic status revealed no differences among the groups, suggesting that the differences obtained on the TQ were not merely a function of diagnosis.

A subsequent study (Yufit and Benzies 1973) obtained similar results while using a tighter experimental design. Subjects were thirty high-intent parasuicides, thirty low-intent parasuicides, thirty nonsuicidal psychiatric controls, and thirty normal controls. All groups were matched on age, sex, race, marital status, and SES, and the three psychiatric groups were additionally matched on diagnosis. The TQ was administered and scored in the manner described above. Results indicated that the high-intent parasuicidal group scored significantly lower than the other psychiatric patients, who in turn scored lower than the normal control group. In addition, the high-intent group had a significantly shorter future extension than the other three groups, who did not differ from each other. These results converge with the findings of Melges and Weiss (1971) and clearly suggest that the highly suicidal individual has a foreshortened and poorly elaborated view of the future that is quite distinct from individuals who are not highly suicidal.

Research in this area was propelled by the development of the Hopelessness Scale (HS; Beck, Weissman, Lester and Trexler 1974). The HS has been widely used because it is simple to administer and has demonstrated reliability and validity. The twenty-item, true–false measure was designed to tap the "system of cognitive schemas whose common denominator is negative expectations about the future'' (Beck et al. 1974, p.864).

A number of studies have consistently reported that suicidal groups receive higher HS scores than other psychiatric groups. For example, Wetzel (1976b) reported that a group of suicide ideators were significantly more hopeless than a parasuicidal group, who were significantly more hopeless than a group of psychiatric controls. Of particular interest to the present discussion are studies that have investigated the relationship between hopelessness, depression, and suicide. The HS correlates about .70 with depression scales such as the BDI (Beck, Weissman and Kovacs 1976; Dyer and Kreitman 1984; Ellis 1985) and both the HS and BDI correlate significantly with suicide ideation (Beck, Kovacs and Weissman 1979) and suicide intent (Minkoff et al. 1973; Kovacs, Beck and Weissman 1975; Petrie and Chamberlain 1983; Dyer and Kreitman 1984). However, when hopelessness is statistically controlled through the use of partial correlations, studies consistently find that the correlation between depression and suicide intent drops to nonsignificant levels; when depression is similarly controlled, however, the correlation between hopelessness and suicide intent remains significant (Minkoff et al. 1973; Kovacs et al. 1975; Beck, Kovacs and Weissman 1979; Kazdin, French, Unis, Esveldt-Dawson, and Sherick 1983; Petrie and Chamberlain 1983; Dyer and Kreitman 1984). This suggests that hopelessness mediates the relationship between depression and suicide.

Several other studies demonstrated that hopelessness is more closely related to suicidal behavior than is depression. In a study of 200 parasuicides, Kovacs, Beck, and Weissman (1975b) reported that hopelessness is a better predictor than depression of whether one engages in parasuicide for manipulative or escape reasons. Higher HS scores were found in individuals who chose parasuicide as an attempt to escape from life. Two studies that directly compared suicidal patients with nonsuicidal depressed patients reported that the suicidal groups were significantly more hopeless than the nonsuicidal groups even though the groups had equivalent levels of depression (Beck, Kovacs and Weissman 1979; Ellis 1986). Beck, Kovacs and Weissman (1979) studied 90 hospitalized ideators who were divided into four groups based on median splits of their HS and BDI scores. The groups with higher HS scores were found to have higher ideation scores irrespective of level of depression. Beck et al. (1976) reported identical findings with a larger sample of 366 parasuicides. Additionally, a multiple regression analysis found that the HS was the best predictor of suicide intent (accounting for 37 percent of the variance) while level of depression did not significantly increase predictive power.

Because of the consistent relationships found between hopelessness, suicidal ideation, and parasuicide, the instrument would appear to be a useful long-term predictor of completed suicide. In order to test this hypothesis, Beck et al.

(1985) conducted a long-term follow-up of 207 patients who were hospitalized for suicidal ideation during the period 1970–1975. All subjects completed the HS, BDI, and SSI within 48 hours of their admission. Following discharge, contact was maintained with patients for at least five years so that the number of individuals who committed suicide within this period could be determined. Of the 207 ideators, 14 (6.9 percent) committed suicide. Of the three instruments administered during hospitalization, only the HS distinguished between suicide completers and noncompleters. A cutoff score of nine on the HS clearly separated the completers from the noncompleters: only one (9.1 percent) of the completers obtained a score below this point. However, as with previous attempts to predict suicide, the practical value of using the HS to predict suicide is quite limited: Of 86 ideators who scored above ten on the HS, 76 did not commit suicide. This false positive rate of 88.4 percent clearly demonstrates that the HS is a poor predictor of completed suicide, although it also establishes hopelessness as another indicator of suicide risk.

Analysis of Studies of Anticipation of the Future

Researchers utilizing the HS have consistently reported that suicidal groups are pessimistic about the future, and that their pessimism is not merely a function of depression. However, the original factor analysis of the HS (Beck et al. 1974) reveals that the scale primarily taps affective and motivational features of one's view of the future, while cognitive features are only minimally assessed. Although the affective experience of hopelessness clearly marks the endpoint of the progression toward suicide, it is the cognitive features of a shortened and poorly elaborated view of the future that are crucial in limiting an individual's ability to consider alternatives other than suicidal behavior (Melges and Weiss 1971; Yufit et al. 1970; Yufit and Benzies 1973).

In the present model of suicidal choice, the nonsuicidal individual has a well elaborated and predominantly positive view of the future. At low levels of suicidal ideation, the individual begins to anticipate negative future outcomes. As suicidal ideation increases, anticipations are inconsistent because of disorganization of the individual's construct system, the extension of the individual's view into the future is decreased, and much of the future appears uncertain. At high levels of ideation, anticipations of the future become consistently negative and the individual experiences depressive hopelessness.

A COGNITIVE MODEL OF SUICIDAL CHOICE

The present model posits that individuals who are not suicidal have a relatively stable construct system, and a predominantly positive view of themselves and the future. Low levels of suicidal ideation may develop as the individual experiences invalidation in important areas of his or her life and begins to incorporate negative elements into a predominantly positive construct system. At this low level of suicidality, self-destructive behavior is considered as just one of a number of alternative solutions. The ideation is likely to be of short duration as the individual effectively adjusts to the demands of the situation and resolves the problem. Low levels of ideation are a relatively common occurrence in the general population.

Certain features of an individual's construct system, such as rigidity or constriction, limit his or her ability to respond optimally to life stresses. In a constricted system, constructs that have a limited applicability are employed such that important events cannot be considered in meaningful terms. A rigid system may utilize more effective constructs, but they are applied in an inflexible manner. Both types of systems are "impermeable" (Kelly 1955, p. 79) in that they are limited in their ability to apply to unexpected turns of events. An individual utilizing either type of system has difficulty making appropriate adjustments to invalidation and is therefore ineffective in problem solving.

In the face of moderate levels of invalidation, which may result either from a single severe stressor or from a series of smaller problem-solving failures, suicidal ideation increases as the individual's construct system loses its coherence and becomes disorganized. During this period of transition between more stable structures, anticipations are inconsistent and vacillate between positive and negative (Neimeyer 1984). The individual experiences anxiety, and views both the present and future as uncertain. Parasuicidal behavior at this point is likely to be a poorly planned low-lethality bid for certainty, and it becomes most likely if other potential solutions carry negative implications for the individual. Suicide itself is viewed as harmful.

If problem solving continues to be ineffective, and invalidation thereby continues, the construct system stabilizes again as anticipations become consistently negative. The individual views himself or herself in predominantly negative terms, experiences hopelessness because alternatives other than death appear untenable, and views death as positive. At this point, the successful completion of suicide is much more likely because the behavior is well planned and is viewed as helpful and effective. See Figure 1 for an illustration of this progression.

It is worth emphasizing that self-injurious behavior is not a simple consequence of an impermeable construct system, poor problem-solving skills, or other cognitive factors. The model presumes that some "noncognitive" stressor, such as a threat to an important relationship or a biologically induced depression, is necessary to start the individual on the path toward suicide. In the absence of such stressors, the individual's problem-solving abilities are not taxed beyond their limits. In addition, there are a number of factors that could abort the progression outlined above. For example, an individual who becomes

Figure 1. Model of suicidal choice.

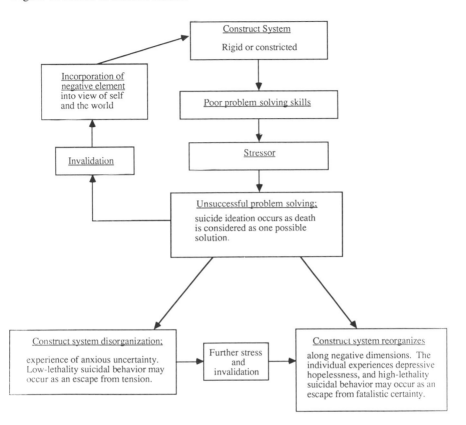

increasingly suicidal as problem-solving attempts fail may eventually implement a strategy that leads to constructive change. Alternatively, the individual may resolve the problem in a way that circumvents personal invalidation, such as by pressuring others to change. Finally, even in the face of an insoluble or unavoidable problem, family members or others may intervene and provide the individual with the support necessary to either extend his or her cognitive and behavioral resources to actively manage the problem or passively ''wait out'' the stressful period until the problem is resolved in some other way.

FUTURE DIRECTIONS

The model outlined in this chapter represents an attempt to integrate three separate lines of research on the cognitive processes of self-destructive adults: those concerned with their cognitive structure, with their problem-solving skills, and with their anticipations of the future. It is our belief that a more complete understanding of suicide can result from a consideration of these cognitive factors in interaction with environmental stressors, rather than from a consideration of either internal or external factors taken alone.

Nonetheless, there is a clear need for research that tests the validity of the proposed model. For example, although the separate components of the model have each received a reasonable degree of support, no empirical research to date has assessed their combined use in predicting suicide ideation or self-injurious behavior. More importantly, the sequence of interactions between cognitive and situational factors proposed by the model needs to be tested in longitudinal research. Such a sequential model, if validated, could have important practical as well as heuristic implications. At a practical level, it could provide a more coherent rationale for intervention efforts, by specifying a relevant set of "targets" for psychotherapy or primary prevention programs. For instance, a counselor confronted with an imminently suicidal client might well concentrate on the most immediate cognitive "link" mediating the suicidal choice, and attempt to offer realistic hope for future relief, perhaps by encouraging the client to imaginally project him- or herself into a future when present difficulties are resolved (Lewinsohn et al. 1985). Once a modicum of hope is instilled, the counselor can more easily shift attention to the logically prior link concerning problem-solving strategies, with the immediate goal of generating additional plausible solutions to the stressful situation the client faces. This form of "alternative therapy" (Bedrosian and Beck 1980) seeks simply to brainstorm as many options for managing the stressor as possible (e.g., discussing the problem with a friend, calling the counselor) to counteract the constricted client's focus on suicide as the "only" way to respond to life's problems.

Once more viable solutions to the immediate stressor are implemented, therapy can then focus on more basic deficits in the client's problem-solving skills and cognitive in an effort to minimize vulnerability to future suicide ideation. Well-developed therapies currently exist for augmenting clients' interpersonal problem solving (Platt, Prout and Metzger 1986), as well as for revising their polarized and dysfunctional thinking about themselves, the world, and the future (Beck, Rush, Shaw and Emery 1979). Moreover, careful attention to constricted, rigid, and fragmented features of their personal construct systems could serve an important preventive role, by helping clients construct a more flexible and integrated identity that would be resilient in the face of future stressors (Neimeyer 1986; Neimeyer and Neimeyer 1987). Thus, by encompassing several cognitive features of demonstrated relevance to suicidal behavior, the present model might also coordinate treatment efforts, by suggesting ways to dovetail the strategies and techniques of some of the most sophisticated cognitive therapies yet devised.

In short, we are encouraged by recent efforts to investigate those cognitive processes that eventuate in the decision to end one's own life. We hope that our review of this research, and our attempt to place it in a larger framework, will contribute to a better understanding of the complex phenomenon of suicide.

REFERENCES

Adorno, T.W., E. Frenkel-Brunswick, D.J. Levinson and R.N. Stanford. 1950. *The authoritarian personality.* New York: Harper.

Bancroft, J.H.H., A.M. Skrimshire and S. Simkin. 1976. The reasons people give for taking overdoses. *British Journal of Psychiatry* 128:538–48.

Beck, A.T., J.H. Davis, C.J. Frederick, S. Perlin, A.D. Pokorny, R.E. Schulman, R.H. Seiden, and B.J. Wittlin. 1972. Classification and nomenclature. In H.L.P. Resnik and B.C. Hathorne, eds., *Suicide prevention in the 70 s.* Washington D. C.: U. S. Government Printing Office.

Beck, A.T., N. Epstein and R. Harrison. 1983. Cognitions, attitudes and personality dimensions in depression. *British Journal of Cognitive Psychotherapy* 1:1–16.

Beck, A.T., M. Kovacs and A. Weissman. 1979. Assessment of suicidal intention: The scale for suicide ideation. *Journal of Consulting and Clinical Psychology* 47:343–52.

Beck, A.T., A.J. Rush, B.F. Shaw and G. Emery. 1979. *Cognitive therapy of depression.* New York: Guilford.

Beck, A.T., D. Schuyler and I. Herman. 1974. Development of suicide intent scales. In H.L.P. Resnik and D.J. Lettieri, eds., *The prediction of suicide.* Bowie, MD: Charles Press.

Beck, A. T., R. A. Steer, M. Kovacs and B. Garrison. 1985. Hopelessness and eventual suicide: A 10-year prospective study of patients hospitalized with suicidal ideation. *American Journal of Psychiatry* 142:559–63.

Beck, A.T., R.A. Steer, and M.G. McElroy. 1982. Relationships of hopelessness, depression and previous suicide attempts to suicidal ideation in alcoholics. *Journal of Studies on Alcohol* 43(9):1042–46.

Beck, A.T., A. Weissman and M. Kovacs. 1976. Alcoholism, hopelessness, and suicidal behavior. *Journal of Studies on Alcohol* 37(1):66–77.

Beck, A.T., A. Weissman, D. Lester and L. Trexler. 1974. The measurement of pessimism: The hopelessness scale. *Journal of Consulting and Clinical Psychology* 42(6):861–65.

Bedrosian, R.C. and A.T. Beck. 1980. Cognitive aspects of suicidal behavior. *Suicide and Life-Threatening Behavior* 9(2):87–96.

Bemporad, J.R. and A.A. Wilson. 1978. A developmental approach to depression in childhood and adolescence. *Journal of the American Academy of Psychoanalysis* 6:325–52.

Bernard, J.L. and M.L. Bernard. 1982. Factors related to suicidal behavior among college students and the impact of institutional response. *Journal of College Student Personnel* 23:409–13.

Cavan, R. 1928. *Suicide.* Chicago: University of Chicago Press.

Clum, G.A., A.T. Patsiokas and R.L. Luscomb. 1979. Empirically based comprehensive treatment program for parasuicide. *Journal of Consulting and Clinical Psychology* 47(5):937–45.

Dew, M.A., E.J. Bromet, D. Brent, and J.B. Greenhouse. 1987. A quantitative literature review of the effectiveness of suicide prevention centers. *Journal of Consulting and Clinical Psychology* 55(2):239–44.

Dyer, J.A.T. and N. Kreitman. 1984. Hopelessness, depression, and suicidal intent in parasuicide. *British Journal of Psychiatry* 144:127–33.

Ellis, T.E. 1985. The hopelessness scale and social desirability: More data and a contribution from the Irrational Beliefs Test. *Journal of Clinical Psychology* 41(5):634–39.

Ellis, T.E. and K.G. Ratliff. 1986. Suicidal characteristics of suicidal and nonsuicidal psychiatric inpatients. *Cognitive Therapy and Research* 10(6):625–34.

Ettlinger, R. 1975. Evaluation of suicide prevention after attempted suicide. *Acta Psychiatrica Scandinavia* 57 (Suppl 260):5–135.

Farrar, C.B. 1951. Suicide. *Journal of Clinical and Experimental Psychopathology* 12:79–88.

Fawcett, J., W. Scheftner, D. Clark, D. Hedeker, R. Gibbons and W. Coryell. 1987. Clinical predictors of suicide in patients with major affective disorders: A controlled prospective study. *American Journal of Psychiatry* 144:35–40.

Freeman, D.J., K. Wilson, J. Thigpen and R.K. McGee. 1974. Assessing intention to die in self-injury behavior. In C. Neuringer, ed., *Psychological assessment of suicidal risk*. Springfield, IL: Charles C. Thomas.

Getzel, J.W. and P.W. Jackson. 1962. *Creativity and intelligence*. New York: Wiley.

Greer, S. and C. Bagley. 1971. Effects of psychiatric intervention in attempted suicide. *British Medical Journal* 1:310–12.

Kelly, G.A. 1955. *The psychology of personal constructs*. New York: Norton.

Kelly, G.A. 1961. Suicide: The personal construct point of view. In N.L. Farberow and E.S. Shneidman, eds., *The cry for help*. New York: McGraw-Hill.

Kovacs, M., A.T. Beck and A. Weissman. 1975a. Hopelessness: An indicator of suicidal risk. *Suicide* 5(2):98–103.

——1975b. The use of suicidal motives in the psychotherapy of attempted suicides. *American Journal of Psychotherapy* 29:363–68.

Kreitman, N. 1977. *Parasuicide*. New York: John Wiley.

Landfield, A. 1976. A personal construct approach to suicidal behavior. In P. Slater, ed. *Explorations of Personal Space*. New York: John Wiley.

Lester, D. 1970. Attempts to predict suicidal risk using psychological tests. *Psychological Bulletin* 74:1–17.

Lester, D., A.T. Beck and B. Mitchell. 1979. Extrapolation from attempted suicides to completed suicides: A test. *Journal of Abnormal Psychology* 88:78–80.

Levenson, M. 1974. Cognitive correlates of suicidal risk. In C. Neuringer, ed. *Psychological assessment of suicidal risk*. Springfield, IL: Charles C. Thomas.

Levenson, M. and C. Neuringer. 1971. Problem-solving behavior in suicidal adolescents. *Journal of Consulting and Clinical Psychology* 37:433–36.

Lewinsohn, P.M., D.O. Antonuccio, J.L. Steinmetz and L. Teri. 1985. *The coping with depression course*. Eugene, OR: Castalia.

Linehan, M.M., P. Camper, J. A. Chiles, K. Strosahl and E. Shearin. 1987. Interpersonal problem solving and parasuicide. *Cognitive Therapy and Research* 11:1–12.

Linehan, M.M., J.A. Chiles, K.J. Egan, R.H. Devine and J.A. Laffaw. 1986. Presenting problems of parasuicides versus suicide ideators and nonsuicidal psychiatric patients. *Journal of Consulting and Clinical Psychology* 54:880–81.

Linehan, M.M. and S.L. Nielson. 1981. Assessment of suicidal ideation and parasuicide: Hopelessness and social desirability. *Journal of Consulting and Clinical Psychology* 49:773–75.

MacKinnon, D.R. and N.L. Farberow. 1976. An assessment of the utility of suicide prediction. *Suicide and Life-Threatening Behavior* 6:86–91.

McLeavey, B.C., R.J. Daly, C.M. Murray, J. O'Riordan and M. Taylor. 1987. Interpersonal problem-solving deficits in self-poisoning patients. *Suicide and Life-Threatening Behavior* 17:33–49.

Melges, F.T. and A.E. Weisz. 1971. The personal future and suicide ideation. *Journal of Nervous and Mental Disease* 153:244–50.

Minkoff, K., E. Bergman, A.T. Beck and R. Beck. 1973. Hopelessness, depression, and attempted suicide. *American Journal of Psychiatry* 130:455–59.

Mishara, B. L., A.H. Baker and T.T. Mishara. 1976. The frequency of suicide attempts: A retrospective approach applied to college students. *American Journal of Psychiatry* 133:841–44.

Neimeyer, R.A. 1984. Toward a personal construct conceptualization of depression and suicide. In F. R. Epting and R. A. Neimeyer, eds. *Personal meanings of death: Applications of personal construct theory to clinical practice.* Washington, D. C.: Hemisphere.

——1985. Personal constructs in depression: Research and clinical implications. In E. Button, ed. *Personal construct theory and mental health.* Cambridge, MA: Brookline.

——1986. Personal construct therapy. In W. Dryden and W. Golden, eds., *Cognitive-behavioral approaches to psychotherapy.* London: Harper & Row.

Neimeyer, R.A. and G.J. Neimeyer. 1987. *Personal construct therapy casebook.* New York: Springer.

Neuringer, C. 1961. Dichotomous evaluations in suicidal individuals. *Journal of Consulting Psychology* 25:455–49.

——1964. Rigid thinking in suicidal individuals. *Journal of Consulting Psychology* 28:54–58.

——1967. The cognitive organization of meaning in suicidal individuals. *Journal of General Psychology* 76:91–100.

——1968. Divergencies between attitudes towards life and death among suicidal, psychosomatic, and normal hospitalized patients. *Journal of Consulting and Clinical Psychology* 32:59–63.

Neuringer, C., and D.J. Lettieri. 1971. Cognition, attitude, and affect in suicidal individuals. *Life-Threatening Behavior* 1:106–24.

Osgood, C.E., G.J. Suci, and P.H. Tannenbaum. 1957. *The measurement of meaning.* Urbana, IL: University of Illinois Press.

Pallis, D.J., J.S. Gibbons and D.W. Pierce. 1984. Estimating risk among attempted suicides: Efficiency of predictive scales after the attempt. *British Journal of Psychiatry* 144:139–48.

Parker, A. 1981. The meaning of attempted suicide to young parasuicides: A repertory grid study. *British Journal of Psychiatry* 139:306–12.

Patsiokas, A.T., G.A. Clum and R.L. Luscomb. 1979. Cognitive characteristics of suicide attempters. *Journal of Consulting and Clinical Psychology* 47:478–84.

Petrie, K. and K. Chamberlain. 1983. Hopelessness and social desirability as moderator variables in predicting suicidal behavior. *Journal of Consulting and Clinical Psychology* 51:485–87.

Platt, J., M.F. Prout, and D.S. Metzger. 1986. Interpersonal cognitive problem-solving therapy (ICPS). In W. Dryden and W. Golden, eds. *Cognitive-behavioral approaches to psychotherapy.* London: Harper & Row.

Platt, J., G. Spivack and M. Bloom. 1971. *Means-end problem-solving procedure: Manual and tentative norms.* Philadelphia: Hahnemann Medical College.

Platt, J., and G. Spivack. 1977. *Measures of interpersonal cognitive problem-solving for adults and adolescents.* Philadelphia: Hahnemann Medical College.

Pokorny, A.D. 1966. A follow-up of 618 suicidal patients. *American Journal of Psychiatry* 122:1109–16.

——1983. Prediction of suicide in psychiatric patients. *Archives of General Psychiatry* 40:249–57.

Rigdon, M.A., F.R. Epting, R.A. Neimeyer and S.R. Krieger. 1979. The threat index: A research report. *Death Education* 3:245–70.

Rigdon, M.A. 1983. Death threat before and after attempted suicide: A clinical investigation. In F. R. Epting and R. A. Neimeyer, eds. *Personal meanings of death: Applications of personal construct theory to clinical practice.* Washington, D. C.: Hemisphere.

Rokeach, M. 1948. Generalized mental rigidity as a factor in ethnocentrism. *Journal of Abnormal and Social Psychology* 43:259–78.

Roy, A. 1982. Risk factors for suicide in psychiatric patients. *Archives of General Psychiatry* 39:1089–95.

Saranson, I., J. Johnson and J. Siegel. 1978. Assessing the impact of life changes: Development of the life experiences survey. *Journal of Consulting and Clinical Psychology* 46:932–46.

Schotte, D.E. and G.A. Clum. 1982. Suicide ideation in a college population: A test of a model. *Journal of Consulting and Clinical Psychology* 50:690–96.

Shneidman, E.S. 1976. *Suicidology: Contemporary developments.* New York: Grune & Stratton.

Slater, P. 1972. *Notes on INGRID 1972.* Unpublished manuscript, St. Georges Hospital, Department of Psychiatry, London.

Smith, K. and S. Crawford. 1986. Suicidal behavior among "normal" high school students. *Suicide and Life-Threatening Behavior* 16:313–25.

U. S. Bureau of the Census. 1987. *Statistical Abstract of the United States:* 107th edition. Washington, D.C.: U. S. Government Printing Office.

Westefeld, J.S. and S.R. Furr. 1987. Suicide and depression among college students. *Professional Psychology: Research and Practice* 18:119–23.

Wetzel, R.D. 1975a. Ratings of life and death and suicide intent. *Psychological Reports* 37:879–85.

——1975b. Self-concept and suicide intent. *Psychological Reports* 36:279–282.

——1976a. Semantic differential ratings of concepts and suicide intent. *Journal of Clinical Psychology* 32:4–13.

——1976b. Hopelessness, depression, and suicide intent. *Archives of General Psychiatry* 33:1069–73.

Wilson, R., P. Christenson, P. Merrifield and J. Guilford. 1975. *Alternate Uses Test.* Beverly Hills, CA: Sheridan Psychological Company.

Withers, L.E. and D.W. Kaplan. 1987. Adolescents who attempt suicide: A retrospective clinical chart review of hospitalized patients. *Professional Psychology: Research and Practice* 18:391–93.

Yufit, R.I. and B. Benzies. 1973. Assessing suicidal potential by time perspective. *Life-Threatening Behavior* 3:270–82.

Yufit, R.I., B. Benzies, M.E. Fonte and J.A. Fawcett. 1970. Suicide potential and time perspective. *Archives of General Psychiatry* 23:158–63.

2

Suicide and Violent Death: Longitudinal Studies

Paul C. Holinger

Suicide is such a complex, multidetermined phenomenon that it is impossible to discuss one aspect of the problem without at least acknowledging contributions in a variety of areas. This chapter will deal specifically with certain issues in psychiatric epidemiology and their clinical correlates; in keeping with a general systems approach other subfields within suicidology deserve mention and will be discussed elsewhere in this volume. For example, biologic investigations (by researchers such as van Praag, Roy, Kety, and Fawcett), clinical, affect, and infant studies (by Freud, Menninger, Kohut, Shneidman, G. Alder, Maltsberger, Basch, Stern, and Tompkins), and sociologic research (by Durkheim and Hendin) and others should at least be noted in order to put the current work into perspective.

The purpose of this chapter is twofold: first, a brief description of the development of the study of longitudinal patterns of suicide and other violent deaths (homicide and accidents) will be presented; and, second, a more detailed investigation of longitudinal patterns of suicide and other violent deaths will be discussed with specific reference to demographics, prediction, and clinical correlations.

LONGITUDINAL PATTERNS OF SUICIDE

Psychiatric epidemiologists have become increasingly interested in understanding longitudinal patterns of suicide, inasmuch as such understanding appears to provide a vehicle by which better intervention and prevention strategies can be developed. Durkheim's (1897) monumental work *Suicide* is perhaps best known for its elucidating demographic variables and hypothesizing various types of suicide. However, Durkheim's work also emphasized the importance of studying longitudinal trends in order to adequately understand suicide and its prevention.

More recently, two researchers have been particularly important in understanding long-term trends in the epidemiology of suicide and other violent deaths: Harvey Brenner (1971, 1979) and Richard Easterlin (1980). Before turning to their work, however, three key terms in longitudinal epidemiologic studies must be defined: age effects, period effects, and cohort effects. Age effects involve changes in age-specific rates of mortality over the life-span of the individual (Holford 1983). For example, in the United States it is well-known that in males, suicide rates increase as age increases, while rates in females increase to mid-adulthood and then decrease in older age (Holinger 1987). Period effects refer to changes in rates of mortality during a particular historical period (Holford 1983). For instance, one sees an increase in suicide rates during periods of economic depression, and a decrease during war (Holinger 1987). A cohort refers to a group of people born at a particular time and followed as they age. Cohort effects involve differences in rates of mortality among these individuals defined by some shared temporal experience, e.g., year or decade of birth (Holford 1983). The "baby boomers," i.e., that group born in the decade after World War II, are an example of a cohort.

Although the definitions of age, period, and cohort effects appear clear enough, in practice it is often difficult to distinguish between a cohort and a period effect. What seems to be a cohort effect may be due to period effects, and vice versa. For instance, a period effect may have an impact on a particular cohort that will appear distinctive because of the circumstances or experiences of that cohort. For example, the Vietnam War was an event that impacted on the entire society but was perhaps most stressful for young adults. Thus, period effects may impact on a particular age group more than on others and thereby act like cohort effects.

Brenner's and Easterlin's work has helped make long-term epidemiologic patterns of violent deaths understandable through their elucidating various period and cohort effects (although they didn't necessarily label them as such at the time). Brenner (1971, 1979) was the first to systematically demonstrate the importance and logical consistency of period effects in psychiatric epidemiology. He focused on a single variable, economic cycles, and related it not only to psychiatric hospitalizations but mortality as well. Brenner found that the worse the economy (as measured by unemployment rates), the higher the rates of suicide, homicide, and, ultimately, other causes of mortality. Long-term data from the United States, England, and Wales tended to demonstrate that suicide and homicide rates showed increases within a year of increasing unemployment, while cardiovascular mortality begins to increase two to three years later and malignancy shortly after that (Brenner 1971, 1979).

The second major recent contribution to be made in the understanding of longitudinal trends in suicide and other violent deaths is that of Easterlin (1980). Easterlin studied the baby boomers, investigating the impact that the size of this cohort had upon both the cohort itself and the rest of society in the United

States. Although Easterlin's work did not directly address the topic of violent deaths to any great extent, his work has profound implications for the field. The Easterlin hypothesis maintains that there is a cause-effect relationship between birth cohort size and economic, social, educational, and political trends. According to Easterlin, when the size of the birth cohort increases, it produces excessive competition for existing and limited resources and institutions, and results in relative deprivation. Easterlin has identified three broad social institutions through which the effects of cohort size operate: family, school, and the labor market.

To summarize this first section on violent deaths and the longitudinal perspective, it can be said that not only are the long-term trends in suicide, homicide, and accidents understandable, but also that many of the key variables producing these trends are identifiable. These major influences on rates are period effects due to the economy, war, and demographics. Finally, in finding that violent death trends are understandable, a congenial concept exists in what is called chaos theory. Chaos theory involves studies of apparently random patterns, and makes order out of disorder. The term "strange attractor" refers to this process of discovering ordered patterns.

VIOLENT DEATHS, DEMOGRAPHICS, AND CLINICAL CORRELATIONS

This section will deal with three issues: violent deaths and their longitudinal patterns; demographics and prediction; and clinical correlations, i.e., relationship between epidemiologic and clinical data.

Violent Deaths and Their Longitudinal Patterns

In turning to the first topic, violent deaths, a definition is necessary: the term violent deaths has been used to refer to the integrated study of suicide, homicide, and accidents (Weiss 1976; Holinger 1987). In attempting to understand self-destructiveness among human beings, it appears that we often unnecessarily limit ourselves by studying only suicide. We may do ourselves a disservice if we do not investigate similar phenomena, such as homicide and accidents. This is the rationale that has led us to examine homicide and accidents in addition to suicide. Needless to say, controversy exists regarding the extent to which homicide and accidents, as well as suicide, may reflect self-destructive tendencies. Homicide data, strictly speaking, refer to those who are killed (not the killers), and Wolfgang's (1968) studies of victim-precipitated homicides, as well as epidemiologic data by Brenner (1971, 1979) and Klebba (1975) tend to provide support for the idea that self-destructive tendencies underlie many homicides. With respect to accidents, some data suggest that deaths due to accidents, including motor-vehicle accidents, may be due to accident-proneness and risk-taking that reflect depression and suicidal tendencies. To summarize, the bulk of both clinical and epidemiologic data seem to suggest that the concepts of excessive risk-taking and victim-precipitated homicide have therapeutic and predictive value, and that homicide and accidental deaths may be psychologically determined by underlying self-destructive tendencies. However, testing these hypotheses is extremely difficult and fraught with methodologic problems, and there is much data that does not support the hypotheses. (For a detailed review of the literature on this controversial topic, see Holinger and Klemen 1980; and *Injury in America*, 1985). It might be noted, though, that giving strongest support to these hypotheses are long-term epidemiologic data for suicide and homicide, which show similar time trends for more than fifty years (Holinger 1987).

In addition to the value of studying accidents and homicide—as well as suicide—as windows to understanding self-destructiveness, another issue must be addressed: the importance of utilizing a longitudinal perspective. Five or 10 or even 20 years are simply not enough data by which to establish longitudinal patterns. One needs decades—40, 50, 60 years at least—in order to sort out the various age, period, and cohort effects involved. (It might be noted that this puts an unusual psychological strain on the investigators, who will probably not live to see their hypotheses tested as adequately as they would like!)

Longitudinal studies of violent deaths have yielded important information that has critical implications for intervention and prevention. For example, as noted above, the most important variables influencing long-term trends in violent mortality appear to be the economy, demographics, and war (Brenner 1971, 1979; Easterlin 1980; Holinger 1987). In addition, the data seem to suggest that a certain proportion of the population is at risk of dying a violent death, but that the type of violent death is dependent on one's age, race, and sex (the "typological" factor). For example, whites are at a much greater risk of dying by suicide, whereas nonwhites are much more likely to die of homicide; young people are more at risk of dying by homicide and older people by suicide, motor-vehicle accidents, and non-motor-vehicle accidents. Thus, race and sex appear to determine the type of violent death from which one is most likely to die; and sex seems to determine the degree of risk of dying from a particular type of violent death (e.g., females have lower rates than males for virtually every type of violent death at every age).

Demographics and Prediction

The above discussion sets the stage for the second topic: the relationship between demographics and violent deaths, and the potential for predicting violent deaths by utilizing demographic variables. Of the three variables that exert major influences on long-term trends—the economy, war, and demographics—

only the demographic variables are suited for long-range prediction and ultimate prevention of violent deaths on a large-scale basis.

There is increasing evidence that demographic variables—i.e., trends in population shifts—may be of use in understanding a variety of social phenomena. Recently, two different types of studies have begun to evaluate demographic variables for their possible explanatory and predictive power on violent death rates in the United States as well as other countries. These two types of investigations have been termed cohort studies and population model studies. Although both examine demographic variables, it is becoming increasingly clear that they are quite different types of investigations: They ask different questions and reach different conclusions.

In discussing cohort studies, it should be reiterated that cohort effects refer to differences in rates of mortality or illness during a particular historical period. Cohort analyses enable one to follow over time a group of people born during specific years. Examples of cohort studies include Easterlin's (1980) work on the baby boom cohort, and Solomon and Hellon (1980) and Murphy and Wetzel's (1980) cohort analyses documenting the increases in suicide among the young during the 1960s and 1970s.

The population model studies a different aspect of demographic influence. The population model examines a specific age group over time (for example, 15–24-year-olds), and it examines the population shifts within that age group. That is to say, the age group stays the same, but the subjects change. Cohort analyses, on the other hand, follow the same group of people, or cohort, over time as it ages.

Population model studies found that increases and decreases in the number and proportion of adolescents in the total population correlated with increases and decreases, respectively, in the suicide rates among adolescents (Hendin 1982; Holinger and Offer 1982). Methodologically, it should be noted that while one would naturally expect the number of suicides to increase with an increase in population, the rate should not necessarily increase. These data were for the United States and covered nearly 50 years. For older adults, the opposite trend was found: increases and decreases in the older adult population were accompanied by decreases and increases, respectively, in their suicide rates.

These findings were subsequently expanded to include all age groups as well as homicide and accidents in addition to suicide (Holinger and Offer 1984, 1987). The data have been clearest for suicide and homicide. The data included all suicides and homicides in the United States for the 50-year period from 1933–1982. Mortality data before 1933 were not included because it was only after 1932 that all states were incorporated into the national mortality statistics (Alaska was added in 1959 and Hawaii in 1960). Significant positive correlations were found between the suicide and homicide rates for 15–24-year-olds

Figure 1. Suicide and Homicide Rates and Percentage of U.S. Population for 15–24 year olds, 1933–1982.
Sources of data: Holinger and Offer 1987.

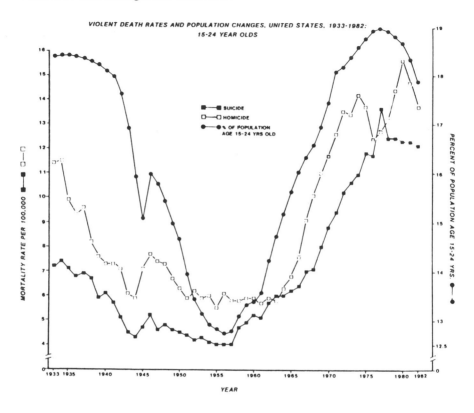

and the proportion of 15–24-year-olds in the U.S. Significant negative correlations were found for most adult age groups (35–64 years). Figure 1 shows the parallel trends for mortality rates among adolescents and their population shifts. Figure 2 presents an example from the adult age groups, with population shifts among 35- to 44-year-olds inversely related to their suicide and homicide rates. In summary, what appears to be emerging is a positive relationship between suicide and homicide and population changes among adolescents; and an inverse relationship between violent deaths and population shifts among adults.

Of all the tasks of science, perhaps prediction and attempts to disprove hypotheses are among the most important. Prediction is possible utilizing the population model inasmuch as there exist approximations of the number of preadolescents in the population. One can thereby predict the numbers of adolescents and adults, and thus make attempts to predict the violent death rates. For example, Figure 3 shows an attempt made several years ago to predict suicide rates for 15- to 24-year-olds, and to disprove the hypothesis. Unlike the cohort studies that predicted continued increases in suicide rates among adolescents, the population model suggested that the rates would level off. These rates have leveled off (Holinger, Offer, Zola 1988), but a predicted decrease has not yet occurred. Needless to say, in keeping with the longitudinal perspective, years and decades will be required to adequately disprove or lend support to the hypothesis relating violent death to population changes.

RELATIONSHIPS BETWEEN EPIDEMIOLOGIC AND CLINICAL DATA

In attempting to understand these results, it appears that with massive increases of adolescents, the entire psychosocial system becomes over-stressed. This occurs on epidemiologic, psychodynamic, and public health levels. For example, with increased competition for jobs, college positions, mental health resources, academic and athletic honors, come increased numbers of psychologically vulnerable adolescents who fail to get such external sources of self-esteem and the mental health services they need. The Institute of Medicine, in evaluating the Easterlin proposal, has termed this reasoning the deprivation hypothesis, and it seems to best explain the data at the present time. For the adults, the findings are different: their rates decrease as their population increases. Why? They are more powerful politically, better able to exert pressure to obtain economic benefits from the government, and more attractive as employees because of experience and schooling. Thus the population increases in the adult groups may lead not so much to increased competition and failure, but rather to greater economic and political benefits.

The findings and discussion above allow us to turn to the relationship between epidemiologic and clinical propositions with particular reference to self-psychology and the work of Heinz Kohut. Without going into detail regarding the various epistemological issues at stake (Gedo and Goldberg 1973; Holinger 1987), it would appear that the bulk of the evidence suggests that epidemiologic and clinical data and hypotheses can each be usefully employed to enhance an understanding of the other—if one is careful to distinguish the different levels of abstraction involved. In the past, the dynamic understanding of suicide has tended to focus on such issues as guilt, ambivalent identifications with the lost object, rage turned against the self, and so on—primarily couched in terms of psychosexual development at an oedipal level—and, indeed, these formulations have been helpful in enhancing the understanding of some of our suicidal patients. More recently, an increased comprehension of dyadic issues and early

Figure 2. Suicide and Homicide Rates and Percentage of U.S. Population for 35–44 year olds, 1933–1982.
Sources of data: Holinger and Offer 1987.

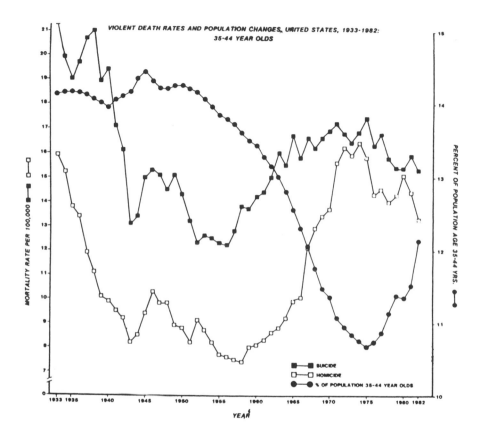

developmental problems has led to a greater depth of understanding of the dynamics of suicide. And still more recently, the work of Heinz Kohut and self-psychology appears to provide a window through which to understand still better patients with what have variously been called narcissistic or selfobject disorders or disturbances in self-esteem regulation (Kohut 1984; Kavka 1976; Reiser 1986). Not only does a self-psychology perspective aid one clinically, but it also may make some of the epidemiologic findings more understandable.

Turning briefly to some clinical phenomena, a few definitions are in order, such as self and selfobject. Kohut defined self as "an independent center of initiative." Exploring the blurring of boundaries that can occur between self and

Figure 3. Suicide Rates (Actual and Predicted) and Population Changes, 15–24 year olds, United States, 1933–2000.
Sources of data: Holinger, Offer, and Zola 1988.

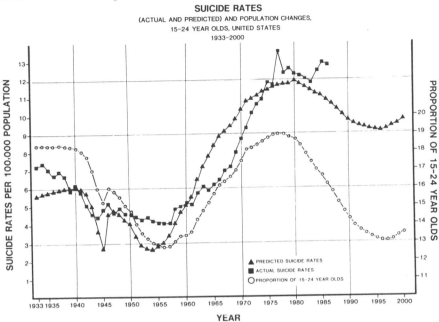

SUICIDE RATES
(ACTUAL AND PREDICTED) AND POPULATION CHANGES,
15–24 YEAR OLDS, UNITED STATES
1933–2000

object in disorders of early development, Kohut began to develop the selfobject concept, or, in order to focus on the internal aspects, selfobject function. The selfobject concept involves the need to provide the organism with functions that it cannot provide for itself. For the infant, this involves providing various physiologic needs such as feeding, changing, temperature regulation, and the "gleam-in-the-eye" admiring—ultimately, of course, these needs become increasingly psychological in nature. Particularly important are the capacities for self-soothing, tension regulation, and self-esteem regulation, which hopefully will become increasingly internalized and less dependent on, and subject to, the external world. Of course, many patients—and perhaps particularly those who become suicidal—do not have these functions internalized, and this leads to a variety of clinical phenomena. For example, one often sees in suicidal patients decreased tension regulation and self-soothing capacities. Rapid regressions and fragmentation occur in the face of frustrations, slights, and failures, as patients suffer disruptions in their narcissistic homeostasis. Rather than guilt and the defense of repression that one encounters in oedipal or psychoneurotic disorders, one sees extreme self-esteem vulnerability—disavowal is the defense, and the overwhelming affect is massive shame and humiliation (Basch 1985). Mortification is perhaps a good term—with its root word meaning death—to convey the horrible sinking feeling, isolation, and despair that these people suffer.

In addition to aiding one clinically, self psychology and the work of Kohut, Basch, Goldberg, and others also enhances the understanding of the impact of demographic shifts on the epidemiology of violent deaths. For example, when an unusually large cohort exists, as happened among adolescents from the late 1950s to the late 1970s, the entire system appears stressed and overburdened on a number of different levels of abstraction. Parents have too many children, schools have too many pupils, businesses have too many job applicants, and the mental health care system too many patients. In these instances, it is the psychologically vulnerable child who will become increasingly at risk due to the increased numbers—those whose compromised internal capacities for tension and self-esteem regulation will increasingly cause them distress as the environment is less and less able to provide the external sources of self-esteem and other needs that might aid in preventing a suicidal outcome. As the number of adolescents increases, there are only a relatively fixed number of athletic positions, academic honors, teacher and parent time, jobs, and so on that might be utilized by those adolescents whose psychological structure is such that they are excessively dependent upon the external world to fulfill their various selfobject needs. All is not lost, however. The intrapsychic work by Kohut (1971, 1977, 1984), infant development research (e.g., Stern 1985), studies on large and small schools by Barker and Gump (1964, 1968), and the epidemiologic investigations noted above all help to better understand the demographic pressures, and suggest a promising variety of intervention and prevention strategies (e.g., see Rosenberg, et al. 1987).

REFERENCES

Barker, R.G. 1968. *Ecological psychology*. Stanford, CA: Stanford University Press.

Barker, R.G. and P.V. Gump. 1964. *Big school, small school*. Stanford, CA: Stanford University Press.

Basch, M.F. 1985. Interpretation. In A. Goldberg, ed., *Progress in self psychology, volume 1*. New York: Guilford.

Brenner, M.H. 1971. *Time series analysis of relationships between selected economic and social indicators*. Springfield, VA: National Technical Information Service.

Brenner, M.H. 1979. Mortality and the national economy. *Lancet* 1:568–73.

Durkheim, E. 1897. *Le Suicide*. Paris: Felix Alcan.

Easterlin, R.A. 1980. *Birth and fortune*. New York: Basic Books.

Gedo, J. and A. Goldberg. 1973. *Models of the mind*. Chicago: University of Chicago Press.

Hendin, H. 1982. *Suicide in America*. New York: Norton.

Holford, T.R. 1983. The estimation of age, period and cohort effects for vital rates. *Biometrics* 39:1311–24.

Holinger, P.C. 1987. *Violent deaths in the United States*. New York: Guilford.

Holinger, P.C. and E.H. Klemen. 1982. Violent deaths in the United States, 1900–1975. *Social Science & Medicine* 16:1929–38.

Holinger, P.C. and D. Offer. 1982. Prediction of adolescent suicide. *American Journal of Psychiatry* 139:302–307.

Holinger, P.C. and D. Offer. 1984. Toward the prediction of violent deaths among the young. In H.S. Sudak, A.B. Ford and N.B. Rushforth, eds., *Suicide in the young*. Boston: John Wright.

Holinger, P.C., D. Offer and E. Ostrov. 1987. Suicide and homicide in the United States. *American Journal of Psychiatry* 144:215–19.

Holinger, P.C., D. Offer and M. Zola. 1988. A prediction model of suicide among youth. *Journal of Nervous & Mental Disease* 176:275–79.

Injury in America. 1985. Washington, DC: National Academy Press. Institute of Medicine. Discussion summary from workshop on forecasting stress-related social problems. National Academy of Sciences, Washington, DC, September 1985.

Kavka, J. 1976. The suicide of Richard Cory. *Annual of Psychoanalysis, Volume 4*. New York: International Universities Press.

Klebba, A.J. 1975. Homicide trends in the United States, 1900–1974. *Public Health Reports* 90:195–204.

Kohut, H. 1977. *The restoration of the self.* New York: International Universities Press.

Kohut, H. 1971. *The analysis of the self.* New York: International Universities Press.

Kohut, H. 1984. *How does analysis cure?* Chicago: University of Chicago Press.

Murphy, G.E. and R.D. Wetzel. 1980. Suicide risk by birth cohort in the United States, 1949–1974. *Archives of General Psychiatry* 37:519–23.

Reiser, D.E. 1986. Self psychology and the problem of suicide. In A. Goldberg, ed., *Progress in self-psychology, Volume 2*. New York: Guilford.

Rosenberg, M.L., R.J. Gelles and P.C. Holinger. 1987. Violence. *American Journal of Preventive Medicine* 3 (supplement to #5):164–78.

Solomon, M.I. and C.P. Hellon. 1980. Suicide and age in Alberta, Canada, 1951–1977. *Archives of General Psychiatry* 37:511–13.

Stern, D.N. 1985. *The interpersonal world of the infant.* New York: Basic Books.

Weiss, N.S. 1976. Recent trends in violent deaths among young adults in the United States. *American Journal of Epidemiology* 103:416–22.

Wolfgang, M.E. 1958. *Patterns of criminal homicide.* Philadelphia: University of Pennsylvania Press.

3

Possible Biologic Determinants of Suicide

Alec Roy

A great deal is known about the social and psychiatric determinants of suicide. In recent years there has been a growing literature suggesting that there may also be biological and genetic determinants of suicidal behavior. This literature is less well known. The purpose of this chapter is to review these areas.

ARE THERE BIOLOGIC RISK FACTORS FOR SUICIDE?

Serotonin

The first study of central monoamine metabolites in patients exhibiting suicidal behaviors was by Asberg et al. (1976). They found a bimodal distribution of levels of the serotonin metabolite 5-hydroxy-indoleacetic acid (5-HIAA) in the lumbar cerebrospinal fluid (CSF) of 68 depressed patients. van Praag and Korf (1971) had made a similar observation. Asberg et al. made the observation that significantly more of the depressed patients in the "low" CSF 5-HIAA group had attempted suicide in comparison with those in the "high" CSF 5-HIAA group (Figure 1). This led to the proposal by Asberg et al. that low CSF 5-HIAA levels may be associated with suicidal behavior.

Subsequently Brown et al. (1979, 1982), in two studies of personality disordered individuals, also found that patients with a history of suicidal behavior had significantly lower CSF 5-HIAA levels than patients without such a history. Since then other studies in personality disordered, schizophrenic, and depressed patients have also reported an association between low levels of CSF 5-HIAA and aggressive and suicidal behaviors, though there have also been negative reports (reviewed in Asberg et al. 1986) (Table 1).

It is of note that low CSF 5-HIAA levels have been found to be particularly associated with violent suicide attempts. In fact, Traskman et al. (1981) reported that CSF 5-HIAA levels were significantly lower only among those patients who had made a violent suicide attempt (hanging, drowning, shooting, gassing,

Figure 1. Suicidal acts in relation to 5-HIAA in CSF. Suicide attempts with sedative drugs (circles); attempts with other means (squares). Patients died from suicide (crosses). From Asberg, M., L. Traskman, and P. Thoren, (1976) 5-HIAA in the cerebrospinal suicide predictor. *Archives of General Psychiatry* 33:93–97.

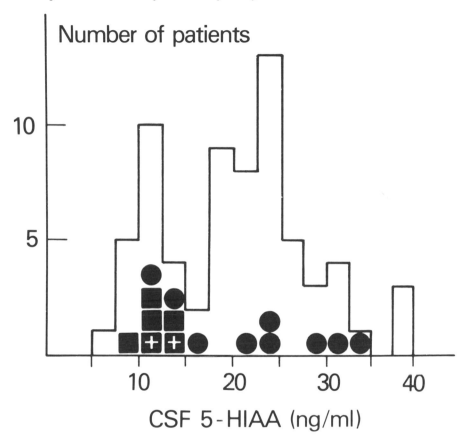

Table 3-1: STUDIES OF CSF 5-HIAA IN RELATION TO SUICIDAL BEHAVIOR

Author	Subjects	Measure of Suicidality	Result
Asberg et al (1976)	68 hospitalized depressed patients	Attempted or completed suicide within index illness episode	Low 5-HIAA in the 15 attempters

Table 3-1 (continued)

Agren (1980)	33 depressed patients	SADS suicidality scale scores	Negative correlation with 5-HIAA and MHPG
Traskman et al (1981)	30 suicide attempters (8 depressed, 22 other psychiatric disorders excluding schizophrenia and alcoholism), 45 healthy controls	Recent attempted or completed suicide	5-HIAA lower in attempters than in controls, HVA lower in depressed attempters only
Leckman et al (1981)	132 psychiatric patients	Nurses ratings of suicidal tendencies	Negative correlations with 5-HIAA
Brown et al (1978)	12 patients with borderline personality disorder	Lifetime history of suicide	Lower 5-HIAA in the 5 attempters
van Praag (1982)	203 depressed patients	Recent suicide attempt	Lower CSF 5-HIAA after probenecid in the 54 suicide attempters
Palanappian et al (1983)	40 hospitalized depressed patients	Suicide item in the Hamilton Rating Scale	Negative correlation with CSF 5-HIAA and HVA
Agren (1983)	110 depressed patients	SADS suicidality scale	Negative correlation to CSF 5-HIAA and MHPG
Roy-Byrne et al (1983)	32 bipolar, 13 unipolar patients in different phases of illness	Lifetime history of suicide attempt	No association with 5-HIAA
Banki et al (1983)	141 female inpatients (36 depressed, 46 schizophrenic, 35 alcoholic, 24 with adjustment disorder; 45 previously reported)	Recent suicide attempt	Negative correlation with 5-HIAA in all diagnostic groups; inconsistent relationship to HVA

van Praag (1983)	10 nondepressed who attempted suicide in response to imperative hallucinations, 10 non-suicidal schizophrenics, 10 controls	Recent suicide attempt	Lower CSF 5-HIAA after probenecid in suicide attempters
Peres de los Cobos et al (1984)	21 depressed patients	Suicide attempt, suicidal ideation rated on the Hamilton Scale and the AMDP system	More attempts and higher suicidality scores in patients with low 5-HIAA
Ninan et al (1984)	8 suicidal, 8 non-suicidal patients, matched for age and sex	Lifetime history of suicide attempt	Lower 5-HIAA in suicidal patients
Roy et al (1986)	26 who had attempted compared with 26 who had not	Lifetime history of suicide attempt	No association with 5-HIAA, HVA or MHPG

From Asberg, M., Nordstrom, P., Traskman-Bendz, L. (1986) Biological factors in suicide. In Roy, A. (Ed.). Suicide, Williams and Wilkins.

several deep cuts), and that levels were not reduced among those who had made a nonviolent suicide attempt (i.e., overdosage) (Figure 2). More recently Banki et al. (1983) also found among 141 psychiatric patients suffering from depression, schizophrenia, alcoholism, or adjustment disorder that levels of CSF 5-HIAA were significantly lower in the violent suicide attempters in all four diagnostic categories.

Dopamine

Some studies have also reported lower CSF levels of the dopamine metabolite homovanillic acid (HVA) among patients who have attempted suicide. Traskman et al. (1981) reported that both violent and nonviolent suicide attempts were associated with significantly lower levels of both CSF 5-HIAA and CSF HVA in comparison with controls (Figure 3). Their depressed suicide attempters showed the lowest CSF levels of 5-HIAA and HVA but the greatest reduction was in fact found with levels of CSF HVA, which showed a reduction of almost 50 percent when compared to controls. As the reduction of CSF HVA levels was significantly greater among their depressed attempters, but not among non-

Figure 2.

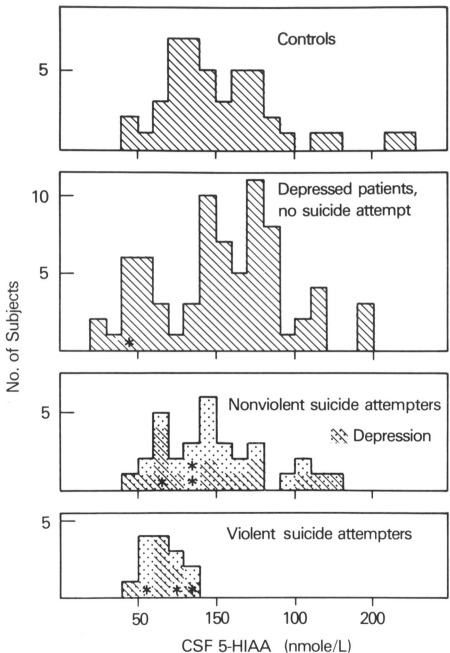

Figure 3. 45
Upper figure:
Differences in CSF monoamine levels (adjusted for age and height) between controls
and violent and nonviolent suicide attempters. Symbols indicate significance levels of
differences from mean of controls at following levels: minus sign, P > .05 asterisk,
P < .05; and three asterisks, P < .001. 5-HIAA indicates 5-hydrocyindoleacetic acid;
HVA homovanillic acid; and MHPG 3-methoxy-4-hydroxy-phenylglycol.
Lower figure:
Differences in CSF monoamine levels (adjusted for age and height) between controls and
depressed and nondepressed suicide attempters. Symbols and abbreviations as explained
above.
From Traskman et al. (1981) Monoamine metabolites in CSF and suicidal behavior.
Archives of General Psychiatry 38: 631–36.

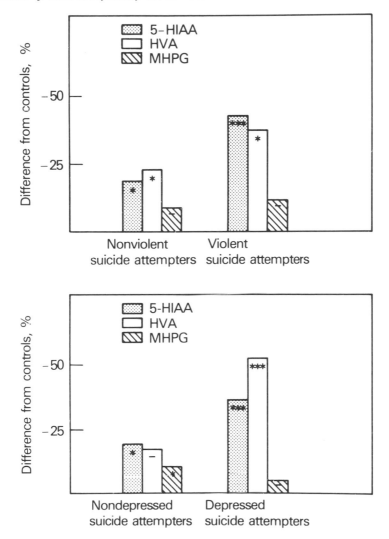

depressed attempters, Traskman et al. suggested that low CSF HVA levels may be more related to depression than to suicide behavior.

Agren (1983) also reported that low CSF HVA levels were associated with the potential lethality of past suicide attempts made by depressed patients and that the contribution of CSF 5-HIAA was quite minimal in comparison to that of CSF HVA. Thus, Agren concluded that CSF HVA levels were even stronger than CSF 5-HIAA levels in explaining past suicidal behavior in depressed patients. Roy et al. (1986) reported similar results. Montgomery and Montgomery (1982) also found a highly significant relationship between CSF HVA levels and a history of attempting suicide ($p < 0.001$) and that the relationship with low CSF 5-HIAA levels was less strong ($p < 0.05$) (Figure 4).

Postmortem Studies

Over the years most postmortem studies of the brains of suicide victims have focused on the serotonin system. Some, but not all, of the neurochemical studies have reported modest decreases in serotonin itself, or of its metabolite 5-HIAA, in either the brain stem or frontal cortex. The few studies that have examined norepinephrine, dopamine, or its metabolite homovanillic acid have tended to be negative (reviewed in Stanley et al. 1986). There have been few postmortem brain studies of the enzymes involved in catecholamine metabolism. No changes in monoamine oxidase (MAO) activity have been reported (reviewed in Mann et al. 1986).

Four of five postmortem brain receptor studies, using ^3H imipramine as the ligand, have reported significant decreases in the presynaptic binding of this ligand to serotonin neurones in suicide victims (reviewed in Stanley et al. 1986). Stanley and Mann (1983), using ^3H spiroperidol as the ligand, have also reported a significant increase in postsynaptic $5\text{-}HT_2$ binding sites among suicide victims who used violent methods to end their lives.

Taken together these postmortem neurochemical and receptor studies tend to support the hypothesis that diminished central serotonin metabolism (as evidenced by reduced presynaptic imipramine binding, reduced levels of 5HT and 5-HIAA, and up-regulation of the postsynaptic $5HT_2$ receptor) is assciated with suicide. However, most of these studies do not compare suicide victims with depressed patients who have died for reasons other than suicide. Thus, the possibility exists that abnormality of central serotonin metabolism found in postmortem studies of suicide victims may apply to depressive illness in general. Also, Mann et al. (1987) recently reported a significant increase in beta adrenergic receptor binding in the frontal cortex of suicide victims (Figure 5).

Violent Offenders

The relationship of low CSF 5-HIAA levels to behavior has been further explored by Linnoila et al. (1983). They examined CSF 5-HIAA levels among 36

Figure 4. Upper figure:
Distribution of CSF HVA in 49 depressed patients.
Lower figure:
Distribution of CSF 5-HIAA in 49 depressed patients.
From Montgomery, S. and D. Montgomery. (1982) Pharmacological prevention of suicidal behavior. *Journal of Affective Disorder* 4:291–98.

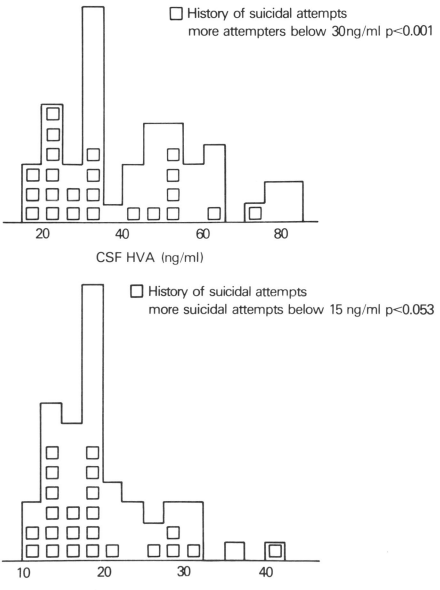

Figure 5. Postmortem Beta-adrenergic binding in frontal cortices of suicide victims. Binding was measured using tritiated dihydroalprenolol. Suicide group differed significantly from controls (P < .05) using two-tailed t test and Mann-Whitney test. From Mann et al. (1987) *Archives of General Psychiatry.*

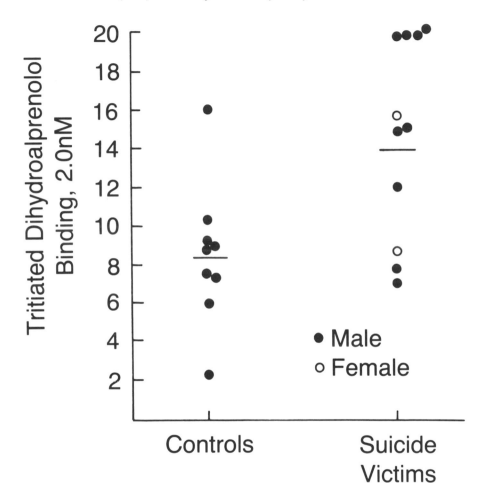

male murderers and attempted murderers undergoing an intensive one to two month court ordered forensic psychiatry evaluation. Impulsiveness was defined by the characteristics of the index crime. Patients with a clear premeditation of their act were classified as nonimpulsive while patients without established premeditation (attacking without provocation and not knowing the victim) were classified as impulsive. The source of this information was the police report concerning the index crime. Using this method, 9 of these 36 violent offenders were classified as nonimpulsive and 27 as impulsive.

Psychiatric diagnoses in the violent offenders were made according to DSM III criteria by a forensic psychiatrist who was not blind to the criminal records of the patients. The impulsive patients had either intermittent explosive or antisocial personality disorder, whereas the nonimpulsive patients had either paranoid or passive aggressive personality disorder. The authors found that CSF 5-HIAA levels were significantly lower among the two groups of impulsive violent offenders than among the nonimpulsive violent offenders.

Also, the 17 offenders (14 impulsive and 3 nonimpulsive) who had committed more than one violent crime had CSF 5-HIAA levels significantly lower than those found among offenders who had committed only one violent crime (mean 67.9 ± 12.1 vs 87.1 ± 23.7 nM, $p < 0.02$). Furthermore, the violent offenders who at some time had attempted suicide were found to have significantly lower CSF 5-HIAA levels than the violent offenders who had never attempted suicide.

Arsonists

In a later study Virkkunen et al. (1987) performed lumbar punctures on 20 male arsonists also undergoing intensive forensic evaluation. Impulsive fire setters were studied because they show relatively little interpersonal aggressive behavior. This allowed an examination of whether low CSF 5-HIAA levels are primarily associated with impulsivity or aggressivity. Impulsiveness in these patients was defined as a sudden uncontrollable urge to set a fire. Arsonists setting fires for economic gain, such as insurance fraud, were excluded from the sample.

The arsonists were matched for age, height, and sex with a subgroup of the previously studied violent offenders and they were also compared with 10 normal controls. The results showed that CSF 5-HIAA levels were significantly lower among the arsonists than among the other two groups. When subjects who had made past violent suicide attempts were excluded from the groups, the arsonists again showed significantly lower CSF 5-HIAA levels than the other two groups.

All of the arsonists also met DSM III criteria for borderline personality disorder and many of them had exhibited occasional explosive behavior. Virkkunen et al. also noted that among the arsonists the motive of revenge was not significantly associated with low CSF 5-HIAA levels and, furthermore, that the arsonists did not consider themselves to be aggressive.

The results of these studies of violent offenders and arsonists have led to the hypothesis that low CSF 5-HIAA levels may be associated with poor impulse control. Although CSF 5-HIAA levels are an imprecise indicator of brain serotonin turnover we, and others, have speculated that some individuals may have a defect in their central serotonin metabolism that manifests itself in poor impulse control leading to either attempts at suicide or violence toward others (Roy et al. 1986a,b; 1987a,b; 1988a).

ARE THERE GENETIC RISK FACTORS FOR SUICIDE?

There are five lines of evidence about the possibility that there may be genetic factors in suicide. There are data from clinical, twin, Iowa 500, Amish, and Copenhagen adoption studies.

Clinical studies

Pitts and Winokur (1983) found that among 748 consecutively admitted patients, 37 reported a possible or definite suicide in a first-degree relative (4.9 percent). In 25 of these 37 cases (68 percent) the diagnosis was an affective disorder. The statistical probability of this distribution occurring by chance was less than 0.02. When the probable diagnosis in the cases of the first-degree relatives who committed suicide were considered, in 24 of the 37 patient-relative pairings both members had affective disorders. Pitts and Winokur estimated that 79 percent of the suicides of the first-degree relatives were associated with probable affective disorder.

Roy (1983) found that a family history of suicide significantly increased the risk of a suicide attempt in a wide variety of diagnostic groups. Almost half (48.6 percent) of the 243 patients with a family history of suicide had themselves attempted suicide. More than half (56.4 percent) of all the patients with a family history of suicide had a primary diagnosis of an affective disorder and more than a third (34.6 percent) had a recurrent unipolar or bipolar affective disorder. Linkowski et al (1985) found that 123 of 713 depressed patients (17 percent) had a first- or second-degree relative who had committed suicide. A family history of suicide significantly increased the risk for a violent suicide attempt. Linkowski et al. concluded that "A positive family history for violent suicide should be considered as a strong predictor of active suicide attempting behavior in major depressive illness."

Among suicide attempters with a primary diagnosis of primary affective disorder Murphy and Wetzel (1982) found that 17 percent had a family history of suicide and 17 percent a family history of suicide attempts. As individuals with affective disorders comprise a larger proportion of suicides than individuals with personality disorders, Murphy and Wetzel predicted that more of their patients with affective disorder could be expected to present a significant suicide risk in the future. Therefore, they concluded that a "systematic family history of such behavior coupled with modern clinical diagnosis would prove useful in identifying those attempters at increased risk for suicide."

Twin studies

Haberlandt (1967) pooled the accumulated data from twin studies from different countries. Of the 149 sets of twins where one twin was known to have committed suicide, there were 9 sets of twins where both twins had committed suicide. All of these 9 twin pairs were identical twins: there was no set of fraternal twins concordant for suicide (P < 0.0001). In 3 of the 9 pairs the twins were also concordant for manic-depression.

Iowa 500 study

In a recent follow-up study, Tsuang (1983) found that the first-degree relatives of the psychiatric patients in the Iowa 500 study had a risk of suicide almost eight times greater than the risk in the relatives of normal controls. The risk of suicide was significantly greater among the first-degree relatives of depressed patients than it was among the relatives of either schizophrenic or manic patients. Among the first-degree relatives of the psychiatric patients who had committed suicide the suicide risk was four times greater than the risk in the relatives of patients who did not commit suicide. The suicide risk was equally high among the relatives of both depressed and manic patients.

The Amish study

Egeland and Sussex (1985) reported on the suicide data obtained from the study of affective disorders among the Old Order Amish community of Lancaster County in southeast Pennsylvania. Several of the important social risk factors for suicide among individuals in the general population such as unemployment, divorced or separated marital status, social isolation, and alcoholism are not commonly found among these Amish.

Twenty-four of the 26 suicide victims over the 100 years from 1880 to 1980 met RDC criteria for a major affective disorder. Eight of the suicide victims had bipolar I, 4 bipolar II, and 12 unipolar affective disorder. A further case met diagnostic criteria for a minor depression. Furthermore, most of the suicide victims had a heavy family loading for affective disorders. For example, among the 8 bipolar I suicide victims the morbidity risk for affective disorders among their 110 first-degree relatives was 29 percent compared with the 1 to 4 percent found among the general population.

Almost three quarters of the 26 suicide victims were found to cluster in four family pedigrees, each of which contained a heavy loading for affective disorders and suicide (Figures 6 and 7). Interestingly, the converse was not true as there were other family pedigrees with heavy loadings for affective disorder but without suicides. It is also of note that morbidity risk for affective disorders among 170 first-degree relatives in other bipolar I pedigrees without suicide was similar to that found in bipolar pedigrees with suicide, also in the 20 percent range. Thus, a family loading for affective disorders was not in itself a predictor for suicide.

Egeland and Sussex concluded that "Our study replicates findings that

52

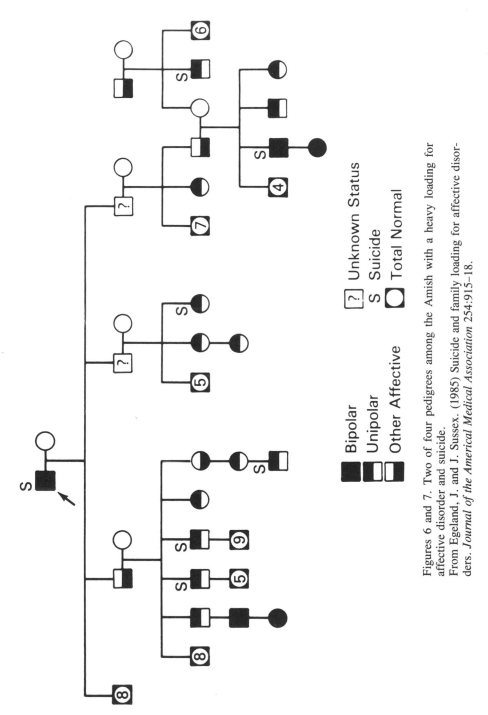

Figures 6 and 7. Two of four pedigrees among the Amish with a heavy loading for affective disorder and suicide.

From Egeland, J. and J. Sussex. (1985) Suicide and family loading for affective disorders. *Journal of the American Medical Association* 254:915–18.

Bipolar
Unipolar
Other Affective

? Unknown Status
S Suicide
○ Total Normal

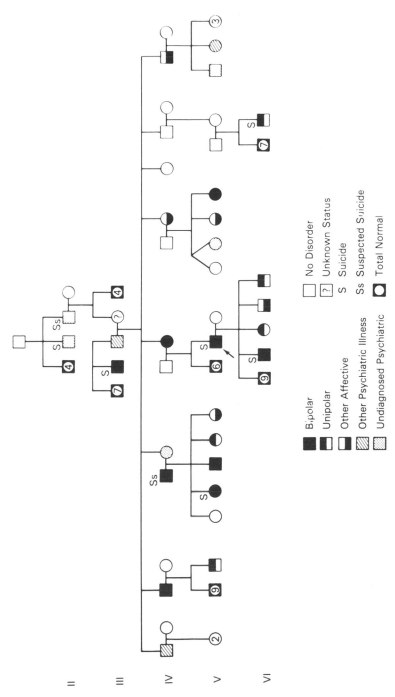

indicate an increased suicidal risk for patients with a diagnosis of major affective disorder and a strong family history of suicide. The number not receiving adequate treatment for manic-depressive illness (among the suicides) supports the common belief that intervention for these patients at risk is recommended.'' Also ''It appears most warranted in those families in which there is a family history of suicide. The clustering of suicides in Amish pedigrees follows the distribution of affective illness in the kinship and suggests the role of inheritance.''

Danish-American Adoption Studies

The strongest evidence for the presence of genetic factors in suicide comes from the adoption studies carried out in Denmark by Schulsinger et al. (1979). The Psykologisk Institut has a register of the 5,483 adoptions that occurred in greater Copenhagen between 1924 and 1947. A screening of the registers of causes of death revealed that 57 of these adoptees eventually committed suicide. They were matched with adopted controls for age, sex, social class of the adopting parents, and time spent both with their biological relatives and in institutions before being adopted. Searches of the causes of death revealed that 12 of the 269 biological relatives of these 57 adopted suicides had themselves committed suicide, compared with only 3 of the 269 biological relatives of the 57 adopted controls (P $<$ 0.01). None of the adopting relatives of either the suicide or control group had committed suicide.

Wender et al. (1986) went on to study the 71 adoptees identified by the psychiatric case register as having suffered from an affective disorder. They were matched with 71 control adoptees without affective disorder. Significantly more of the biological relatives of the adoptees with affective suicide disorder had committed suicide than their controls. It was particularly adoptee suicide victims with the diagnosis of ''affect reaction'' who had significantly more biological relatives who had committed suicide than controls. This diagnosis is used in Denmark to describe an individual who has affective symptoms accompanying a situational crisis that is often an impulsive suicide attempt. These findings led Kety (1986) to suggest that a genetic factor in suicide may be an inability to control impulsive behavior that has its effect independently of, or addictively to, psychiatric disorder. Affective disorder or environmental stress may serve ''as potentiating mechanisms which foster or trigger the impulsive behavior, directing it toward a suicidal outcome.''

CONCLUSION

Suicide, like so much else in psychiatry, tends to run in families. The family member who has committed suicide may serve as a role model to identify with when the option of committing suicide becomes one possible solution to intolerable psychological pain. However, the family, twin, Amish, and adoption studies reviewed here suggest that there may be genetic factors in suicide. In many suicide victims these will be genetic factors involved in the genetic transmission of manic-depression. However, the Copenhagen adoption studies strongly suggest there may be a genetic factor for suicide independent of, or additive to, the genetic transmission of affective disorder. Kety's suggestion that this may be an inability to control impulsive behavior is compatible with the data reviewed earlier, suggesting that diminished central serotonin turnover may be associated with poor impulse control.

REFERENCES

Bushsbaum, M., R. Coursey and D. Murphy. 1976. The biochemical high-risk paradigm: Behavioral and familial correlates of low platelet monoamine oxidase activity. *Science* 194:339–41.

Egeland, J. and J. Sussex. 1985. Suicide and family loading for affective disorders. *Journal of the American Medical Association* 254:915–18.

Haberland, W. 1967. Aportacion a al genetica del suicido. *Folia Clinica International* 17:319–22.

Kety, S. 1986. Genetic factors in suicide. In A. Roy, ed., *Suicide*. Baltimore, MD: Williams and Wilkins.

Leckman, J., D. Charney, C. Nelson, G. Heninger and M. Bowers. 1981. CSF tryptophan, 5-HIAA and HVA in 132 patients characterized by diagnosis and clinical state. *Recent Advances in Neuropsychopharmacology* 31:289–97.

Linkowski, P., V. de Maertelaer and J. Mendlewicz. 1985. Suicidal behavior in major depressive illness. *Acta Psychiatrica Scandinavia* 72:233–38.

Montgomery, S. and D. Montgomery. 1982. Pharmacological prevention of suicidal behavior. *Journal of Affective Disorders* 4:291–98.

Oreland, L., A. Wiberg, M. Asberg, L. Traskman, L. Sjostrand, P. Thoren, L. Bertilsson and G. Tybring. 1981. Platelet MAO activity and monoamine metabolites in cerebrospinal fluid in depressed and suicidal patients and in healthy controls. *Psychiatry Research* 4:21–29.

Palaniappan, V., V. Ramachandran and O. Somasundaram. 1983. Suicidal ideation and biogenic amines in depression. *Indian Journal of Psychiatry* 25:286–92.

Pitts, F. and G. Winokur. 1964. Affective disorder. Part 3 (Diagnostic correlates and incidence of suicide). *Journal of Nervous and Mental Disease* 139:176–81.

Roy, A. 1983. Family history of suicide. *Archives of General Psychiatry* 40:971–74.

Roy, A. 1986. Genetics of Suicide. *Annals of the New York Academy of Sciences* 487:97–105.

Roy-Byrne, P., R. Post, D. Rubinow, M. Linnoila, R. Savard and D. Davis. 1983. CSF 5-HIAA and personal and family history of suicide in affectively ill patients: A negative study. *Psychiatry Research* 10:263–74.

Schulsinger, F., S. Kety, D. Rosenthal, and P. Wender. 1979. A family study of suicide. In M. Schov and E. Stromgren, eds., *Origin, prevention and treatment of affective disorders*. London: Academic Press, 227–87.

Traskman, L., M. Asberg, L. Bertilsson and L. Sjostrand. 1981. Monoamine metabolites in CSF and suicidal behavior. *Archives of General Psychiatry* 38:631–36.

Tsuang, M. 1983. Risk of suicide in the relatives of schizophrenics, manics, depressives, and controls. *Journal of Clinical Psychiatry* 44:396–400.

van Praag, H.M. 1982. CSF 5-HIAA and suicide in non-depressed schizophrenics. *Lancet* I:977–78.

van Praag, H.M. 1982. Depression, suicide and the metabolism of serotonin in the brain. *Journal of Affective Disorders* 4:275–90.

Wender, P., S. Kety, D. Rosenthal, F. Schulsinger, J. Ortmann and I. Lunde. 1986. Psychiatric disorders in the biological and adoptive families of adopted individuals with affective disorders. *Archives of General Psychiatry* 43:923–29.

4

Serotonin And Suicide: A Functional/ Dimensional Viewpoint

Martin L. Korn, Serena-Lynn Brown, Alan Apter and Herman M. van Praag

In the 1950s, a new era in psychiatric research began with the introduction of several new distinct classes of pharmacological agents efficacious in the treatment of previously refractory psychiatric disorders. Such drugs included the neuroleptics for the treatment of psychotic disorders, and the tricyclic antidepressants and the monoamine oxidase inhibitors for the treatment of depression. While these drugs were employed in the treatment of diverse psychiatric illnesses, all were soon demonstrated to exert specific effects on central nervous system (CNS) monoamines such as noradrenaline (NA), dopamine (DA) and serotonin (5-hydroxytryptamine; 5-HT). Since that time, a major methodological thrust of research in biological psychiatry has involved the attempt to identify biological variables (and in particular monoamine dysfunctions) corresponding to well-delineated psychiatric syndromes. For example, 5-HT has been implicated in the pathogenesis of the affective disorders (van Praag et al. 1970), anxiety disorders (Kahn et al. 1988), schizophrenia (Bleich et al. 1988) and obsessive compulsive disorder (Zohar et al. 1987), among other syndromes, leading to a "serotonergic hypothesis" for each of these disorders.

The proliferation of evidence indicating 5-HT dysfunction in these heterogeneous syndromes has lead some to characterize such findings as nonspecific and chaotic (van Kammen 1987). We believe otherwise. We have previously argued (van Praag and Leijnse 1965; van Praag et al. 1975, 1987, 1988) that the near-exclusive reliance of biological psychiatric research on a nosological/syndromal model is too restricted and should be complemented by a functional/dimensional approach. The tenets of that approach can be defined as follows: (1) Psychological dysfunctions are to be considered as the elementary units of classification in psychopathology; (2) Psychiatric diagnosis is a two-tiered process—first, determination of a syndrome, and next, dissection of that syndrome into the constituent psychological dysfunctions; and (3) In biological psychiatric re-

57

search, correlations between psychological and biological dysfunctions should be sought for.

The frequently replicated finding of decreased CSF 5-hydroxyindoleacetic acid (5-HIAA), the major metabolite of 5-HT, in suicide attempters irrespective of psychiatric diagnoses supports the validity of this approach. This chapter will trace the evolution of our understanding of 5-HT disturbances in suicide and will present a reinterpretation of those data employing a functional/dimensional approach.

Serotonin and Suicide

Van Praag et al. (1970) reported that depressives exhibited decreased baseline 5-HIAA as well as diminished post-probenecid 5-HIAA accumulation in CSF, suggesting a decrease in CNS 5-HT metabolism in these individuals. Those patients with lowered 5-HIAA predominated the group of so-called "vital depressives" (van Praag et al. 1965), a syndrome that is closely analogous to the DSM-III diagnosis of major depression-melancholic type. Low 5-HIAA subjects, however, could not be distinguished symptomatically from vital depressives with normal levels, and in "neurotic" depressives a decrement in 5-HIAA levels was less prevalent. Several other groups have confirmed this association with and without the use of probenecid (Asberg et al. 1984; Traskman et al. 1984), lending support to the notion that 5-HT is involved in mood disturbances.

Asberg et al. (1976) demonstrated a bimodal distribution of CSF 5-HIAA in depressed patients that differed from the normative distribution of the metabolite observed in controls. Moreover, they demonstrated that depressives with and without lowering of CSF 5-HIAA were distinguishable in that the low 5-HIAA group had a significantly higher incidence of suicidal acts compared to depressives with normal 5-HIAA (40 percent vs. 15 percent). When the data was further analyzed to distinguish so-called violent attempts (hanging or drowning) from nonviolent attempts (drug overdose and superficial wrist cutting), violent suicides were confined to the low group. Two eventually successful suicides were both in the low-metabolite group, suggesting that this biological variable might serve as predictor of suicidal behavior.

There have been a number of replications and extensions of this original finding (see Table 4.1). Banki and Arato (1983) looked at 62 female inpatients with major depression, schizophrenia, and alcohol dependence as well as other disorders and found that CSF 5-HIAA was diminished in violent suicide attempters as compared with both nonviolent suicide attempters and nonattempters. This effect was independent of primary diagnosis. Asberg et al. (1981) reported on a prospective study involving patients of several diagnoses with a history of a suicide attempt. Of those patients with low 5-HIAA, 22 percent eventually committed suicide. This was markedly greater than the 2 percent suicide rate found in all patients admitted to the intensive care unit with a suicide attempt. van Praag (1982) looked at 203 patients with depression of varying symptomatology and found an increased number of suicide attempts in the low CSF 5-HIAA group. The number of violent suicides was not increased in the low 5-HIAA group. Oreland et al. (1981) also found diminished 5-HIAA in depressed and nondepressed suicide attempters, as did Traskman et al. (1981). Traskman et al. (1981)—but not Oreland et al. (1981)—noted an association with violent but not nonviolent attempts. Lopez-Ibor et al. (1985) similarly found decreased CSF 5-HIAA in depressed inpatients with suicide attempts as did Palaniappan et al. (1983). Vestergaard et al. (1978) as well as Roy-Byrne et al. (1983) were unable, however, to confirm a relationship between 5-HIAA and suicide.

Table 4.1: CSF 5-HIAA in Suicide Attempters (SA) Positive Studies

Investigator	Subjects	CSF 5-HIAA
Asberg et al. 1976	68 Depressed	Decreased in violent SA
Agren 1980	33 Bipolar & Unipolar	Unipolar-negative correlation with SA; bipolar-no correlation with SA
Asberg et al. 1981	148 Depressed	22% succesful SA within 1 year in low 5-HIAA patients
Banki et al. 1981	33 Depressed females	Increased suicidal behavior in low 5-HIAA patients
Traskman et al. 1981	8 Depressed & 22 non-depressed SA	Low in violent attempters
Oreland et al. 1981	19 Depressed & non-depressed SA	Low in SA compared to depressed non-SA & normal controls
van Praag 1982	203 Depressed	Low in SA; violent attempters evenly distributed
Agren 1983	110 Depressed unipolar & bipolar	Negative correlation with past SA in unipolar but not bipolar
Banki and Arato 1983	62 Inpatients with mixed diagnoses	Decreased in violent SA
Palaniappan et al. 1983	40 Depressed	Low in SA

Table 4.1 (continued)

Ninan et al. 1984	8 Schizophrenic SA	Low compared to non-suicidal schizophrenics
Lopez-Ibor et al. 1985	21 Depressed	Low in SA
Vestergaard et al. 1979	56 Unipolar & bipolar	No difference between high and low groups
Roy-Byrne et al. 1983	13 Unipolar; 32 bipolar	No difference between patients with & without SA

Considering these data, several authors have suggested that diminished serotonergic function is related to a suicidal state (and, in particular, violent suicidal states) rather than to depression per se. As van Praag (1985) suggests, however, this conclusion may be premature. The relationship between suicidal behavior and depression is quite complex, with depressive features frequently being present around the time of the suicide attempt and dropping significantly after the event (van Praag and Plutchik 1985). Most studies do not take this relationship into account and measure biological parameters at varying times after the event, when the affective state could be at variance from that present at the time prior to the suicide attempt.

In order to better delineate the relationship between suicide, diagnosis, and CSF 5-HIAA, van Praag (1983) studied nondepressed schizophrenics who attempted suicide secondary to command auditory hallucinations and found 5-HIAA to be low compared to schizophrenics with no suicidal history. Ninan et al. (1984) also found that schizophrenics who made a suicide attempt demonstrated decreased 5-HIAA as compared to nonsuicidal schizophrenics. This effect was independent of depression ratings. In schizophrenics with a lifetime history of suicidal behavior who were currently not suicidal, CSF 5-HIAA has been reported as not differing from normal subjects (van Praag 1986). Those schizophrenics who reported suicidal ideation but had no history of suicide attempts also had normal CSF 5-HIAA levels. This lends support to the notion that lowered CSF 5-HIAA levels correspond to recent suicide attempts rather than to suicidal thoughts in these patients.

In affective disorders, however, the situation may be more complex. Van Praag (1986) studied 52 melancholic, nonpsychotic depressives with either a recent suicide attempt, a past history of a suicide attempt without recent suicidal behavior, or suicidal ideation with no history of attempts. In contrast to the schizophrenic group, those with a recent attempt as well as those with past attempts demonstrated depressed post-probenecid 5-HIAA levels. Those with only suicidal ideation had normal levels. The conclusion was drawn that, in affective disorders, low CSF 5-HIAA is a trait marker related to increased risk of suicidal behavior. Ideation itself was not associated with low CSF 5-HIAA levels in schizophrenics nor affectively disordered patients. Obviously, in biological suicide research, suicidal ideation, recent suicide attempts, and lifetime history of suicide attempts should not be lumped together.

In an effort to define the psychological profile of individuals with low levels of 5-HIAA in CSF, depressed and/or suicidal patients with low metabolite levels were compared to a cohort with normal 5-HIAA on the Rorshach by Rydin et al. (1982). Those with diminished 5-HIAA demonstrated increased anxiety, hostility, and difficulties handling interpersonal conflict. Banki et al. (1981) looked at 33 severely depressed female inpatients and found that low 5-HIAA correlated with increased anxiety, suicidal behavior and insomnia.

To summarize, the serotonergic system was initially implicated as involved in the pathogenesis of depression as a nosological entity. The demonstration by Asberg et al. in 1976 of low CSF 5-HIAA in depressed violent suicide attempters and the subsequent confirmation of these data in diverse patient groups by other investigators suggests that low 5-HT metabolite levels correspond to some aspects of suicidal behavior, independent of diagnostic entity. Exactly which features of the suicidal state are associated with decreased CSF 5-HIAA levels remains an area of ongoing investigation.

Since suicide is often defined as aggression turned inward, and since there appears to be a strong correlation between suicidality and aggression, the role of 5-HT in outwardly directed aggression will be considered next.

SEROTONIN AND OUTWARDLY DIRECTED AGGRESSION

5-HT has been implicated as important in several types of aggressive behavior and has been widely studied in animal aggression (for review see Valzelli 1981). In animals, Moyer (1976) has delineated seven types of aggressive behaviors: the neuroanatomical and neuropsychopharmacological substratum underlying each of these types is presumed to be different.

Research investigating the role of biological factors in aggression in humans has been difficult to carry out because of its intermittent expression, generally short duration, and the numerous intervening variables for which it is hard to control (e.g., drugs and alcohol). Despite this, there have been several recent studies implicating the serotonergic system in aggressive disorders. Brown et al. (1979) looked at 26 military men with personality disorders who were being evaluated for suitability for further service. CSF 5-HIAA correlated -0.78 with current and past histories of aggressive behavior while 3-methoxy-4- hydroxyphenylglycol (MHPG) correlated $+0.64$ with this behavior. Subjects receiving a diagnosis of a personality disorder associated with greater amounts of behavioral impulsivity (i.e. antisocial, explosive, immature, and hysterical) had lower 5-HIAA and higher MHPG than those with diagnoses corresponding to less behavioral impulsivity (i.e. passive-aggressive, passive-dependent, schizoid, obsessive-compulsive, and inadequate). Personality disordered individuals with a history of suicide attempts demonstrated decreased 5-HIAA levels compared to those with no history of suicide. In a second study, Brown et al. (1982) demonstrated negative correlations between CSF 5-HIAA and aggression scores on the MMPI as well as with a history of suicide attempts in 12 individuals diagnosed as borderline personalities.

Other studies have tended to confirm the link between 5-HIAA and increased outward directed aggression and hostility (see Table 4.2). Bioulac et al. (1980) found that XYY individuals with high aggression scores had decreased CSF 5-HIAA. Treatment with 5-HTP lead to clinical improvement. Lidberg et al. (1984) reported on three cases of individuals who demonstrated aggression toward family members, eventually murdering a child. All demonstrated low 5-HIAA levels. Lidberg et al. (1985) compared 16 men convicted of criminal homicide, 22 men who had attempted suicide, and 39 controls. Metabolite levels were reduced in both suicidal men (especially in those using violent means) and men who had killed a sexual partner. Interestingly, homicidal men who had not murdered a sexual partner had normal 5-HIAA levels. The authors suggest that this discrepancy might be explained by the degree of impulsivity or intense negative affect involved in familial homicidal acts.

Table 4.2: CSF 5-HIAA in Outwardly Directed Aggression/Impulsivity

Investigator	Subjects	CSF 5-HIAA
Brown et al. 1979	26 Mixed personality disorders	Correlation of −0.78 with history of aggression
Bioulac et al. 1980	6 Aggressive XYY patients	Decreased compared to normals, improvement with 5HTP
Brown et al. 1982	12 Borderline personality disorders	Decreased in aggressive subjects
Linnoila et al. 1983	36 Violent criminals	Low in impulsive offenders
Lidberg et al. 1984	3 SA who killed children	Low in all 3

Lidberg et al. 1985	16 Homicidal men	Low in men who had killed a sexual partner
Virkkunen et al. 1987	20 male arsonists	Low compared to violent offenders & normal controls

Linnoila (1983), in an attempt to separate out violent from impulsive behavior, studied 36 murderers and attempted murderers selected for crimes of "unusual severity." Those who had committed "impulsive murders" (i.e., without premeditation) had significantly lower levels of CSF 5-HIAA than "nonimpulsive" murderers. Multiple murderers had lower levels of 5-HIAA than single murderers and impulsive murderers with a history of suicide attempts had the lowest levels of all. All impulsive offenders had a history of disturbed childhood behavior or were judged to have met criteria for conduct disorder as a child. The authors concluded that this study supports the hypothesis that low 5-HIAA levels correspond to impulsivity rather than violence per se. Caution should be observed in interpretation of this data, however, as all of the subjects met criteria for alcohol abuse and decreased CSF 5-HIAA has been demonstrated in alcoholics shortly after intoxication as well as during abstinence (Ballenger et al. 1979.) Subsequently, Virkhunen et al. (1987) found that 20 arsonists had lower CSF 5-HIAA levels than habitually violent offenders and normal controls. Since arsonists are considered to be particularly impulsive in their criminal behavior, the authors suggest that these results lend support to the association between lowered 5-HIAA and impulsivity.

In summary, data from several studies in individuals with varying diagnoses suggest a relationship between lowered CSF 5-HIAA and problems with regulation of aggression and/or impulsivity. This effect appears to exist independently from disturbance of mood. As van Praag (1985) notes, however, a decrement in serotonergic function may be related to both disorders of mood as well as of aggression. This might offer a biological explanation for the frequently observed association between these two states.

SEROTONIN AND ANXIETY

Although evidence exists in the animal literature indicating a role for 5-HT in anxiety regulation, this area of investigation has remained relatively neglected in humans (for review see Kahn et al. 1988). There is increasing evidence, however, suggesting that 5-HT may play a role in the modulation of this affect. Treatment studies have demonstrated that 5-hydroxytryptophan (5-HTP, the immediate precursor to 5-HT) and the 5-HT reuptake inhibitor clomipramine are efficacious in the treatment of panic disorder (Kahn et al. 1987). It should be noted, however, that these agents are not 5-HT-specific, but studies are currently being conducted using more selective 5-HT reuptake inhibitors. In addition, ritanserin (a 5-HT2 receptor antagonist) and buspirone (a new anxiolytic drug that has been shown to decrease serotonergic transmission) are efficacious in the treatment of generalized anxiety disorder (Ceulemans et al. 1985; Taylor et al. 1985).

There are no studies of CSF 5-HIAA in patients with anxiety disorders. However, there is some data in other patient groups to suggest that decreased CSF 5-HIAA correlates with increased anxiety. Banki et al. (1981) found a negative association between anxiety in depressed female inpatients and CSF 5-HIAA. Low 5-HIAA was also associated with insomnia and suicidal behavior in this study. Rydin et al. (1982) compared Rorschach ratings of depressed and/or suicidal patients with low CSF 5-HIAA to matched patients with normal CSF 5-HIAA. Individuals with diminished 5-HIAA demonstrated increased anxiety in addition to hostility and difficulties handling interpersonal conflict.

Recently, using the relatively specific 5-HT receptor agonist m-chlorophenyl-piperazine (MCPP), we found behavioral (Kahn et al. 1988) as well as neuroendocrine evidence (Kahn et al. 1988) suggesting that the 5-HT receptor may be hypersensitive in panic disorder. Using the neuroendocrine challenge paradigm (Murphy et al. 1986), we were able to show increased cortisol release with the administration of oral MCPP in panic patients compared to normal controls and patients with major depression. Since MCPP is a direct 5-HT receptor agonist, and since cortisol appears to be under partial serotonergic control, this increase in cortisol release suggests that these receptors may be supersensitive in this disorder. In accordance with this hypothesis, MCPP increased anxiety levels in panic disorder and not in major depression or in normal controls. It should be noted that Charney et al. (1987), using 0.1 mg/kg MCPP administered intravenously, found no differences in cortisol release between panic disorder patients and normal controls. However, we believe that the dose employed in this study was too high to detect supersensitivity of the 5-HT receptor, since anxiety was induced in normal controls at this dosage as well.

Thus, several studies have provided evidence that 5-HT is involved in the regulation of anxiety. Recent data, in fact, suggests that 5-HT may play a central role in panic disorder. However, the specificity of these data has not yet been studied. It could very well be that this finding is dimensionally rather than nosologically specific, and that the 5-HT dysfunction will be shown to be related to the psychological dimension of anxiety rather than to a particular diagnostic entity.

RELATIONSHIPS AMONG SUICIDE, AGGRESSION, AND ANXIETY

Violence and suicide have repeatedly been shown to be closely related. Depending upon the population studied, from 7 percent to 48 percent of those patients with a history of violent behavior have also made suicide attempts in the past. This is reported to be true for psychiatric emergency room patients (Skodal and Karasu 1978), prepubertal children (Pfeffer et al. 1983), and prisoners (Plutchik et al. 1976). Inamdar et al. (1982), for example, reported on the prevalence of violent and suicidal behavior in 51 hospitalized psychotic adolescents. Of these subjects, 66.7 percent reported a history of violent behavior, 43.1 percent reported a suicidal history, and 27.5 percent had demonstrated both behaviors. Tardiff and Sweillam (1980) found that in psychiatric patients with either suicidal ideation or a recent suicide attempt, 14 percent of males and 7 percent of females had demonstrated assaultive behavior prior to admission. Weissman et al. (1973) found that a sample of female suicide attempters exhibited more overt hostility both during the psychiatric interview as well as in interpersonal relationships as compared to a matched group of nonsuicidal depressed women.

At our institution we have confirmed the robust association between suicide and violent behavior. In a diagnostically diverse group of psychiatric inpatients admitted to a large municipal hospital, 40 percent had a history of a suicide attempt, 42 percent had engaged in past violent behavior, and 23 percent had histories of both types of behavior (Plutchik et al. 1985). Ratings of impulsivity correlated $+0.43$ with suicide risk and $+0.63$ with violence risk. Although several environmental, life history, affective, and behavioral variables were found to be associated with both suicide and violence risk, partial correlations revealed some items that were differential predictors of each measure. Suicide risk was found to best be predicted by depression, hopelessness, and the number of life problems, while violence risk was best predicted by impulsivity, legal difficulties, and menstrual problems.

The relationship between anxiety and inwardly and outwardly directed aggression has received scant attention in the psychiatric literature. We recently found evidence that anxiety, suicidality, and violent behavior are highly correlated (Apter et al. 1988). Sixty psychiatric inpatients were evaluated for suicide risk, risk of violence, and extent of anger and anxiety. Measures of anxiety correlated significantly with suicide risk ($r = +0.62$, $p < 0.001$) and violence risk ($r = +0.30$, $p < 0.05$). Since suicide and violence risk were highly correlated ($r = +0.62$, $p < 0.001$), partial correlations were performed with suicide and violence risk partialed out. The correlation of anxiety with suicide risk remained the same. However, the correlation of anxiety with violence risk became negative ($r = -0.28$, $p = 0.06$), just failing to reach significance.

Thus, it appears that anxiety, suicidality, and violence are highly correlated, regardless of diagnostic entity. Such a conclusion might be expected, considering previously discussed work indicating that 5-HT dysfunction has been implicated in the pathogenesis of each of these phenomena. A major question that still remains, however, concerns whether the correlation between 5-HT and suicidality is a "real" one, or whether it is a derivative of an underlying relationship between 5-HT dysfunction and anxiety.

CONCLUSION

In tracing the evolution of our theoretical understanding of the relationship between 5-HT and psychiatric disorders, we noted that, initially, low CSF 5-HIAA was identified as a disturbance in a subgroup of depressed patients. However, serotonergic disturbances including low CSF 5-HIAA were also found in a wide variety of other psychiatric syndromes, suggesting that these findings were not specific for depressive disorders. Asberg et al. (1976) then noted that in a group of depressed individuals, low CSF 5-HIAA was more highly associated with violent suicidal behavior than with depression per se. Subsequent research in this area also demonstrated lowered CSF 5-HIAA in both nondepressed nonpsychotic and nondepressed psychotic suicide attempters as well. These data suggested the notion that low CSF 5-HIAA is most highly correlated with suicidal behavior rather than depression, and thus that disturbances of 5-HT might be more closely associated with the manifestation of a particular psychopathological dimension (e.g., self-directed aggression) rather than with a nosological category per se. In addition, other data on individuals with a variety of psychiatric diagnoses suggest a relationship between lowered CSF 5-HIAA and problems with regulation of outwardly directed aggression and/or impulsivity. Thus, decreased CSF 5-HIAA appears to correlate with the psychopathological dimension of disturbed aggression regulation, regardless of direction or psychiatric diagnosis.

More recently, there is some data to suggest the presence of 5-HT disturbances (in particular, low CSF 5-HIAA and disturbed 5-HT challenge tests) in individuals with high anxiety ratings across several diagnostic entities. Therefore, it may be that decreased CSF 5-HIAA indicating lowered 5-HT metabolism in the CNS correlates with both dimensions (i.e., aggression regulation and anxiety). Both dimensions could relate to 5-HT in an independent manner. Alternatively, the anxiety dimension may be the common denominator in all such patients with low CSF 5-HIAA, the relation to aggression being a derivative one.

We have recently demonstrated intercorrelations between aggressive and anxious affects in psychiatric inpatients demonstrating inwardly and outwardly directed aggression (Apter et al. 1988). The relationship between these affects and serotonergic dysfunction remains to be further elucidated. Interrelationships between these variables are certainly a possibility in view of the cerebral distribution of 5-HT. Serotonergic fibers originating in the dorsal and median raphe nucleus project to multiple areas of the limbic system and cortex including the septum, amygdala, hypothalamus, hippocampus, and forebrain. Different 5-HT projections could modulate different psychological functions such as anxiety, mood, and aggression. Interrelationships between these projections might explain clustering of symptoms such as anxiety and depression or aggression and impulsivity.

The research cited above in the area of 5-HT and suicidality certainly indicates the appropriateness of the functional/dimensional approach in biological psychiatry. This viewpoint will of necessity lead to increased rigor in the quantitative and qualitative assessment of psychological functioning through psychometric and behavioral analysis and measurement. Despite our technical sophistication in assessing biological parameters and our evolving ability to reliably and validly assess psychiatric disorders via standardized diagnostic instruments, we continue to rely primarily on relatively crude psychometric scales. Many of these scales were developed several decades ago and are frequently criticized for their lack of precision. Yet they remain widely employed for reasons of historical continuity. Impulsivity, for example, has been posited as a central manifestation of serotonergic dysfunction. Unfortunately, most researchers have relied on diagnostic category (e.g., borderline personality disorder) or characteristics of a behavioral act (e.g., arson) to separate impulsive from nonimpulsive individuals. Clearly, this method is problematical, since not all individuals with a particular diagnosis or exhibiting a specific behavior act in an impulsive manner. Impulsivity is a poorly defined, multidimensional construct with behavioral, cognitive, and affective concomitants that has proven difficult to reliably assess. It is certainly conceivable that a disturbance of 5-HT will correspond to some but not all aspects of impulsivity, but until better diagnostic criteria are developed, this will be extremely difficult to ascertain.

The introduction of new somatic treatments three to four decades ago forced a radical reevaluation of our nosological system. The hope that a specific biological ''marker'' would be discovered for these specifically defined entities has not been fulfilled to date. We are presently in an era when further biological specificity is being achieved and biological sophistication is growing. Our neuroimaging techniques, for example, allow for in vivo analysis of neuroanatomical features; our ligands probe specific receptor subtypes for which drugs are being developed. Psychopathological sophistication should also be growing by the incorporation of a dimensional vantage point as well. Research investigating the role of 5-HT in suicidal behavior suggests that dysfunctions within such specific neurotransmitter systems may be more specific to symptom complexes or dimensions rather than to diagnostic entities themselves. As we continue to gain precision in our ability to delineate physiological factors contributing to psychiatric disorders, it is imperative that our measurement of psychological functions keep pace. Lacking this, the biological revolution in psychiatry may indeed appear chaotic.

References

Apter, A., R. Plutchik, S. Sevy, M.L. Korn, S. Brown and H.M. van Praag. 1988. Anxiety, impulsivity and depressed mood: Relation to suicide and violent behavior (Submitted).

Apter, A., H.M. van Praag, R. Plutchik, S. Sevy, M. Korn and S.L. Brown. 1988. The relationships between a serotonergically linked series of psychopathological dimensions (Submitted)

Asberg, M., L. Bertilsson, E. Rydin, C. Schalling, P. Thoren and L. Traskman-Bendz. 1981. Monoamine metabolites in cerebrospinal fluid in relation to depressive illness, suicidal behaviour and personality. In B. Angrist, G.D. Burrows, M. Lader, O. Lingjaerde, G. Sedvall and D. Wheatley, eds., *Recent Advances in Neuropsychopharmacology*, Oxford: Pergamon Press.

Asberg, M., L. Bertilsson, B. Martensson, G.P. Scalia-Tomba, P. Thoren and L. Traskman. 1984. CSF monamine metabolites in melancholia. *Acta Psychiatrica Scandinavia* 69:201-19.

Asberg, M., L. Traskman and P. Thoren. 1976. 5-HIAA in the cerebrospinal fluid: A biochemical suicide predictor? *Archives of General Psychiatry* 33:1193-97.

Ballenger, J.C., F.K. Goodwin. L.F. Major and G.L. Brown, 1979. Alcohol and central serotonergic metabolism in man. *Archives of General Psychiatry* 36:224-27.

Banki, C.M. and M. Arato. 1983. Amine metabolites, neuroendocrine findings and personality dimensions as correlates of suicidal behavior. *Psychiatry Research* 10:253-61.

Banki, C.M., G. Molnar and M. Vojnik. 1981. Cerebrospinal fluid amine metabolites, tryptophan and clinical parameters in depression: Part 2. Psychopathological symptoms. *Journal of Affective Disorders* 3:91-99.

Bleich, A., S.L. Brown, R. Kahn and H.M. van Praag. 1988. The role of serotonin in schizophrenia. *Schizophrenia Bulletin* (in press).

Bioulac, B., M. Benezech, B. Renaud, B. Noel and D. Roche. 1980. Serotonergic functions in the 47, XYY syndrome. *Biological Psychiatry* 15:917-23.

Brown, G.L., M.H. Ebert, P.F. Goyer, D.C. Jimerson, W.J. Klein, W.E. Bunney and F.K. Goodwin. 1982. Aggression, suicide and serotonin: Relationships to CSF amine metabolites. *American Journal of Psychiatry* 139:741-46.

Brown, G.L., F.K. Goodwin, J.C. Ballenger, P.F. Goyer and L.F. Major. 1979. Aggression in humans correlates with cerebrospinal fluid amine metabolites. *Psychiatry Research* 1:131-39.

Ceulemans, D.L.S., M.L.J.A. Hoppenbrouwers, Y.G. Gelders and A.J.M. Reyntjens. 1985. The influence of ritanserin, a serotonin antagonist, in anxiety disorders: A double-blind placebo controlled study versus lorazepam. *Pharmacopsychiatry* 18:303-305.

Charney, D.S., S.W. Woods, W.K. Goodman and G.R. Heninger. 1987. Serotonin function in anxiety. II. Effects of the serotonin agonist MCPP in panic disorder patients and healthy subjects. *Psychopharmacology* 92:14-24.

Inamdar, S.C., D.O. Lewis, G. Siomopoulos, S.S. Shanok and M. Lamela. 1982. Violent and suicidal behavior in psychotic adolescents. *American Journal of Psychiatry* 139:932-35.

Kahn, R.S., G.M. Asnis, S. Wetzler, and H.M. van Praag. 1988. Neuroendocrine evidence for serotonin receptor hypersensitivity in patients with panic disorder. *Psychopharmacology* (in press).

Kahn, R.S., H.M. van Praag, S. Wetzler, G.M. Asnis, and G. Barr. 1988. Serotonin and anxiety revisited. *Biological Psychiatry* 23:189-208.

Kahn, R.S., H.G.M. Westenberg, W.M.A. Verhoeven, C. Gispen-de Wied and W. Kamberbeek. 1987. Effect of a serotonin precursor and uptake inhibitor in anxiety disorders: a double blind comparison of 5-hydroxytryptophan, clomipramine and placebo. *International Clinical Psychopharmacology* 2:33-45.

Kahn, R.S., S. Wetzler, H.M. van Praag, G.M. Asnis and T. Strauman. 1988. Behavioral indications for serotonin receptor hypersensitivity in panic disorder. *Psychiatry Research* (in press).

Lidberg, L., M. Asberg and U.B. Sundquist-Stensman. 1984. 5-Hydroxyindoleacetic acid in attempted suicides who have killed their children. *Lancet*, ii:928.

Lidberg, L, J.R. Tuck, M. Asberg, G.P. Scalia-Tomba and L. Bertilsson. 1985. Homicide, suicide and CSF 5-HIAA. *Acta Psychiatrica Scandinavia* 71:230-36.

Linnoila, M., M. Virkhunen, M. Scheinin, A. Nuutila, R. Rimon and F.K. Goodwin. 1983. Low cerebrospinal fluid 5-hydroxyindoleacetic acid concentration differentiates impulsive from nonimpulsive violent behavior. *Life Sciences* 33:2609-2614.

Lopez-Ibor, J.J., S.R. Jeronimo, and J.C. Perez de los Cobos. 1985. Biological correlations of suicide and aggressivity in major depressions (with melancholia): 5-Hydroxyindoleacetic acid and cortisol in cerebral spinal fluid, dexamethasone suppression test and therapeutic response to 5-hydroxytryptophan. *Neuropsychobiology* 14:67-74.

Moyer, K.E. 1976. *The psychobiology of aggression.* New York: Harper and Row.

Murphy, D.L., E.A. Mueller, N.A. Garrick and C.S. Aulakh. 1986. Use of serotonergic agents in the clinical assessment of central serotonin function. *Journal of Clinical Psychiatry* 47 (4)(suppl):9-15.

Ninan, P.T., D.P. van Kammen, M. Scheinin, M. Linnoila, W.E. Bunney and F.K. Goodwin. 1984. CSF 5-hydroxyindoleacetic acid levels in suicidal schizophrenic patients. *American Journal of Psychiatry* 141:566-69.

Oreland, L.A., M. Wiberg, L. Asberg, L. Traskman, P. Sjostrand, P. Thoren and G. Tybring. 1981. Platelet MAO activity and monoamine metabolites in CSF in depressed and suicidal patients and in healthy controls. *Psychiatry Research* 4:21-29.

Palaniappan, V., V. Ramachandran and O. Somasundaram. 1983. Suicidal ideation and biogenic amines in depression. *Indian Journal of Psychiatry* 25:286-92.

Pfeffer, C.R., R. Plutchik and M. Mizruchi. Predictors of assaultiveness in latency age children. *American Journal of Psychiatry* 140:31-35.

Plutchik, R., C. Climent and F. Ervin. 1976. Research strategies for the study of human violence. In W.L. Smith and A. Kling, eds., *Issues in Brain/Behavior Control.* New York: Spectrum Books.

Plutchik, R., H. van Praag and H.R. Conte. 1985. Suicide and violence risk in psychiatric patients. *Biological Psychiatry* 20:761-63.

Roy-Byrne, P., R. Post, D. Rubinow, M. Linnoila, R. Savard and D. Davis. 1983. CSF 5-HIAA and personal and family history of suicide in affectively ill patients: A negative study. *Psychiatry Research* 10:263-74.

Rydin, E., D. Schalling and M. Asberg. 1982. Rorschach ratings in depressed and suicidal patients with low levels of 5-hydroxyindoleacetic acid in cerebrospinal fluid. *Psychiatry Research* 7:229-43.

Skodal, A.E. and T.B. Karasu. 1978. Emergency psychiatry and the assaultive patient. *American Journal of Psychiatry* 135:202-205.

Tardiff, K. and A. Sweillam. 1980. Factors related to increased risk of assaultive behavior in suicidal patients. *Acta Psychiatrica Scandinnvia* 62:63-68.

Taylor, D.P., M.S. Eison, L.A. Riblet, and C.P Vandermaelen. 1985. Pharmacological and clinical effects of buspirone. *Pharmacology Biochemistry and Behavior* 23:687-94.

Traskman, L., M. Asberg, L. Bertilsson and P. Thoren. 1984. CSF monamine metabolites of depressed patients during illness and after recovery. *Acta Psychiatrica Scandinavia* 69:333-42.

Valzelli, L. 1981. *Psychobiology of aggression and violence.* New York: Raven Press.

van Kammen, D.P. 1987. 5-HT, a neurotransmitter for all seasons? *Biological Psychiatry* 22:1-3.

van Praag, H.M. 1982. Biochemical and psychopathological predictors of suicidality. *Biblthca Psychiatrica* 162:42-60.

van Praag, H.M. 1982. Depression, suicide and the metabolism of serotonin in the brain. *Journal of Affective Disorders* 4:275–90.

van Praag, H.M. 1983. CSF 5-HIAA and suicide in non-depressed schizophrenics. *Lancet* ii:977–78.

van Praag, H.M. 1985. The linkage between depression and aggression. A biological hypothesis. In *Stukken van de puzzel. Over de klinische psychiatrie en haar grensgebieden.* (Pieces of the puzzle. On clinical psychiatry and its borderlands.) Festschrift for Prof. W.K. van Dijk. J.W.B.M van Berkestijn, R. Giel and R.H. van de Hoofdakker, eds. Van Dendersen, Groningen, pp. 155–72.

van Praag, H.M. 1986. (Auto)aggression and CSF 5-HIAA in depression and schizophrenia. *Psychopharmacology Bulletin* 22(3):669–73.

van Praag, H.M., R.S. Kahn, G.M. Asnis, S. Wetzler, S.L. Brown, A. Bleich and M.L. Korn. 1987. Denosologization of biological psychiatry or the specificity of 5HT disturbances in psychiatric disorders. *Journal of Affective Disorders* 13:1–8.

van Praag, H.M., R. Kahn, G.M. Asnis, S. Wetzler, S. Brown, A. Bleich and M. Korn. 1988. Beyond nosology in biological psychiatry. 5-HT disturbances in mood, aggression and anxiety disorders. In M. Briley and J. Fillion, eds., *New Concepts in Depression.* London: Macmillan Press.

van Praag, H.M., J. Korf, J.P.W.F. Lakke and T. Schut. 1975. Dopamine metabolism in depressions, psychoses, and Parkinson's disease: The problem of the specificity of biological variables in behavior disorders. *Psychological Medicine* 5(2):138–46.

van Praag, H.M., J. Korf and J. Puite. 1970. 5-Hydroxyindoleacetic acid levels in the cerebrospinal fluid of depressive patients treated with probenecid. *Nature* 225:1259–1260.

van Praag, H.M. and B. Leijnse. 1965. Neubewertung des syndroms. Skizze einer funktionellen pathologie. *Psychiatria Neurologia Neurochirurgia* 68:50–56.

van Praag, H.M. and R. Plutchik. 1985. An empirical study on the "cathartic effect" of attempted suicide. *Psychiatry Research* 16:123–30.

van Praag, H.M., A.M. Uleman and J.C. Spitz. 1965. The vital syndrome interview. A structured standard interview for the recognition and registration of the vital depressive symptom complex. *Psychiatria Neurologia Neurochirurgia* 68:329–46.

Vestergaard, P., T. Sorensen, E. Hoppe, O.J. Rafaelsen, C.M. Yates and N. Nicolaou. 1978. Biogenic amine metabolites in cerebrospinal fluid of patients with affective disorders. *Acta Psychiatrica Scandinavia* 58:88.

Virkunen, M., A. Nuutila, F.K. Goodwin and M. Linnoila. 1987. Cerebrospinal fluid monamine metabolite levels in male arsonists. *Archives of General Psychiatry* 44:241–47.

Weissman, M., K. Fox and G. Klerman. 1973. Hostility and depression associated with suicide attempts. *American Journal of Psychiatry* 130:450–55.

Zohar, J., E.A. Mueller, T.R. Insel, R.C. Zohar-Kadouch and D.L. Murphy. 1987. Serotonergic responsivity in obsessive-compulsive disorder. *Archives of General Psychiatry* 44:946–51.

5

Suicide, Depression and Economic Conditions

René F. W. Diekstra

This chapter concerns the strength and the nature of the association between unemployment and suicidal behavior. Since the recent increase in suicide rates in the majority of northwest and central European countries has coincided with an increase in unemployment, the hypothesis has been put forward by several authors that unemployment could be the principal agent of the rise in suicide.

There is a large variation in death rates from suicide in countries throughout the world. Of the countries that report to the World Health Organization (WHO) and whose suicide rates are published in the 1987 *World Health Statistics Annual* (WHO 1987) or are available in the WHO data bank for at least one year after 1979, the range of suicide rates spans from practically zero (where there are no deaths from suicide) in countries like Malta and Egypt to the remarkably high figure of 661 per million in Hungary (see Table 1).

Table 1. Mortality by suicide in countries reporting to WHO (1980 or later) per million of population

Country	M	F	Country	M	F	Country	M	F
Falklands			Puerto Rico	176	23	Cape Verde	44	6
Maldives	1000	—	Scotland	166	60	Martinique	44	13
Hungary	661	259	Uruguay	159	-	Bahrain	40	6
Surinam	436	128	New Zealand	157	50	Mauritius	40	16
Finland	430	113	El Salvador	148	61	Paraguay	33	15
Austria	421	158	Singapore	147	107	Dominica	28	—
Sri Lanka	377	197	Netherlands	146	81	Mexico	25	7
Denmark	351	206	Korea	139	49	Barbados	25	15
France	331	127	Hong Kong	137	107	Panama	22	5
Switzerland	330	132	Portugal	136	51	Saint Vincent	20	0
Belgium	326	153	Northern Ireland	131	39	Grenadine	17	

71

Czechoslovakia	292	92	England and Wales	121	57	Santa Lucia	17	0
Japan	278	149	Trinidad & Tobago	121	50	Iran	16	4
Fed.Rep. Germany	266	12	Italy	110	43	Belize	13	—
Sweden	250	115	Chile	107	18	Kuwait	12	5
Bulgaria	232	94	Argentina	105	34	Bahamas	10	—
Yugoslavia	228	97	Ireland	92	39	Guatemala	9	1
Poland	220	44	Venezuela	76	20	Philippines	5	4
Norway	208	74	Israel	75	35	Syria	2	—
Luxembourg	207	74	Costa Rica	74	15	Papua New Guinea	1	2
Iceland	206	58	Thailand	69	62	Egypt	0	0
Canada	205	54	Spain	68	23	Malta	—*	6
United States	197	54	Greece	57	25	Dem.Rep. Germany	—*	—
Australia	182	51	Ecuador	55	36	Cuba	—*	—

* no figures reported in WHO Statistics Annual 1987

The global picture of suicide mortality clearly shows a consistent pattern. Arab countries have relatively low rates of suicide. The same holds true for Latin American countries. The European countries and countries populated in the majority by people of European descent, such as Australia, the United States, and Canada tend to have relatively high rates. Within the European countries there is a discernible pattern. Southern European countries have relatively low rates while northern and middle European countries usually tend to have higher rates. The Asians have rates more evenly distributed across the range.

The consistency of the global picture of suicide mortality is not only of a geographical but also of a chronological nature. An analysis of the suicide rates of the 62 countries that reported to WHO both in 1960 and at least one of the years 1980 to 1986 indicate that over that period their rank order has only slightly changed. This is true despite the often substantial changes in suicide rates within countries. It appears that more countries (42) have witnessed an increase than a decrease (20) over the past quarter of a century. The average percentage change is about + 37 percent with a range of − 82 percent to + 437 percent.

Relatively large increases can be seen in most countries in northwest and central Europe. Countries populated mainly by people of European descent, show a similar trend, though generally less sizeable. Striking is the fact that

Latin countries, both around the Mediterranean and on the American continent have witnessed decreasing suicide rates. For the Asian countries the picture is mixed, with relatively large increases for Southeast Asia (Sri Lanka, Thailand, and Singapore) and no changes or decreases for the Far East (Hong Kong, Japan, and the Philippines).

The strikingly consistent global distribution of suicide mortality rates (and of recent changes in those rates) contradicts the suggestion made time and again (WHO 1982) that differences in classification or death certification procedures (or changes in those procedures) are the first and foremost factors of international variation in suicide statistics. Without ignoring any influence of certification procedures, it seems more plausible that differences in social, psychological, and even biological factors between populations and ethnic groups lie at the heart of differences in national suicide rates as well as explaining the trends in those rates.

Since the recent increase in suicide rates in the majority of northwest and central European countries has coincided with important socioeconomic developments among which unemployment figures most prominently, it has been hypothesized by several authors (Platt 1984) that unemployment or loss of employment could be a principal causal agent of the current rise in suicide mortality in those countries.

This chapter reviews the evidence for this hypothesis, drawing on the available literature and on two studies in one particular country, the Netherlands. Departing from the point of view that unemployment can be considered both socially and individually a stressful event or stressor to which people may react with self-destruction, a causal role, if any, of employment should be demonstrable for all categories of suicidal behavior, both those with fatal outcome (suicides) and those with nonfatal outcome (attempted suicides or parasuicides) (Platt 1984).

SUICIDAL BEHAVIOR: DISTINCTIONS AND DEFINTIONS

At present there are no internationally standardized and accepted definitions of the main types of suicidal behavior. Although most authors agree on the existence of two main types, usually distinguished by their (fatal or nonfatal) outcome, the terms to designate them may differ as well as the criteria for inclusion or exclusion of behaviors under a specific type. Suicidal acts with a nonfatal outcome are either labeled suicide attempts, attempted suicides, parasuicides, or acts of deliberate self-harm, depending upon the country of origin of the author(s) or the school he adheres to. While those terms are often used as synonyms, several authors also distinguish between attempted suicide and parasuicide, the former implying an intention (however vague and ambiguous) to do away with oneself while the latter also encompasses so-called "contraintentioned'' acts, meaning that the individual uses the semantic blanket of ''Suicide'' with a conscious absence of any lethal intention.

In a recent WHO copublication (Diekstra et al. 1989) the following set of definitions has been proposed:
Suicide:

(a) An act with a fatal outcome;
(b) that is deliberately initiated and performed by the deceased himself
(c) in the knowledge or expectation of its fatal outcome;
(d) the outcome being considered by the actor as instrumental in bringing about desired changes in consciousness and social conditions.

Attempted suicide:

(a) A nonhabitual act with a nonfatal outcome;
(b) that is deliberately initiated and performed by the individual involved in expectation of such an outcome;
(c) that causes self-harm or without intervention from others will do so or consists of ingesting a substance in excess of its generally recognized therapeutic dosage;
(d) the outcome being considered by the actor as instrumental in bringing about desired changes in consciousness and/or social condition.

Like every general definition, these have to be used with certain legends or inclusion/exclusion criteria. For example, a person who lies on a railway track in order to be killed by the next train but who is rescued in time, or a person who jumps off a bridge in order to drown him/herself but is then quickly pulled out of the water by others, might not yet have injured him/herself. However, such an act should certainly be considered a case of attempted suicide according to the definition above. Furthermore, a person who is not a habitual drinker of alcohol or a user of tranquilizers who all of a sudden takes a large amount of alcohol or an overdose of tranquilizers, does so deliberately and at the same time fulfills criterion (d) of the attempted suicide definition (assuming the act is not simply undertaken to find out how alcohol or tranquilizers feel). However, if that same person had clearly taken precautions to prevent his/her act from resulting in death, such as by taking a substance that provokes throwing up of a later-to-be-taken substance such as alcohol or tranquilizers, he/she should be considered a case of parasuicide. A habitual user of excessive quantities of alcohol or a habitual user of dangerous quantities of hard drugs is not to be considered a case of parasuicide if found unconscious as a result of an overdose (assuming that other information indicating lethal intent such as a suicide note is not present). A person who in an acutely psychotic state jumps out of a window with the unnatural assumption that he is able to fly, and then as a result of the fall, dies, is not to be considered a case of suicide, since that behavior does not fulfill all of the criteria of the definition of suicide.

Consequently, suicidal ideation should be broken down into two categories: a) ideation of suicide and, b) ideation of parasuicide. In order to avoid terminological confusion here, it seems sensible to label the two categories as suicidal and parasuicidal ideation.

These definitions are based on the following assumptions. First of all, attempted suicides are not simply failed or bungled suicides, for there are important epidemiological, etiological, and motivational differences between attempted and completed suicides. Secondly, the prefix "para" in parasuicide should be taken to refer to acts that are intended by the actor to resemble suicidal acts while both in terms of outcome and motivation they are not. As to the first point, available research evidence (Van Egmond and Diekstra 1989) suggests characteristic differences between suicide and attempted suicide in relation to the methods of self-harm that have been used, clinical aspects (such as psychiatric diagnosis and treatment), psychological features, and personality patterns. Also there are differences in terms of age and sex of the persons involved and in relation to emotional precipitants of the behavior. As to social antecedents, such as unemployment or loss of work, suicide and parasuicide populations seem to overlap considerably.

As to the second point, most studies tend to adopt somewhat idiosyncratic nominal definitions of suicide/attempted suicide/parasuicide; it is not unusual to find studies in which attempted and parasuicide are brought together under the same heading, thereby making comparisons between different investigations more or less problematic. It is with these precautions in mind that the reader should approach the present state of knowledge with regard to the relationship between suicide and unemployment as reviewed in the remainder of this chapter.

UNEMPLOYMENT AND SUICIDAL BEHAVIOR: THE LITERATURE

Over the last decade several reviews of the literature on the relationship between unemployment and suicide have been published (for an overview see: Platt 1984; Pritchard 1988). In order to appreciate the similarities and dissimilarities in the conclusions drawn from these reviews, it is necessary to take into account that a) studies on the association between unemployment and suicidal behavior show a high degree of diversity in design and, b) depending upon design characteristics and methods of analysis used, both type and strength of the association may vary (Platt 1984).

Aggregate cross-sectional studies, for example, provide no evidence for a consistent relationship between suicide and unemployment, while aggregate longitudinal studies do point to a positive relationship in a number of countries in the western hemisphere (though for some countries the evidence is negative).

Even the general conclusion drawn by Platt (1984) and confirmed by other reviewers, that there is firm evidence of an association between unemployment and suicidal behavior, but that the nature of this relationship remains highly problematic, might still be considered premature. The association appears relatively straightforward for men, but for women the evidence is quite equivocal or even negative, at least for some countries such as the United Kingdom and West Germany (Pritchard 1988) as far as suicide is concerned. For attempted suicide or parasuicide in some parts of the United Kingdom there appears to be a clear positive relationship with unemployment both in males and females.

Since the social and economic consequences of unemployment differ from country to country and often also from community to community (to be unemployed might be relatively normal in one place and quite abnormal in another), findings such as the ones presented above cannot be considered sufficient evidence on which to build a (para) suicide-unemployment case. But even if one goes along with Platt's conclusion of an association between the two phenomena, the question of the nature of this relationship remains largely unanswered. The assumption of a direct causal relationship between unemployment and suicide seems both theoretically unsound and empirically invalid.

Only a small percentage of those unemployed commit or attempt suicide or engage in parasuicidal acts, while among suicides and parasuicides a large percentage are not unemployed. Therefore, unemployment might (and almost certainly does) have its place in the causal link of events leading up to suicidal behavior in certain individuals or social groups, but not in others. Several authors (Diekstra et al. 1986) have forwarded the hypothesis that unemployment might play the role of moderator or intermediate variable between psychiatric illness and suicide. Their reasoning is that the suicides' work loss results not so much from broad social and economic trends as from the fact that their psychiatric morbidity interfered with their capacity for work, resulting in work loss with its attendant disadvantages, so that mental illness at once stimulated in them suicidal thinking and at the same time took away from them an effective protection against suicidal behavior.

This hypothesis might still hold even if one assumes that under unfavorable economic circumstances such as recession the psychiatric ill carry a relatively high risk for losing their jobs.

Although most of the literature reviews mentioned point to the plausibility of this hypothesis, not one of them presents research data that support it or indicate in what way it could be tested.

Psychiatric Disorder, Unemployment, and Suicidal Behavior

The evidence for a positive association between mental illness and the risk of fatal or nonfatal suicidal behavior is convincing. Although the estimated absolute percentages may differ from study to study, most studies on the topic concur in the conclusion that the majority of persons dying by their own hand suffer from an ascertainable mental disorder at the time of their death. Of the suicides suffering from a mental illness, most are diagnosed as patients of depressive disorders. In a recent review of the literature (Diekstra 1989) the present state of knowledge with regard to the relationship between depression and suicide was summarized as follows:

—15 to 20 percent of patients suffering from major depression finally die by their own hand;

—50 to 60 percent of persons committing or attempting suicide suffer from depressive disturbances.

Given these data it seems safe to assume that there is a positive association between changes in the prevalence and incidence of depressive disturbances in a population and (possibly but not certainly lagged) changes in the suicide rate of that population. Given the scarcity of data on the epidemiology of depression, no aggregate longitudinal studies are available that have validly tested this hypothesis on the population level. The same holds true for the individual level. Understandably, direct tests of the depression-unemployment-suicide sequence are not available.

This is even more understandable if one accepts the more refined model proposed by some authors (Diekstra et al. 1986) in which mental illness (such as depression) may lead to unemployment, which in turn might increase the severity of the depressive disturbance that then becomes the breeding ground for suicidal tendencies.

One difficulty with all of the models linking mental illness, unemployment, and suicide has to do with the fact that most authors, particularly if they are sociologists, approach suicide only in the sense of an act with a fatal outcome (suicide in the narrow sense), while in fact a suicidal death is the outcome of a process in which suicidal ideation, threats, gestures, and nonfatal attempts usually precede that outcome. Furthermore, in the majority of cases the suicidal process will not end in self-inflicted death but—by whatever forces—will be halted before death can occur.

The fatality of a suicide attempt often depends on factors such as whether or not others—by coincidence—discover and interfere with the attempt, the unpredictable (or at least unpredicted) interaction of suicide methods used, or the limited knowledge of some actors with regard to the method used and so on.

It follows then that if an association between unemployment and suicidal behavior exists in reality, that association—on a population level—will generally be closer in the case of attempted than of committed suicides. In addition, it might well be that attempted suicide, so common in persons suffering from emotional or mental disorders, through its social sequelae might in itself become a factor of unemployment or work loss so that the unemployment-suicide association is, mirabile dictu, at least partially caused by suicidal behavior!

In the following I will present the results of two studies that have attempted to assemble information relevant to these issues. In the first study we investigated the relationship between indices of emotional disturbance, unemployment, attempted suicide, and suicide over the period 1975-1986 for one country, the Netherlands.

In the second study, while controlling for the mental illness variable by using a sample of psychiatric patients, we investigated the relationship between unemployment and suicidal behavior, in casu attempted suicide. The design also allowed for establishing the effect of previous suicidal acts on work record.

STUDY 1: EMOTIONAL PROBLEMS, UNEMPLOYMENT, AND SUICIDAL BEHAVIOR IN THE NETHERLANDS 1970–1987

In this study we analyzed trends in 1) rates of suicide and of attempted suicide; 2) unemployment rates; 3) subjectively experienced emotional disturbances. The study covers the period of 1970–1987 (1985 for attempted suicides) in the Netherlands. It is one of the very few (possibly the only) country to date where data on attempted suicide on a national level are available.

Materials and Methods

The mortality rates for suicide (ICD code, 8th and 9th Revision: E950–959) over the period 1975-1986 were directly obtained from The Central Bureau of Statistics (Statistics Police and Justice) for men and women separately and for the age range 15 years and over.

The rates for attempted suicide were obtained from two sources that partially overlap allowing for cross-checking. The first source was the Foundation for Health Care Information (SIG), a national hospital inpatient register that records all cases of discharge (episodes, not persons) from general hospitals in the country after admission for attempted suicide (ICD code, 8th and 9th revision: E950–959). The second source was the Sentinel Stations (Continuous Morbidity Registration). These Sentinel Stations constitute a sample of general practices in the country, covering about one percent of the population, that is a fairly accurate representation of the total population in terms of age, sex, geographical distribution, and level of urbanization (Diekstra and van Egmond 1989).

Comparison of the rates of hospital discharged cases of attempted suicide over each year revealed for five years sizeable differences, with the rates provided by the Foundation always being considerably higher than those reported by the Sentinel Stations. Since there are strong indications of underreporting by general practitioners of hospital admitted cases of suicide attempts from among their own patients (Diekstra and van Egmond 1989) the rates reported by the Foundation were used for further analysis in the study.

The data used in this study on emotional disturbance were obtained from the Social and Cultural Planning office of the Netherlands. In 1975 this agency started a study titled Cultural Changes in the Netherlands, in which, among other things, indicators of subjectively experienced psychoemotional complaints are monitored by sample surveying, using samples of approximately 2000 persons in each monitor year. Data are available for the years 1975, 1979–1981, 1983 and 1986. Of the nine items on emotional or psychological complaints only two can be considered to be indicative of depressive symptoms or depressive mood disturbance according to generally accepted nosological standards (ICD-10 draft, WHO 1988). The two items are: (1) Are there things that make you feel depressed? and (2) Do you sometimes have the feeling that life is without sense and purpose? (three answer categories, no, yes, and ?)

Two categories of data on unemployment were used: a) the number of persons unemployed as percent of the workforce, and b) rate of unemployed per 1000 of adult population.

First we shall present the results of the analyses of trends on suicide and attempted suicide over the period under observation. Next the findings on the relationship between those trends, unemployment and emotional disturbance variables will be presented.

Changes in Suicide and Attempted Suicide 1970–1987

Trends in suicide rate   Figures 1 and 2 show the trendlines in suicide rates for men and women in the period 1970–1987.

For men (figure 1) the rate has been gradually rising from 1970 onward—it peaked around 1983 and has been leveling off somewhat since then. While the percent change for all age groups taken together is about 22.5 percent, there is considerable variation between groups. Persons aged 20 to 39 years show almost a doubling of their rates, while those 50 to 79 years of age have 1987 rates at the level of their rates in 1970 or even slightly below.

The youngest age group shows a trend similar to the overall trend.

For women (figure 2) the picture is pretty much similar to the one found for men. The ratio of the male-female suicide rate did hardly change over the total period and continues to center around 160 to 170 male suicides for every 100 female suicides. There are, however, substantial differences between the age

FIGURE 1. Suicide in the Netherlands. Trends for Males 1980–1987 (rate per 100,000)

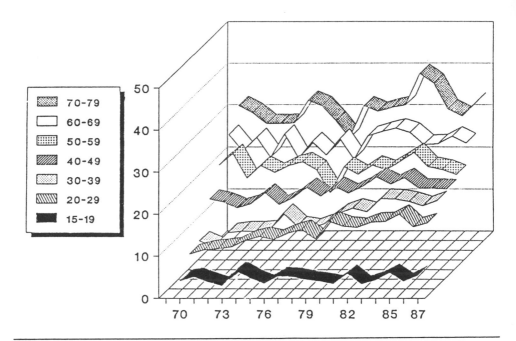

Source: CBS

groups in this respect. Both for the very young (15–19) and the very old (80 and over) there are about 300 male suicides for every 100 female ones.

Among men incidence of suicide tends to increase with age, with the peak rate found among 80-plus years old. Among women the suicide rate usually also increases with age, but the peak age is equally often found in either the 60–69 years old or the 70–79 years old, depending upon the year under consideration. Remarkable is the strong decline in the suicide rate in women 80 and over (minus 60 percent contrasted with an increase in males 80 and over of about 10 percent).

Trends in the suicide attempt rate   Figures 3 and 4 show the trendlines in rates of attempted suicide for men and women. For men (figure 3) the rate has gradually been rising from 1970 onward until it peaked around 1983 and thereafter has been slightly decreasing. The percentage change for all age groups taken together is about 100 percent, and there is little variation between age groups

FIGURE 2. Suicide in the Netherlands. Trends for Females 1980–1987 (rate per 100,000)

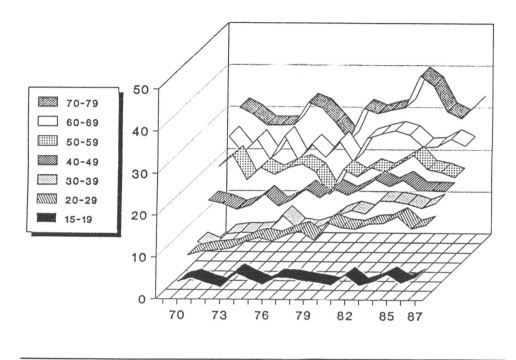

Source: CBS

in this respect, with the exception of persons aged 50 to 69 years showing a more moderate rise.

For women (figure 4) the picture is similar to the one found for men, except for the fact that in the age group 60–69 the rate shows a steady increase over the whole of the period and peaks in the latest year of reporting, 1985. The ratio of the male-female suicide attempt rate is almost exactly the opposite of the one for suicide. Here we find around 160 to 170 female attempts to every 100 male attempts, and again this ratio did hardly change over the whole over the period. For the youngest age group (15–19), however, the ratio is significantly different from the general trend. Here we find about 250 to 300 female attempts for every 100 male attempts.

FIGURE 3. Attempted suicides in the Netherlands by age. Trends for Males 1970–1985 (hospital discharges)

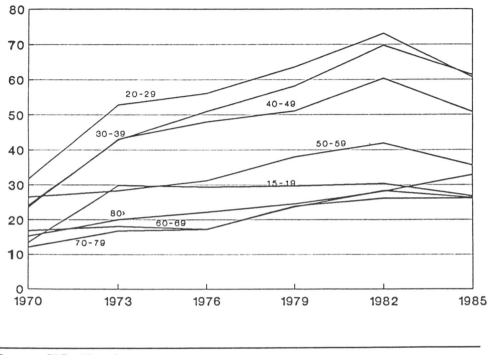

Source: SIG, Utrecht

For men and women the rate of suicide attempts peaks in the first part of life, that is to say in the 20 to 49 years age groups. While for men the most vulnerable age in this respect is between 20 to 29 years, vulnerability for nonfatal suicidal behavior among women appears to last longer because they show a broad age top covering the whole of the age range 20 to 49 years. Thereafter a steady decline in rates can be observed for women, while for men the oldest group (80 and plus) shows a rate that is at the level of the 60 to 79 years old.

The incidence of both suicide and attempted suicide seems to decrease slightly since 1982–1983 in men and in women, after a strong and steady rise over the preceding decade or so. However, the changes observed are still too small and the period of observation too short to draw any definite conclusions about contemporary downward trends.

FIGURE 4. Attempted suicides in the Netherlands. Trends for Females 1970–1985 (hospital discharges)

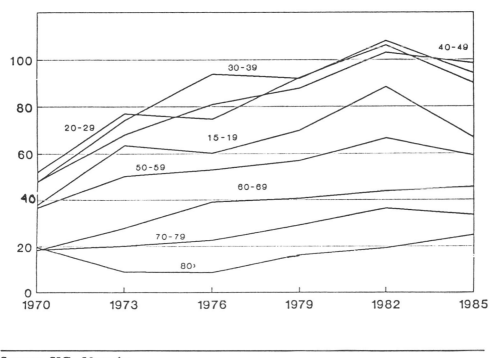

Source: SIG, Utrecht

A question of particular concern here is what factors can be held responsible for the upward jump in both suicides and suicide attempts in the 1982–1983 period. Given the fact that the most recent economic recession in Western European countries reached its lowest point in that period as well, the possibility of a relationship between both developments seems to be worth studying.

Suicide, attempted suicide and unemployment 1974–1985

Figure 5 graphically shows the developments in suicide and unemployment rates over the period 1974–1985. In figure 6 the trendlines are shown (best fit trendline through datapoints based on least square fit). Clearly both suicide and unemployment rates present a similar picture over the study period. As to be expected, the association between suicide and unemployment is close among males, while among females there appears to be a tenuous relationship.

The same sex difference is found for the association between attempted sui-

FIGURE 5. Unemployment and Suicide 1974–1985 Trends (unemployment as percent of workforce)

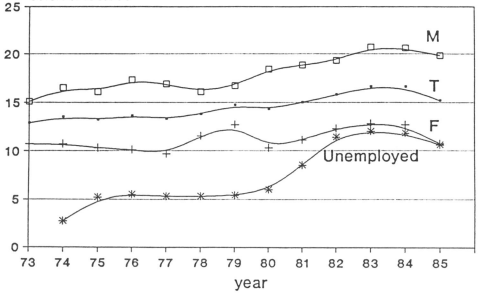

M = males, F = females, T = total

cide and unemployment (see figure 7), although here the association between the female rate and unemployment is closer than in the case of suicides.

It is noteworthy that for all rates and for both sexes the peak year is 1983.

Association with Emotional Disturbance

Figure 8 depicts the developments over time of the indicators of emotional disturbance. Both for females as well as for males the correlation between both indicators is relatively small (although somewhat bigger for males than for females). Only the depressed mood indicator shows a development similar to the one found for suicidal behavior and unemployment.

A plausible explanation for these findings might be the fact that the second indicator ("Do you sometimes have the feeling that life is without sense and purpose") does not precisely tap personal feelings of stress and depressive mood, because the word *life* might be interpreted to mean "life in general" and not so much "one's own life." Furthermore, the question can be answered truthfully in the affirmative by referring to feelings that existed in the past only.

FIGURE 6. Unemployment and Suicide 1974–1985 Trends (unemployment as percent of workforce)

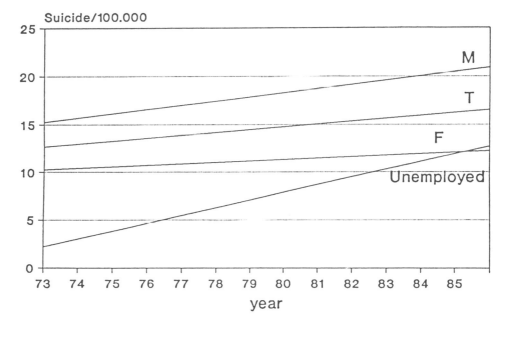

M = males, F = females, T = total

It is for those reasons that we used only the depressed mood indicator in further analyses.

Figures 9 and 10 show there is a close association between changes in depressed mood, suicide, attempted suicide, and unemployment among males. Among females the correlation between those variables is considerably lower (although each one-by-one correlation reaches a statistically acceptable level of significance).

Our data show that there exists an association between changes in depressed mood, unemployment, and incidence of suicide and attempted suicide and that this association is particularly close for males, but less for females. Although our study does not provide information on possible explanations, the observed sex difference might well be interpreted to mean that depressed mood has a different meaning and possibly even a different etiology in men than in women. Women, for example, may more often experience and admit dysphoric feelings, while men may less often be inclined to, unless a relatively severe state has

FIGURE 7. Unemployment and Attempted Suicide 1974-1985 Trends (unemployment as percent of workforce)

M = males, F = females

already been developed. Another explanation might be that depressed mood in men might more often be related to economic and work conditions than in women.

Our data also do not provide any conclusive evidence about the (causal) links between depressed mood, unemployment, and suicidal behavior. It is for that reason that we undertook a study in which suicidal and nonsuicidal psychiatric patients were compared with regard to an array of personality and social variables, including employment status, and their linkages.

Study 2: A Social Learning Model of the Suicide-Unemployment Association

It has been widely established and generally accepted that the best predictor of future suicidal behavior appears to be a history of similar behavior (previous suicidal attempts, plans, threats, or ideation) in response to life events in the past (van Egmond and Diekstra 1989). Consequently, suicidal behavior as a way of coping with a life event, such as unemployment, seems first and foremost

FIGURE 8. Emotional Disturbance 1975–1986 Trends (meanscores)

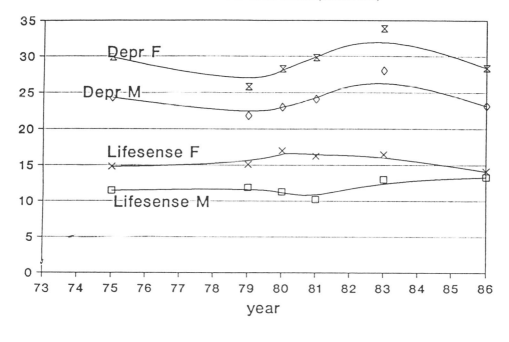

M = males, F = females

to be a function of the individual's response or behavior repertoire, which of course is acquired in the process of socialization or social learning. The closeness of the association between suicide and unemployment therefore will vary from culture to culture or social group to social group and might also vary within social groups over time depending upon the socialization of suicidal responses.

Since socialization processes affect all individuals in a specific culture, independent of their specific personality make-up, the association between suicide and unemployment may be influenced by—but is not necessarily dependent upon—the existence of particular personality characteristics, such as psychiatric or psychological morbidity or intelligence quotient.

In the second study the relationships between suicidal behavior (attempted suicide) on the one hand and behavior repertoire, unemployment, and personality characteristics on the other hand were investigated in such a way that the relative importance of each of those variables interacting with the other ones in causing suicidal behavior could be established.

FIGURE 9. Suicide, Unemployment and Disturbance 1974–1985 Trends (unemployment as percent of workforce, depression meanscore)

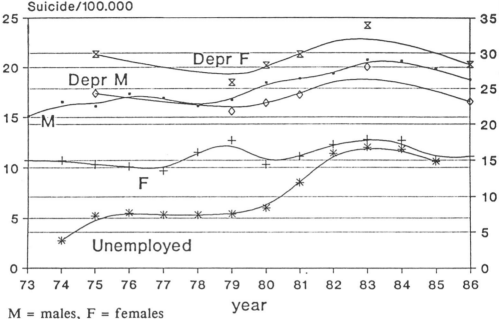

M = males, F = females

Method

The study utilized 580 psychiatric inpatients, admitted to the psychiatric ward of a general hospital in the Netherlands, of whom 109 had been admitted because of suicide attempt. The study group consists of all patients admitted to and discharged from the ward in two consecutive years. The psychiatric facilities of the hospital (in- and outpatient clinic) serves an area of almost 150,000 persons, that in terms of age and sex distribution as well as socioeconomic status can be considered as representative for the whole of the country.

From each of the subjects in the study during admission anamnestic data, demographic data, objective psychological test scores (paper and pencil personality tests, intelligence tests, and neuropsychological tests) as well as experts ratings of psychiatric and psychological morbidity using a standard protocol were collected (Diekstra 1986).

Data analysis

The interrelationships between demographic, behavioral, and personality vari-

FIGURE 10. Attempted Suicide, Unemployment, and Disturbance 1974–1985 Trends (unemployment as percent of workforce, depression meanscore)

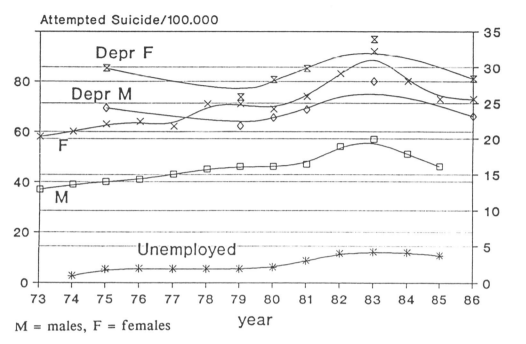

M = males, F = females

ables in the causation of suicidal behavior were analyzed by means of an interaction analysis technique. For this purpose, Sonquist's Automatic Interaction Detector (AID) procedure was used (Sonquist 1970):

> The . . . technique may best be regarded as a step-by-step application of a univariate analysis-of-variance model. An attempt is made to split up a sct of investigation units (subjects, interviewers) into a series of non-overlapping subsets, of which the means account for more of the variance in the dependent variable than any other series of subsets. The classes of multi-categorical variables are regarded as point and the total group is divided into subgroups according to a certain criterion on the most important variable. Each subgroup is now further divided with respect to its most important variable and this process is continued until the number of observations or investigations units reaches a certain minimum or until the variance accounted for remains below a certain minimum. Every division is performed on a basis of maximizing the explained variance. The result is a tree structure which may have all subclasses of the variables as terminal points.
> (See Diekstra 1973, pp. 173–74 for a further description of the technique.)

The predictor variables used in this type of analysis are shown in table 2.

Table 2. Variables in AID-analysis

*1—personality variables	—MMPI-scale-scores[1] (clinical scales, validity scales, Welsh's A- and R-scale and Barron's Es-scale, total of 16 scales) —ABV-scale-scores[2] (neuroticism, neurotic-somatic reactivity, extraversion, test-taking-attitude, total of 4 scales) —WAIS-subtest[3] and total-scores (total of 14 scores)
2—demographic variables	—Sex, age, marital status, sibling position, social class, employment status, education
3—social history variables	—Broken home, recent loss or problems of other kind, physical illness, 'alcohol-, drug-, farmaca-abuse, delinquency, homosexuality, previous suicidal behavior in subject or relatives', prior psychiatric admissions, recent psychiatric patients among relatives, ratings of problem areas by psychologist
4—dependent variable	—Admission in general hospital because of suicidal behavior
Number of predictors is 57	

[1] Minnesota Multiphasic Personality Inventory
[2] Amsterdamse Biografische Vragenlijst (Amsterdam Biographical Inventory)
[3] Wechsler Adult Intelligence Schedule (Subtest Blockdesign).
* for list of item-definitions write to author.

Some of the demographic characteristics of the group under investigation are shown in table 3 (Diekstra 1986). Figure 11 shows the results of the AID analysis with demographic, behavioral, and social history variables, personality variables and employment status as predictors. The resulting configuration explains 38 percent of the variance in the dependent variable and indicates clearly that behavior repertoire characteristics (previous suicidal behavior, drug/alcohol abuse) of the individual herself and/or of persons within the social context are the most powerful predictors of the dependent variable. Given the presence of a suicidal repertoire, being unemployed almost doubles the risk of (future) suicidal behavior.

It is noteworthy that none of the personality variables appears in the resulting configuration as contributing significantly to its predictive power. A possible explanation for this finding might be that some of these variables are "hidden" under behavioral variables such as prior suicidal behavior, since there is for example a relatively high correlation between depressive mood disturbance and suicidal behavior.

FIGURE 11. AID total group social history and demographic data   91

(somacide/somacidal = suicide/suicidal*)

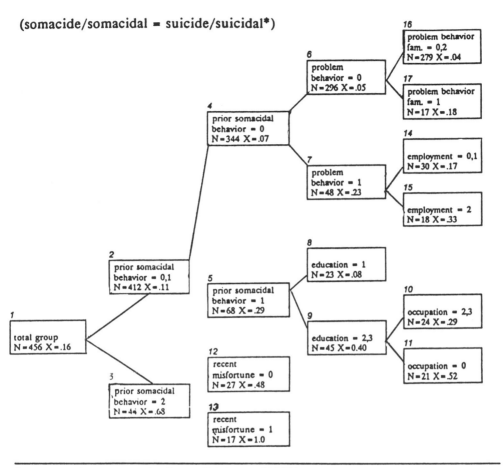

---

* proposed new terminology, Diekstra (1989)

Addenda figure 11:
-X means percentage of suicide attempts   X = 16 means: 16% suicide attempts
e.g.
-prior suicidal behavior: 0 = no
                                           1 = threats/communications
                                           2 = attempts
-problem behavior (Fam.):   0 = no
                                           1 = drug-/farmaca-/alcohol addiction
                                           2 = suicide threats/attempts/death in
                                           relatives

-unemployment: 0 = not applicable
                                            1 = employed
                                            2 = unemployed
-education: 1 = high
                                            2 = intermediate
                                            3 = low
-occupation: 0 = no
                                            1 = high
                                            2 = intermediate
                                            3 = low
-D-, Mf. scale (MMPI), Blockdesign (WAIS): distribution divided in five categories 1–
5: low to high score.

Table 3. Demographic characteristics of suicidal, non-suicidal and total group

	Total group (n = 580)	Suicidal group (n = 109)	Non-suicidal group (n = 471)
1. mean age	34.9	29.3	40.6
	%	%	%
2. male/female ratio	43.1/56.3	30.6/67.2	45.9/53.8
3. marital status:			
—single	48.5	62.2	45.6
—married	47.3	35.7	49.7
—divorced	1.2	2.0	1.1
—widowed	3.0	0.0	3.6
4. employment status:			
—employed	78.9	77.0	79.2
—unemployed	21.1	23.0	20.8
5. previous suicidal behavior			
—suicidal attempts	15.1	59.0	4.9
—suicidal threats	2.5	2.2	2.6
—suicidal thoughts	10.4	17.3	9.2

CONCLUSIONS

The results of this second study seem to confirm our hypothesis that unemployment is not directly related to the occurrence of suicidal behavior. Although it is shown that being unemployed increases the probability of suicidal behavior, it does only so in the presence of a "suicidal behavior repertoire." The most powerful predictive components of such a repertoire for future suicidal behavior are (in rank order):

(1) previous suicide attempts;
(2) previous threats with suicide;
(3) behavior equivalent or similar to suicidal behavior, such as drug and alcohol abuse;
(4) the presence of (1), (2) and (3) among significant others (particular family members).

This finding indicates that (future) suicidal behavior as a response to life events or subjective experiences is learned "by practice" or vicariously (observation of others) or (more probable) by both.

In cultures (such as many western countries today) or subcultures (such as psychiatric institutions) where attitudes toward suicidal behavior are relatively permissive (Diekstra and Kerkhof 1989) and the incidence and visibility of suicidal acts relatively great, any life event that involves an important loss with a concomitant high probability of dysphoric or depressive mood disturbance, economic recession causing an increase in unemployment will in turn cause an increase in fatal and nonfatal suicidal acts. This should not be taken to mean that personality characteristics do not play a role at all, for they influence the probability of work loss as well as of the occurrence and intensity of dysphoric mood disturbance following such a loss.

REFERENCES

Barraclough, B. 1988. International variation in the suicide rate of 15–24 years old. *Soc. Psychiat.* 23:75–84.

Bayet, A. 1922. *Le suicide et la morale.* Paris. Alcon.

Diekstra, R.W. 1973. *Crisis en gedragskeuze (Crisis and behavioral choice).* Amsterdam: Zwets & Zeitlinger.

Diekstra, R.F.W. 1982. Epidemiology of attempted suicide in the EEC. In Wilmotte, J. and J. Mendelwicz, eds. *New trends in suicide prevention.* Bibliotheca Psychiatrica. Basel: Karger, pp. 1–16.

Diekstra, R.F.W. 1985. Suicide and suicide attempts in the European Economic Community: an analysis of trends with special emphasis on trends among the young. *Suicd. Lifethr. B.* 15:402–21.

Diekstra, R.F.W. et al. 1986. *Health Council* of the Netherlands. Rapport inzake suicide (Report on Suicide), December 1986, *Health Council of the Netherlands,* The Hague.

Diekstra, R.F.W. and B. Moritz 1987. Suicidal behaviour among adolescents. In Diekstra, R.F.W. and K. Hawton, eds., *Suicide in Adolescence.* Dordrecht/Boston: Nijhoff, pp. 7–24.

Diekstra, R.F.W. 1987. The complex psychodynamics of suicide. In Diekstra, R.F.W. and K. Hawton, eds., *Suicide in Adolescence.* Dordrecht/Boston: Nijhoff, pp. 30–55.

Diekstra, R.F.W. 1988. City lifestyles. *World Health* June: 18–19.

Diekstra, R.F.W. and M. van Egmond 1989. Suicide and attempted suicide in general practice: 1979–1986. *Acta Psychiatr. Scand.,* 79:268–75.

Diekstra, R.F.W. (in press). The epidemiology of depressive disorders and suicidal behavior in the adolescents and young adults. *Psychobiology*

Egmond, M. van, and R.F.W. Diekstra 1988. The predictability of suicidal behavior: the results of a meta-analysis of published studies. In Diekstra, R.F.W., R.A. Maris, S. Platt, A. Schmidtke, G. Sonneck, eds., *Suicide Prevention: The role of attitude and imitation.* Leiden, the Netherlands: Brill.

Frazier, Sh. 1986. US task force on youth suicide. Paper read at WHO Meeting on Preventive Strategies in Suicidal Behavior, October 4, 1986.

Hafner, H. and S. Schmidtke 1987. Suizid and Suizidversuche-Epidemiologie und aetologie. *Nervenheilkunde* 6:49–63.

Headley, L.A. 1983. *Suicide in Asia and the Near East.* Los Angeles, CA: University of California Press.

Holinger, P.C., D. Offer and M.A. Zola 1988. A prediction model of suicide among youth. *J. Nerv. Ment. Dis.* 176:275–79.

Kelleher, M.J. and M. Daly 1988. Suicide in Cork and Ireland. Paper 2nd European Conference Suic. Res. Edinburgh (U.K.).

Kreidman, N.S. 1977. *Parasuicide.* Chichester: Wiley.

Mahler, H. 1987. Epidemiology, Health Promotion and Health for all by the year 2000. Paper XI Scientific meeting Int. Epid. ASS., Helsinki.

Pitchard, C. 1988. Suicide, unemployment and gender in the British Isles and European Economic Community (1974–1985). *Social Psychitr.* 23:85–89.

Platt, S. 1984. Unemployment and suicidal behavior: A review of the literature. *Soc. Sci. Med.* (19) 2:93–115.

Platt, S. 1988. *Data from Royal Infirmary.* Edinburgh.

Simmons, K. 1987. Task force to make recommendations for adolescents in terms of Suicide Risk. *Jama* 257:3330–32.

Sonquist, J.A. 1970. Multivariate model building the validation of a search strategy. *ISB.* University of Michigan.

Syer-Solursh, D. 1986. *Personal Communications.*

WHO. 1982. *Changing patterns in suicide behavior.* Copenhagen: WHO/Euro, reports and studies, 74.

WHO. 1987. *World Health Statistics Annual.* Geneva: World Health Organization.

WHO. 1988. *Correlates of youth suicide.* Div. Ment. Health. Geneva: World Health Organization, techn. doc.

Wisse, J. 1933. *Selbstmord und Todesfurcht bei den Naturvölkern.* Zutphen: Thieme.

6

Abused Women and Revenge Suicide: Anthropological Contributions to Understanding Suicide

Dorothy Ayers Counts

In many non-Western societies suicide is not considered a deviant or criminal act, nor is it evidence of mental illness; instead it may be an appropriate response to specific, culturally defined situations. For example, in Micronesia suicide is the most common cause of death among young men and, Marshall (1979) argues, may be the only way in which a shamed person can successfully avenge himself against his tormentors. In Papua New Guinea, the Fore regard suicide to be the ''right course of action'' under certain circumstances (Berndt 1962), while the Gasmata-Arawe people of West New Britain commonly choose suicide in response to a frustrated love affair, a forced marriage, the death of a relative, sickness, or adultery (Hoskin, Friedman and Cawte 1969).

There are a variety of ways in which the notion that suicide is an acceptable option may be communicated in other cultures. It may be so much a part of everyday life that it is a theme in children's play—as it is in Arawe where children take turns knotting a noose around their necks and dropping limply to the ground in a dramatization of suicide by hanging (Hoskin, Friedman and Cawte 1969). Or it may be a motif in oral literature as is true in Kaliai, West New Britain, where myths, legends, and folk tales recount the conditions under which people may legitimately kill themselves, describe the methods to be used, and spell out the rules that a person committing suicide should follow in order to communicate a powerful message by the act (Counts 1980).

REVENGE SUICIDE

The insight that suicide may be a socially patterned act that conveys a cultural meaning is a major contribution that the cross-cultural approach of anthropology makes to the study of suicide. I shall, in this chapter, discuss the understanding that anthropology brings to the phenomenon of revenge suicide, self-killing that has the intent of harming another person. Most of the data that I cite comes from Melanesia, especially from Papua New Guinea because much of the anthropological research on revenge suicide has been done there. The research done in other cultures indicates that the patterns found in Melanesia are not unique but are repeated in societies in other parts of the world.

The relationship between self-killing and the desire to kill someone else has long been acknowledged by psychoanalytic theory. Karl Menninger (1938), for example, has noted that suicide contains three elements: a desire to kill, a desire to be killed, and a desire to die. Almost forty years ago Simpson (1951) said that "The most widely accepted view today in psychoanalysis is that suicide is most often a form of 'displacement'; that is, the desire to kill someone who has thwarted the individual is turned back on the individual himself" (p. 24).

The angry despair that leads a person to destroy himself in order to harm another may arise in circumstances where an abused or shamed individual has no other way of striking back at those who have wronged him. In Papua New Guinea, a person who is publicly shamed may be expected to kill himself, while in Truk a young man who has been pushed "over the brink of despair" by close kinsmen who have rejected him in an emotional confrontation may kill himself as an act of vengeance against his tormentors who "suffer guilt thereafter" (Marshall 1979). The prevalence of this culturally patterned response is discussed by Epstein (1984) who notes that one way a humiliated person may discharge his shame is by directing aggression inward against himself to ensure that everyone, including the person who wronged him, feels pity for him. Suicide is, in many societies, one culturally acceptable way of committing aggression toward oneself while redirecting it toward someone else.

The first anthropologist to call attention to the presence of revenge suicide in other cultures was Jeffreys (1952) who called it *samsonic suicide* after the Biblical figure who pulled down a building around his own head in order to kill his enemies. Revenge suicide has been reported among the Zaire of Africa (Wymeersch 1976), the Aguaruna Jivaro of Peru (Siverts 1982; Brown, 1982, 1986), the Trukese of Micronesia (Marshall 1979), and the Fore (Berndt 1962), the Hagen (Strathern, 1972), the Maenge (Panoff 1977), the Maring (Healey 1979), the Gainj (Johnson 1981), and the Lusi-Kaliai (Counts 1980, 1984, 1987) of Papua New Guinea.

In those societies where revenge suicide is an acceptable option there is a cultural pattern that (1) identifies certain types of persons for whom revenge suicide is appropriate; (2) sets out the criteria that are necessary for revenge suicide to occur and the circumstances in which it is an appropriate, reasonable, and even expected response; and (3) establishes the rules governing the way a person should commit suicide, including the method that should be followed, the location where it should be done, and the way in which the suicide can convey to survivors the identity of the individual(s) responsible for the act. The cultural pattern is, of course, not the same for all societies where revenge suicide is common, but there are a number of similarities that are found cross-culturally.

First, revenge suicide is frequently adopted as a mode of social interaction by powerless people who lack an effective, more direct way of affecting the behavior of others. These powerless people are often women (see, for example, Brown 1982, 1986; Healey 1979; Counts 1980, 1984, 1987). In Muslim countries, for example, it is reported that women threaten suicide ". . . in order to pressure their families into accepting their will" (Fluehr-Lobban 1977, p. 135), while in India suicide may be a Havik Brahmin woman's only recourse because she has ". . . no formal power" (Ullrich 1977, p. 101). Suicide is more commonly practiced by women than by men in many Papua New Guinea societies. Among the Maenge of New Britain, for example, revenge suicide occurs chiefly among two categories of person, orphans and women: ". . . precisely those [categories] whose members have the fewest opportunities to pour out their aggressiveness" (Panoff 1977, p. 55). According to Panoff the Maenge do not consider suicide to be proper behavior for everyone; rather, it ". . . is a type of death appropriate only to 'rubbish men' and women" (p. 50).

Second, there are at least two criteria that must be met in order for revenge suicide to occur. There must be a tradition that holds someone other than the victim responsible for the act—the society must recognize the existence of a culpable party—and there must be some culturally recognized mechanism to punish the guilty person(s). This mechanism may be part of the religious system, as is the belief that the ghost of the suicide has the power to torment the living provocateur (Jeffreys 1952), or it may be a social instrument—for example the indigenous political system may impose a penalty on the person who provoked the suicide or sanction the right of the survivors to exact compensation from or take revenge on the guilty party. Anthropologists report that these criteria are present in a number of societies. Westermarck (1908) remarks, for instance, that among the Tshi-speaking people of the Gold Coast of Africa, a person who drives another person to suicide is judged to be culpable. He says:

> Should a person commit suicide, and before so doing attribute the act to the conduct of another person, that other person is required by native law to undergo a like fate. The practice is termed "killing oneself upon the head of another," and the person whose conduct is supposed to have driven the suicide to commit the rash act is visited with a death of an exactly similar nature—unless, indeed, the family of the suicide be pacified with a money compensation. (Westermarck 1908, p. 13)

Women of the Aguaruna of Amazonian Peru who commit suicide often do so with punitive intent because it is one way that they can inflict hardship on their male relatives. According to Brown:

> The very kinsmen who may be unwilling to intervene on a woman's behalf when she is alive are galvanised into action when she kills herself. They subject her husband's behaviour prior to the death to the closest scrutiny. When the husband can

be held accountable—say, because he beat the woman without sufficient reason—her family will attempt to exact compensation in goods or cash. If the husband refuses to negotiate with his dead wife's kin, they may assume a warlike posture. (Brown 1986, Pp. 320–21)

In Malaita a woman who had been sexually assaulted could, by forcing her own kin to kill her, also bring about the death of her assailant (Akin 1985). An East Kwaio woman who entered the sacred area surrounding the men's house was, in early days, killed by her male kin. A woman who had been shamed by being raped would climb onto the roof of the men's house and demand death, at the same time explaining the reason why she wished to die and naming the man who had raped her. As a result, "the rapist himself was seen as the girl's actual murderer, and in every case he was hunted down and killed" (Akin 1985, Pp. 200–201).

Revenge suicide is widely reported in Papua New Guinea. In West New Britain Province, for example, the Lusi-Kaliai say that a person who commits suicide has been "killed with talk" and respond to the death in precisely the same way as they do other forms of homicide (Counts 1980, 1984, 1987). There are commonly known procedures that a Lusi-Kaliai woman who intends to commit revenge suicide should follow. She should warn others of her intent rather than killing herself impulsively or in secret. She should dress herself in her finest clothing, kill herself in the presence of others or where others will be sure to find her body, and communicate to others the identity of the individual she holds responsible for her death. This message is so critical to the successful implementation of a revenge suicide that survivors may report that it has been communicated by the suicide's ghost. If she follows these procedures, a woman can reasonably expect her survivors to consider her to have been killed by shameful slander and/or abuse. When they agree on the identity of the party responsible for the death, the victim's kin retaliate in the same way they do to any other form of homicide (Counts 1980). At the very least the person held responsible by community opinion for slander or abusive treatment leading to suicide expects to compensate the survivors with payments of pigs, cash and shell money, and he or she may also reasonably expect the dead person's kinsmen to seek revenge by either physical violence or sorcery even if they accept the compensation payments. If they do not avenge her death, her survivors may see her ghost wandering near the edge of the village at dusk, reminding them that they have not done their duty.

Elsewhere in Papua New Guinea, the Huli hold the husband of a woman who commits suicide because of his ill-treatment "as responsible as if he had murdered her" (Frankel 1986), while the Jale of the highlands of Irian Jaya (the western, Indonesian portion of the island of New Guinea) believe that suicides are vengeful acts intended to hurt those who are held responsible for the death.

These guilty persons feel regret and self-reproach following the death and are expected to pay compensation to the dead person's kin (Koch 1974). A Fore woman who has been humiliated and who has no socially accepted recourse may kill herself in order to punish the one who offended her because her death will "set in motion the machinery of revenge" (Berndt 1962).

A Gainj woman who kills herself following physical abuse or shaming by her husband can inflict both supernatural harm and mundane disaster on him (Johnson 1981). In her discussion of the Gainj rules for revenge suicide and the effects of the death on the provocateur, Johnson says:

> Gainj women do not kill themselves discreetly. They do it at a time which will preclude their being rescued (usually just before dawn), in a way that leaves no question as to intent (hanging from a tree), and in locations that demand public acknowledgement (usually next to a well-travelled path). It is perhaps the only time in a woman's life when she creates a public event, one calculated, moreover, to thoroughly humiliate her husband. . . . Thus the husband of a suicide loses assets— his wife, the brideprice he paid for her and the compensation he now must pay, and status. He is a man who has been thoroughly and publicly bested by a woman. (Johnson 1981, p. 332)

SUICIDE AND DOMESTIC VIOLENCE

As the above examples make clear, revenge suicide is practiced by powerless people, often women, who have been humiliated or physically abused and who have few if any other options for shifting the burden of shame onto their tormentors and exacting vengeance for the pain and mortification they have suffered. More specifically, the cross-cultural evidence suggests that there is in many societies a significant and complex relationship between female suicide and domestic violence, particularly wife battering.

In Papua New Guinea domestic violence seems to be a normal and expected part of marital relationships (Toft 1985; Toft and Bonnell 1985; Toft 1986), while suicide is widely accepted as a solution to personal problems. A study by Pataki-Schweizer (1985) notes that suicide is common in many Papua New Guinea societies and that it occurs more frequently among females than males. He finds that "Interpersonal conflict, often between spouses, appears as a major precipitant and 'shame,' while often present, does not appear to be the prime or dominant factor" (p. 142).

In Kaliai, West New Britain Province, Counts (1987) reports that wife beating is an expected aspect of the marital relationship. However, a Lusi-Kaliai woman who is beaten unjustifiably or in an unacceptable way, or who is struck repeatedly without a chance to explain herself to her husband, may experience the state of anger, shame and despair that the Lusi-Kaliai call *ailolo sasi*. In this case, she expects her relatives to be sensitive to her pain and humiliation and to champion her against her husband. If she is denied that support, she may kill

herself. Although a Lusi-Kaliai wife may respond to abuse by committing suicide, a death that does not follow the socially constructed pattern for suicide
may be controversial. Counts describes two cases in which death was ambiguous
because the women did not follow the rules for suicide. As a result, some
villagers believed that the women did not kill themselves but died as a result of
injuries received during beatings administered by their husbands (Counts 1987).

Among the Gainj of Papua New Guinea only married women commit suicide.
Although a Gainj husband has the duty to beat his wife if she gives cause by
failing in her domestic duties or if she "exhibits willfulness," women may
respond to being battered by killing themselves (Johnson 1981). "In every case
I recorded, " observes Johnson, "a woman killed herself either after a fight
with another woman in which her husband championed the other woman's
cause, or after public physical abuse from her husband" (p. 326). According
to Johnson, a woman's suicide threats may cause her husband to make conces-
sions to her privately; he cannot do so publicly without acknowledging her
power over him, a situation that a Gainj man would find intolerable. "Indeed,"
says Johnson, "the standard public response of men to suicide threats is, 'there's
a rope nearby.' " (p. 333).

Among the Maring of Papua New Guinea only women commit suicide
(Healey 1979). The major context in which suicide occurs "is after severe, and
physically violent, domestic arguments" (p. 95). In three of six cases analyzed
by Healey, women killed not only themselves but their young daughters after
violent arguments with their husbands. Healey says:

> Destruction of a child in suicide is particularly vengeful, for not only is the husband
> deprived of a wife, but also of children who can care for him in his old age, and
> who will forge new affinal alliances for him. Further, he must provide the customary
> death-payments for both wife and child to the woman's agnates, and face the anger
> and possible vengeance of his affines by physical attack or witchcraft (Healey 1979,
> p. 96)

There is, says Healey, some support for the explanation "that women kill
their daughters to save them from what is perceived to be inevitably an unhappy
future." He recounts the case study of a woman who killed herself because,
among other reasons, "she suffered the public degradation of being spat upon
and beaten by a man who had no clear rights to do so . . .": that is, by men
who were not members of her husband's clan and who, therefore, had no rights
over her. While being spat upon may not seem to be in the same league as
receiving a severe beating, Healey notes that spitting is considered especially
insulting and shaming. One should not spit at pigs and dogs much less at people:
"To be spat at in public is to endure the shame of being treated as less than a
beast" (p. 98).

Both wife beating and suicide are common in the Mount Hagen area of Papua

New Guinea (Strathern 1972). Strathern has data on 29 cases of accomplished suicide; 22 of these cases were women, 20 were married women. A Hagen woman may kill herself because her husband does not pay compensation to her parents for beating her or because she is forced by her parents to return to a husband she wishes to leave. Strathern discusses in some detail how a man may fatally injure his wife, perhaps without intending to, during an episode of marital violence and says that a man is especially likely to kill a promiscuous wife or a woman who is a suspected poisoner. But, says Strathern, "murdering her is also a quasi-suicidal act on the husband's part, for he has destroyed something of potential value to himself. Here the distinction between other-inflicted and self-inflicted injury is not an absolute one" (P. 256).

In his investigation of five suicides among the Managalase of Papua New Guinea, McKellin (1985) reports that the only case of female suicide for which he has data occurred after the woman was struck by her husband. Her family charged that the husband constantly argued with her and hit her, and McKellin interprets her suicide as being the only means she had to escape from an unsatisfactory marriage because her family did not support her against her husband while she was living.

In a study of suicide among Fijian Indians, Haynes (1984) found that where families gave reasons for the death, marital and family problems accounted for 41 percent of female suicides. She says, "Violence was inferred in many cases, either actual assault or fear of it: physical chastisement was recorded in some cases because of conflict with their spouse or with their family, with women usually the victims" (P. 435).

The relationship between wife beating and suicide also exists in South American societies. For example, among the Aguaruna of northern Peru, women kill themselves more frequently than men in a ratio of from 2:1 to 3:1 (Brown 1986). The Aguaruna do not consider suicide to be a socially acceptable reaction to difficult circumstances. Rather, suicide is said to be the result of the victim's inferior ability to think, but Aguaruna women are believed to have inferior reasoning capacity and they have less ability to reach their personal goals. In 31 percent of the cases of female suicide, the victims' relatives said that the motive for death was because the woman was scolded or beaten by either her kinsman or her spouse for failure to perform domestic duties (Brown 1982). According to Brown, women have little control over their marital situation:

. . . men are often reluctant to protect their daughters or sisters from abuse by a brutal husband, except perhaps during the initial trial period of a marriage. This state of affairs changes dramatically when a women kills herself, for then her kinsmen angrily demand an explanation from her husband—and they also seek compensation or exact retribution through a vengeance killing. Women thus use the implicit or explicit threat of suicide to gain leverage over their husband, as a way of preventing beatings or discouraging the formation of a polygynous household. . . . in some cases the husband may face actual physical danger if his wife's family holds him responsible for her death. (Brown 1982, pp. 7–8)

Female suicide is so common among the Aguaruna that it has lost its effectiveness as a way of influencing male behavior: men become inured to it. Brown comments:

> [T]he current high frequency of suicide among Aguaruna women tends to vitiate the coercive power of suicide threats because men can no longer see a clear connexion between their own behaviour and the suicidal behaviour of women. 'It doesn't matter how you treat your wife,' one bewildered man told me. 'Women now just kill themselves for no reason.' (Brown 1986, p. 326)

Wife beating is also common in African societies and may be associated with suicide. Mushanga (1977–1978), himself an African sociologist at the University of Nairobi, suggests that women who are beaten to death by their husbands are, in fact, involved in a type of self-killing. After analyzing the data provided in Bohannan's volume on African homicide and suicide, Mushanga concludes:

> Victims do facilitate their own deaths in many ways. Sometimes the victim invites the offender to kill her or she may use offensive and provocative language which may enrage the husband. . . . Some cases of victim-precipitated homicides in which the wife is the victim result from direct invitation. In one case, a woman, wife of the accused, took a stick and began beating her husband while encouraging him to kill her. . . . It would appear that the new ideas about women's liberation in communities that are generally traditional may create situations in which the wife may directly or indirectly bring about her own death. This may happen as a result of a woman's attempt to assert her own rights, which may conflict with cultural patterns of behaviour and socially accepted responses of a wife towards her husband. (Mushanga 1977–1978, p. 484)

If Mushanga's analysis is correct and African wives are behaving in a way that they know will likely result in their being beaten to death, then they may indeed be involved in a kind of suicide. If this is so, then there are details that Mushanga does not provide that are critical for an understanding of this behavior.

(1) Is this culturally patterned behavior that is taught or exemplified in legend and by gossip?
(2) If so, what are the rules that a woman should follow to allow her to communicate something by her death?
(3) What message is communicated by the manner of her death?
(4) What response may an African woman who dies in this way reasonably expect from other members of her society?

If a woman is expected by other members of her culture to facilitate her death in this way under certain circumstances, and if there are rules that govern her behavior in this event, and if her relatives take vengeance on her husband or demand compensation from him, then this may be a variant on samsonic suicide. If not, then further research is required to determine if the deaths are indeed self-precipitated and, if they are, to place them in their cultural context.

There is also evidence linking wife beating and suicide in North America. As a result of their research on battered women, Back, Post, and Darcy (1982) conclude that the incidence of suicide attempts is higher among beaten women than among those who are not abused and recommend that routine questions about spouse abuse be incorporated into psychiatric evaluation procedures.

In a study of alternatives that are available to North American women who are abused by their husbands, Pagelow (1984) notes that some beaten women react by fighting back, although this is—as she says—"a dangerous gamble." Others try to escape, but if this fails many "resign themselves to their 'fate' and wait for their own death or that of their abusive spouses" (p. 318). Citing an earlier study, she reports that almost all of her survey sample contemplated suicide while 23 percent of them attempted it at least once. Others turn their violence on their husbands, contemplating killing their spouses. "Some of these," she notes, "attempt it, and a few succeed" (p. 318).

In her interviews with fifty suicidal women, Stephens (1985) found that twelve of the fifty were involved in a relationship with a man that included physical abuse. For three of these women, violence was a constant threat "and the suicide effort was both an attempt to escape the brutal situation and to have some kind of revenge" (p. 86). Stephens concludes that:

> The high incidence of battering in this sample requires further investigation. Clearly, the majority of battered women do not attempt suicide—otherwise the rates of female suicide attempting would be much higher than they are—but it appears that a high percent of suicidal women are in battering relationships. The relationship between battering and suicide attempting should be a top priority for researchers. (Stephens 1985, p. 88)

Finally, in a report on their study of the relation of marital separation and divorce to suicide, Jacobson and Portuges (1978) found that perceived verbal attacks by the spouse increase suicide potential—they recommend research on whether this is also true of physical aggression.

WHERE DO WE GO FROM HERE? NEEDS FOR FUTURE RESEARCH

Although there has been virtually no cross-cultural research focussing on the relationship between wife abuse and female suicide, the data that does exist suggests that there is a widespread, significant, and complex relationship between the two forms of violence and that this association exists in all types of societies, small-scale as well as complex industrialized ones.

As Stephens argues, the link between domestic violence and suicide should receive top priority for research, but researchers should be aware that this relationship is a complicated one and that it is essential to know the cultural context in which suicide occurs in order to understand its meaning. For example, does the society recognize suicide as a reasonable act by women who are abused, as the society defines abuse? Second, researchers should carefully examine the circumstances in which death occurs. If suicide is an appropriate response for a woman who suffers from abuse, does the particular death under study meet the criteria for revenge suicide? Did it follow the rules? If not, then there may be other explanations for the death. Possibly the woman was motivated by other factors, such as feelings of guilt or shame that were not directly related to the abuse. For instance, Chowning (1985) reports that among the Kove of West New Britain, ". . . a woman beaten excessively by her husband may commit suicide, but this seems to happen only when she thinks that the beatings are connected with loss of affection, because he is interested in someone else" (P. 82).

It is also possible that a death that occurs in the context of domestic violence is not culpable suicide but covert homicide. A variant of this explanation, one suggested by Mushanga (1977–1978), is that in some cases a woman who is beaten to death by her husband may have actually arranged her own death. Mushanga's examples and the ambiguous deaths reported by Counts (1987) are situations that mirror each other; in one case, deaths that are officially defined as suicide are suspected homicides. In the other circumstance, deaths that clearly seem to be the result of homicide are said to have been in fact "victim-precipitated." In neither of these cases can the line between suicide and homicide be clearly drawn. Finally, there is the possibility that the suicide may be a direct response to the beating itself: a woman may kill herself because she is in despair and no longer able to bear the pain of physical abuse.

Inquiry into the cultural context of wife beating generally, and the complicated relationship between wife battering and suicide specifically, should be top priority for research by anthropologists as well as by other social scientists concerned with domestic violence or the study of suicide. As a closing reminder of the complexity of the problem, we should observe that in some societies it may be the husband rather than the wife who commits suicide after an episode of wife beating. Hezel (1984) who has done research on Trukese suicide reports that men who thrash or verbally abuse their wives sometimes kill themselves following the violent episode, while there "is no recorded case of a wife committing suicide because of a disagreement with her husband" (P. 199). The people of each culture can be expected to make a unique assessment of the combination of shame, desire for vengeance, and despair that lead to self-killing. It is critical that we understand that assessment and the context in which it is reached in order to comprehend the meaning of suicide.

REFERENCES

Akin, D. 1985. Suicide and women in East Kwaio, Malaita. In F.X. Hezel, D.H. Rubinstein, & G. M. White, eds., *Culture, youth and suicide in the Pacific*. Honolulu: Pacific Islands Studies Program, 198–210.

Back, S.M., R.D. Post, and G. Darcy. 1982. A study of battered women in a psychiatric setting. *Women and Therapy* 1: 13–26.

Berndt, R.M. 1962. *Excess and restraint*. Chicago: University of Chicago Press.

Brown, M.F. The dark side of progress. 44th International Congress of Americanists, Manchester, England, September 1982.

Chowning, A. 1985. Kove women and violence. In S. Toft ed., *Domestic violence in Papua New Guinea*. Boroko: Papua New Guinea Law Reform Commission, P. 72–91.

Counts, D.A. 1980. Fighting back is not the way. *American Ethnologist* 7: 332–51.

Counts, D.A. 1984. Revenge suicide by Lusi women. In D. O'Brien & S. Tiffany, eds., *Rethinking women's roles*. Berkeley: University of California Press, P. 71–93.

Counts, D.A. 1987. Female suicide and wife abuse. *Suicide & Life-Threatening Behavior* 17: 194–204.

Epstein, A.L. 1984. *The experience of shame in Melanesia*. London: Royal Anthropological Institute of Great Britain and Ireland.

Fleuhr-Lobban, C. 1977. Agitation for change in the Sudan. In A. Schlegel, ed., *Sexual stratification*. New York: Columbia University Press, P. 127–43.

Frankel, S. 1986. *The Huli response to illness*. Cambridge: Cambridge University Press.

Haynes, R.H. 1984. Suicide in Fiji. *British Journal of Psychiatry* 145: 433–38.

Healey, C. 1979. Women and suicide in New Guinea. *Social Analysis* 2: 89–106.

Hezel, F.X. 1984. Cultural patterns in Trukese suicide. *Ethnology* 23: 193–206.

Hoskin, J.O., M.I. Friedman, and J.E. Cawte. 1969. A high incidence of suicide in a preliterate-primitive society. *Psychiatry* 32: 200–10.

Jacobson, G., and S.H. Portuges. 1978. Relation of marital separation and divorce to suicide. *Suicide & Life-Threatening Behavior* 8: 217–24.

Jeffreys, M.D.W. 1952. Samsonic suicide or suicide of revenge among Africans. *African Studies* 19: 118–22.

Johnson, P.L. 1981. When dying is better than living. *Ethnology* 20: 325–34.

Koch, K.F. 1974. *War and peace in Jalemo*. Cambridge: Harvard University Press.

McKellin, W. 1985. The meanings of Managlase suicide. Association for Social Anthropology in Oceania, Salem, Massachusetts.

Marshall, M. 1979. *Weekend warriors*. Palo Alto: Mayfield.

Menninger, K. 1938. *Man against himself*. New York: Harcourt, Brace & World.

Mushanga, T.M. 1977–78. Wife victimization in East and Central Africa. *Victimology* 2: 479–85.

Pagelow, M.D. 1984. *Family violence*. New York: Praeger.

Panoff, M. 1977. Suicide and social control in New Britain. *Bijdrogen: Tot de Taal-Land-en Volkenkunde* 133: 44–62.

Pataki-Schweizer, K. J. 1985. Suicide in contemporary Papua New Guinea. In F.X. Hezel, D. Rubinstein, and G.M. White, eds., *Culture, youth and suicide in the Pacific*. Honolulu: Pacific Islands Study Program, 139–51.

Simpson, G. 1951. The aetiology of suicide. In E. Durkheim *Suicide*. New York: Free Press, P. 13–34.

Siverts, H. Broken hearts and pots. Forty-fourth International Congress of Americanists, Manchester, England, September 1982.

Stephens, B.J. 1985. Suicidal women and their relationships with husbands, boyfriends and lovers. *Suicide & Life-Threatening Behavior* 15: 77–90.

Strathern, M. 1972. *Women in between*. London: Seminar Press.

Toft, S. 1985. *Domestic violence in Papua New Guinea*. Boroko: Papua New Guinea Law Reform Commission.

Toft, S. 1986. *Domestic violence in urban Papua New Guinea*. Boroko: Papua New Guinea Law Reform Commission.

Toft, S., and S. Bonnell. 1985. *Marriage and domestic violence in rural Papua New Guinea*. Boroko: Papua New Guinea Law Reform Commission.

Ullrich, H.E. 1977. Caste differences between Brahmin and non-Brahmin women in a south Indian village. In A. Schlegel, ed., *Sexual stratification*. New York: Columbia University Press, P. 94–108.

Westermarck, E. 1908. Suicide. *Sociological Review* 1:12–33.

Wymeersch, P. 1976. Moord en zelfmoord. *Tijdschrift voor Sociale Wetenschappen* 21: 331–48.

7

Media Impacts on Suicide

Steven Stack

The field of sociology produces more than 200 studies on suicide per decade. The literature through the early eighties has been reviewed elsewhere (Stack 1982). Since that review, there has continued to be three significant research streams representing each of three theoretical traditions: that on the classic Durkheimian (1966) model; the status integration model (Gibbs and Martin 1964); and the suggestion-imitation model (Phillips 1974).

Recent research has tended to replicate Durkheim's findings on divorce and suicide (e.g. Stack 1985, 1989; Trovato 1986, 1987; Breault 1986). In like manner, recent work has tended to support the Durkheimian tradition that religion reduces the propensity toward suicide (Breault 1986). That the economic anomie produced by unemployment is associated with suicide, has continued to be supported in the sociological work (see Platt 1984 for a review). In contrast, status integration theory has been questioned by some recent work (Stafford and Gibbs 1985; Stack 1987b).

The suggestion-imitation model of Phillips (1974) has probably received the most attention in the last five years (see Phillips 1986 for a review of the work through 1985). This chapter reviews the most recent work on the imitation model. It then suggests points of departure for future work in this research stream.

RECENT RESEARCH DEVELOPMENTS: MEDIA EFFECTS ON SUICIDE

Several issues face the current researcher who works on media effects on suicide. First, there is considerable debate over whether or not media stories have to deal with real persons, as opposed to fictional persons, in order to have an effect. Second, Baran and Reiss (1985a,b) called for theory and research on exactly what types of suicide victims should be expected to trigger imitative suicides. For example, should there be differential effects for villains vs heroes? Should we match victims and the audience at risk by age to control for modeling influences? Third, as Stack (1987a) has pointed out, research needs to take into

The work on this paper was partially supported by grant 41510 from the National Institute of Mental Health.

account the mood of the audience. Some work has been done that tries to tap the receptivity of the audience to imitation. It is possible, for example, that stories might have more of an impact in bad economic times when the mood of depression in the audience is relatively high. Fourth, all previous work has focused on the post-World War II era, an era with all three channels of the media (printed, radio, and television) present. It is not clear if the impact of the media would hold for periods without the electronic media to echo the messages of the printed media.

Real vs Fictional Suicides

While there is not much doubt that news stories about the suicides of real people can have an impact on suicide in the real world, there has been much debate over the impact of fictional stories. A path-breaking work by Phillips (1982) found that suicidal behaviors in the soap operas had a significant impact on the incidence of national suicide. Measurement errors, however, were found in this seminal work: When these errors were corrected, the results indicated no relationship between the media and suicide (Kessler and Stipp 1984). A study of the media impact of a soap opera suicide on suicide in Britain also found no effect (Platt 1987).

Next there came a series of studies on the instance of the four made-for-television films on teenage suicide in late 1984 to early 1985. Focusing on the New York City metropolitan area, Gould and Shaffer (1986) found a significant impact between these fictional films and the suicide rate. They called for additional replication works outside of the New York area. A year later Gould (1987) reported one such effort at replication for several cities spread across the United States that failed on the whole to replicate the results. Berman (1987) was also unable to replicate the Gould and Shaffer study for 19 coroner's offices covering a sample of American cities, coast to coast. Phillips and Paight (1987) inspected the impacts for the populations of two complete states, California and Pennsylvania. They too were unable to replicate the original Gould and Shaffer (1986) study. They called for work on a still larger population. Stack (1988a) answered the call of these authors and studied the possible impact of the films on the whole American population. No significant effect was found; instead the suicide count for teenagers went down in the two weeks after the suicide films. Further analysis removed the rural population to see if possibly the effect was restricted to urban populations. Still, there was no effect. Several other analyses were done where the population was progressively restricted to larger and larger cities similar to New York City. No evidence of an imitation effect was detected. Stack (1988a) concludes that the Gould and Shaffer (1986) findings were probably restricted to the New York area due to some contextual factor, more or less specific to New York. A scrutiny of local New York papers revealed that at the time of the first films there was substantial press coverage of real life suicides. One exhaustive work on suicide clusters termed this one of the most well publicized clusters of the 1980s (Coleman 1987). Stack argues that in order for films about teenage suicide to have an impact on suicide in the real world, real teenage suicides have to be publicized at the same time. Possibly future research may find cities other than New York where the films did have a significant impact. If so, it may be due to a simultaneous coverage of real teen suicide.

The finding that suicide stories must involve real rather than fictional characters in order to have an impact on suicide, is consistent with related experimental evidence. Berkowitz (1984) reviewed evidence indicating that depictions of real as opposed to fictional violence were most apt to elicit aggression among subjects in laboratory settings.

One study that does support an imitation effect is that done in West Germany by Schmidtke and Hafner (1986). The authors found that a publicized, six-part television film series, "Death of a Student," was significantly associated with increases in suicide. The study was restricted to suicide on the railways, the location of the suicide in the film, thereby controlling for the method of suicide. This may explain the discrepancy between their study and the United States based research.

Research on Audience Identification with the Suicide Victim

Most research to date has lumped a wide variety of suicide victims together into aggregated indexes. It would seem that certain social types or categories of victims might promote more identification in the audience than other types. A series of studies has shed some light on the issue of which categories of stories might trigger the most imitative suicides.

Drawing on Tarde's (1903) laws of imitation, Stack (1987a) argued that identification between the audience and the suicide victim was more apt to occur if the victim was of high rather than low social status; that is, imitation follows the law of the inferior copying the behavior of the superior. Stack further contended that imitation was more apt to occur if the suicide victim was well known, i.e., if the audience had some familiarity with him/her from the recent past. Such persons are termed "celebrities." A publicized story about a celebrity suicide, then, is the social type most apt to breed mass identification and, hence, imitative suicides.

There are, however, a number of different social types of celebrities. Stack (1987a) differentiated among different categories of celebrities including economic, political, villain, artist, and entertainment celebrities. Stack contended that, given that nationalism plays a part in the identification process, foreign celebrities in any of these categories will probably not spark identification and suicide imitation in the American population. This, in a preliminary analysis, proved to be the case.

In an analysis of monthly time series data from 1948–1983, Stack (1987a) found that only two types of celebrity suicides were significantly associated with increases in the national monthly suicide rate. First, publicized suicides of entertainers were associated with an increase of 217 additional suicides in the month of the publicity. These included the cases of film star, Marilyn Monroe, and television star, Freddie Prinze. Second, publicized suicides of political celebrities were associated with an increase of 50 suicides. These included the suicides of James Forrestal, the secretary of defense, and United States senators such as Hunt of Wyoming. As anticipated, celebrity-villain suicides were unrelated to increases in suicide. These included those of a mobster and a political official who was about to go on trial for accepting bribes. Surprisingly, economic celebrity suicides did not, evidently, spark enough identification to trigger suicides.

By far the strongest imitation effect found by Stack to date is that of what he calls "star suicide," the suicide of an entertainment celebrity like Monroe. Stack borrowed from Dyer's (1979) theory of the star in order to explain the powerful effect of star suicide on imitative suicide. A star promotes an unusual degree of mass identification since he/she represents both the ordinary and the unusual at the same time. The audience identifies with the star on two levels: the star is like the audience in the ordinary roles (e.g., father, lover) that he/she plays on the screen, but different in that in real life he/she has high status. The star promotes mass audience identification through the celebration of the ordinary.

Identification may proceed along lines in addition to celebrity status. Stack (1987a) contended that the suicidal audience might conceivably identify with celebrities who are experiencing the same types of life's problems as the audience. For example, the suicidal population is known to have a relatively high incidence of poor physical and mental health and marital problems. Stack found, however, that these types of suicidogenic conditions had to be combined with entertainment or political celebrity status in order to trigger imitative suicides. This study, however, was restricted to celebrity suicides, only a small portion of all publicized suicides. The results may be different for a study that includes noncelebrity suicides. Possibly, there is also some downward identification with noncelebrity suicides.

Stack (1987d) explored the impact of publicized suicide stories where the victim had severe marital trouble. These stories were divided into three subgroups: star suicides, suicides preceded by the murder of one's spouse, and a residual category of all other cases of publicized suicides where the victim had marital difficulties. Stack found that all three types of publicized suicides were significantly associated with increases in the monthly suicide rate. Hence, when noncelebrities are included in the analysis, victims' marital troubles per se are found to be associated with suicide. These troubles may be serving as points of identification for the suicidal population.

A recent study implies that imitation effects may be the strongest for young people. Phillips and Carstensen (1986) found that the incidence of teenage suicide increased after television news stories on suicide. The stories, however, involved very few teenage victims. This suggests that age identification—at least for American teenagers—may not be important; they identify with aspects of the suicide victim other than the victim's age.

Another stream of work has documented the importance of age identification in imitation effects. Schmidtke and Hafner (1986) found that the increase in suicide after the showing of the television film "Death of a Student," was strongest for young males; the effect declined as older age cohorts' suicide rates were analyzed. Stack (1987g) analyzed the impact of all publicized television news stories on elderly suicide. Controlling for the other variables in the model, months with a publicized suicide story were associated with a rise of elderly suicide amounting to 10 elderly suicides. When the analysis was restricted to only those stories about elderly victims, the effect increased to 19 additional elderly suicides. The stories on the elderly victims, often containing references to the living problems of the elderly such as poor physical health, were thought to promote more identification among members of the elderly audience.

Phillips and Carstensen (1988) analyze the impact of television news stories on suicide in California for 1968–1985. Care was taken to omit one-network stories since these are known not to affect suicide. Multiprogram suicide news stories had the greatest impact on teenage suicides (22 percent increase), followed by that for 50–64 year olds (8 percent), 40–49 year olds (6.9 percent), and 20–29 year olds (7 percent). The impact of the stories on males and females was about the same (6.1 vs 6.8 percent), and the impact on married vs not married was similar as well (7.4 vs 7.8 percent). The increase in the Werther Effect was greater for blacks than whites (12.7 vs 5.8 percent). Phillips and Carstensen (1988) did not, however, match the demographic characteristics of the victims in the stories with the suicide groups in the real world. Possibly, for example, stories about divorced people would trigger even more suicides among the nonmarried group.

Phillips, Carstensen, and Lundie (1989) test the impact of aspects of story content on possible identification and teenage suicide. Videotapes of 32 news stories were inspected to obtain story content. Aspects of story content investigated were: presence of a photo of the victim, photo of the suicide, method reported, mention of family or friends of the victim, suicide central or peripheral to the story, suicide committed in the United States or not, nationality of the victim, celebrity status of the victim, victim related to a celebrity, sex of victim, and definite vs apparent suicide. None of these aspects of story content was found to be significantly related to teen suicide. The authors conclude that the key determinant of imitative suicide is probably the amount of publicity, not the content of the story (at least for teenagers). They did not, however, inspect the age of the victim as a point of identification for the audience. Possibly, teens would identify more with teen victims than older victims. Teen victims, are, however, uncommon in televised news stories.

An unexplored area in media effects on suicide concerns murder-suicide stories. Some authors argue that since a behavior other than suicide is included in these stories, the stories will probably not trigger suicide. Hence, the murder-suicide stories are often dropped from the analysis in some studies (Phillips and Carstensen 1986). It may be premature to drop these for both theoretical and empirical reasons. Stack (1987c) argues that murder-suicide stories may trigger suicide from the standpoint of Menninger's (1938) theory of suicidal behavior. Menninger viewed most suicides as a mixture of the desire to die and the desire to kill a tormenter. If so, murder-suicides should promote substantial identification among members of the suicidal population since murder-suicides perfectly match the motivational structure of the suicidal personality.

Stack (1987c) analyzed the cases of spectacular murder-suicides and mass murder-suicides. These cases involved the killing of two or more persons followed by the suicide of the victim. Stack reported a substantial increase in suicide during the months of these stories. The results seem consistent with the general logic of Menninger's theory.

The Mood of The Audience: An Intervening Factor

The mood of the audience is a factor neglected in just about all published work on the subject. From the standpoint of Blumer's (1969) symbolic interactionist perspective on media effects, however, this mood variable is critical. For example, if a suicide story appears in a month where the economy is strong, the family is in good shape, and the level of religiosity is high, we might expect a small impact on suicide given the high degree of economic and social support in the mass audience. In contrast, if the economy is weak and marked by rising mass unemployment, if the family is losing its vitality as indicated by a rising divorce rate, and if religious support systems are falling off, then the audience should be more receptive to suicide stories.

Three studies have explored this role of audience mood. Stack (1987f) uses an international war, World War I, as an index of high social integration and low suicidal mood. He contends that stories appearing during an all-out popular war should have little impact on imitative suicide. An analysis of monthly data from 1910–1920 found that this was the case. Peacetime stories increased suicide whereas wartime stories did not.

In one of the few works on suicide in mid-life, Stack (1987h) found no evidence for an imitative effect in an analysis of television news stories. The television news stories concerned people who suicided in mid-life. Stack contends that the reason for the lack of an imitative effect is that of three broad age groups (the young, the middle-aged, and the elderly) the middle-aged are lowest in suicidogenic life conditions. For example, they are not the lowest in physical health, and they are considerably better off financially than the young. Hence, those at mid-life are seen as not being in a receptive mood to imitate publicized suicides.

Stack (1987e) used the state of the economy as an index of audience mood. It was contended that in times of high unemployment the societal mood would move toward a depressed, pessimistic state. Given increases in suicidal mood, the audience should be prone to imitating suicide. Stack compared a multiplicative or interaction model—where the effects of stories in bad economic times follow a multiplicative function—with a model that does not take into account such interaction effects, an "additive" model. There was no appreciable difference in the explanatory value of the two models. For example, they explained the same amount of variance in suicide. Stack cautioned, however, that the reason may have been due to the fact that not a single suicide story involved an unemployed person. Only one story involved a person with financial difficulties and that was a very rich executive officer of a multibillion-dollar multinational corporation. The mass audience probably would not identify with this individual. Stack concluded that we need a fresh data set with some examples of publicized suicide stories that involve unemployed persons in the context of bad economic times. Only then can we fully test the adequacy of contextual factors related to the economy.

Research on the Pre-Television Period

Radio was not easily available until the early 1920s. Hence, work on the media and suicide before that period is based on only one of the three media channels: printed media. The electronic media (radio and television) were totally absent. The absence of the electronic media puts the theory of imitation to a difficult test. Without radio and television to back up its messages to a national audience, the degree of newspaper publicity may not be quite enough to result in imitative suicides.

In an analysis of the monthly suicide rate from 1910 to 1920, Stack measured national coverage in terms of a story making page one in three selected newspapers. He found that months with a publicized suicide story had 48 more suicides than months lacking such stories. Even though the stories in the printed media could not be reinforced by the electronic media, the stories still had a significant impact on suicide in the real world.

All research from other periods has been based on relatively small amounts of media coverage of suicide. Typically, there are no more than one or two publicized suicide stories per year. While this research generally indicates that suicide increases after a publicized, real suicide story, it is unclear from this research if hyper-amounts of media coverage would be associated with hyper-increases in suicide. It is possible that, given a relatively small suicidal population pool, repeated coverage of suicide in the press may reach a point of diminishing returns on suicidal behavior. Persons on the edge of suicidal behavior might imitate suicide early on, leaving fewer and fewer left to imitate dozens of suicide stories that follow. On the other hand, hyper-coverage of suicide may lead to a disinhibition effect where the public becomes more accepting of suicide. Hence, the pool of suicidal people itself might increase as suicide is seen as more legitimate or as less wrong since so many people are doing it. As Berkowitz (1984) pointed out, exposure to depictions of violence are associated with the exaggerations in the perception of how many people are engaged in the behavior. Repeated stories on suicide might continue to add to the suicide problem.

Stack and Gundlach (1988) analyzed data from a period of record high suicide coverage by the *New York Times*. The *Times* published over 100 suicide stories during 1913–1914 (whereas in the post-World War II period they published about two a year). Focusing on the audience at risk, the population of the city of New York, the authors reported a nonlinear relationship. Months with 3 or more suicide stories had a significantly higher rate of suicide. Months with only 1 or 2 publicized suicides did not have a higher suicide rate. There was also a ceiling effect in that the imitation effect did not increase proportionately after the floor of 3 stories per month was reached. It was estimated that the period of hyper-coverage by the *Times* was associated with an increase of 98 suicides.

POINTS OF DEPARTURE FOR FUTURE RESEARCH

Each of the four areas discussed in the first part of this chapter leave issues unaddressed. These issues can serve as points of departure in future work.

Real vs. Fictional Suicides

Phillips (1974) coined the term the Werther Effect to describe the process by which a publicized suicide story has an impact on suicide in the real world. Possibly the case of the novel based on a fictional character has some implications for work on fictional suicide and imitative suicides. Werther, a character in an eighteenth-century German novel, was said to have triggered a wave of suicides. This was, however, a wave among the educated elite. Some dead persons were found with a copy of the novel nearby or even in their hands. Such a Werther Effect was based on prolonged exposure; reading a book takes longer than watching an hour-and-a-half television film frequently interrupted by commercials. Possibly, the multiple part "Death of a Student" had an effect on West German teenage suicide due to the amount of coverage. It may take repeated television episodes to achieve the level of character development one would get from reading a full-length novel. Also, reading a full-length novel may represent more of a receptivity and commitment to suicide ideation than the casual watching of a television film. Future work might inspect the incidence of a Werther Effect by studying suicides among today's educated elite, the group most apt to be reading book-length materials with a prosuicide message. I am reminded of a time when I drove a suicide attempter to an emergency room in a university town. The attending physician made a point out of telling the suicide attempter not to read any novels by Sartre or Camus. Evidently, there was a pattern of association between reading these existentialist authors and perceived suicide risk. Possibly future work might uncover a Werther Effect at this level.

Audience Identification

Further work needs to be done to address Baran and Reiss' (1985a,b) call for distinguishing social types apt to trigger or not to trigger imitative suicides. For example, publicized altruistic suicides (Durkheim 1966) may not be apt to increase imitative suicides. There are numerous cases of this type of suicide, including Jan Palach, who suicided in protest of the Soviet invasion of Czechoslovakia and the suicides in protest of the Vietnam War. Work is needed to see if these, in fact, have no influence on suicide. I would contend that since suicidal people generally do not suicide to further a collective cause, they would not identify with such altruistic suicide victims.

Almost all of Stack's work on differential identification has been done using monthly datasets. Further work is needed using the daily count of suicide. Stack may be minimizing imitative effects to the extent that these effects are of a shorter term than a month. Nevertheless, using daily counts of suicide has its disadvantages. These include not being able to control for sociological conditions such as unemployment and only being able to study the period since 1972, the first year for which daily suicide counts are available (Stack 1987j). The latter problem involves not being able to study a full range of social types of suicide victims due to lack of enough cases.

Another solution to the problem of an inadequate number of national suicide stories for building taxonomies of social types, is to study suicide at the local level. New York City would be a good choice because publicized suicide stories are easy to locate, given that its main newspaper has an adequate index (*New*

York Times Index). While approximately a dozen American cities now have newspaper indexes under the Bell and Howell indexing system (e.g., Los Angeles, Houston, San Francisco), these indexes do not have a complete list of suicide stories under the subject Suicide. New York City's population of eight million makes it as large, or even larger, than many European nations. Studying suicide at the local level would also allow for generating more cases of the suicides of common people to facilitate tests of the process of audience downward identification with noncelebrities. National stories, in contrast, are disproportionately about high status and celebrity-type victims.

Audience Mood: A Contextual Factor

One problem with the work to date on the role of the economic context on imitative suicide is that the victims of the publicized stories were all employed (Stack 1987e). This problem could be resolved by using data from the Great Depression. Preliminary analysis has found instances of numerous publicized suicides of unemployed persons in this period (Stack 1988b). These data, then, would provide the test that was missing in the previous study based on the 1968–1980 period (Stack 1987e).

Work is needed on other structural conditions that are thought to be predictive of a suicidal mood. These conditions include the state of the family—measurable in terms of such indicators as the incidence of divorce and illegitimacy—and religiosity. These conditions are often difficult to measure in small units of time. For example, the monthly data on divorce are available only from the late 1960s. Analyses, then, may have to be based on broad time spans known to be high and low on a specific mediating condition. The period of known high church attendance and low divorce of the 1950s could be compared to the high divorce, lower church attendance period of the 1970s. It is anticipated that the publicized stories of the 1950s would have less of an impact on imitative suicide than the stories of the 1970s.

Pre-Television Period

Work on the pre-television period has probably been hampered for at least two reasons. First, it is difficult to obtain a list of suicide victims given that the *New York Times Index* did not publish such under its Suicide subject heading during the 1930s and 1940s. Hence, the researcher needs to read the front page of each and every newspaper to construct a list of potential suicide victims who might have made national news. For 1940–1949, *Facts on File: An Index to International News,* can be used as an index of national coverage, as a check on the *New York Times.* For information from before 1940, the serious researcher will have to search at least the front page of several other papers to obtain a list of publicized stories. For the 1900–1929 period, however, the *New*

York Times did include a list of suicide victims, making research on this period easier. A second problem is that the suicide data are not available for the nation as a whole before 1933. The data series, then, have to be appropriately adjusted.

There are still a number of issues that can be addressed with these data. Stack's (1987f) finding that wartime suicide stories during World War I had no effect on suicide, needs to be replicated for World War II. For the Second World War, the electronic medium of radio was available to echo the stories in the printed media. The war lasted much longer and involved more casualties and military personnel. In addition, there were significant military setbacks in the early years of the war that may have brought out mass depression given the sacrifices and commitment of the audience to the war effort. It is possible that suicide stories involving the depressed relatives of soldiers killed in times of defeat may trigger imitative suicides. In contrast, suicide stories not involving such persons and that were reported in times of major Allied victories may have had no impact on national suicide rates.

The great stock market crash of October 1929 provides an interesting context for a natural experiment. Data from this period could be analyzed to see if the publicized suicides were associated with an increase in suicide from that time. A substantial increase might be expected.

The 1920s was a period of great economic expansion and relatively low unemployment. In this context, it might be anticipated that publicized suicide stories would have little impact on suicide. Future work is needed to test this assertion.

OTHER RESEARCH NEEDS

Given the infrequency of publicized suicide stories in the United States, work with fresh data from other nations would be welcome. Monthly, weekly, and daily suicide counts are needed to assess imitation theory given the short time frame of imitation effects. Unfortunately, such data are not available in some nations. Schmidtke and Hafner (1986) report that such data are not available from the West German government. Instead, they had to confine their analysis to railway suicides since the only data available was from the railroad companies.

Essentially all of the work on suicide has been based on a somewhat narrow view of media coverage. Either the measure of media coverage has been restricted to the electronic media (e.g., Baran and Reiss 1985a) or restricted to the printed media (e.g., Wasserman 1984; Stack 1987a). Since media coverage in one media channel is not a perfect predictor of coverage in another, work is needed that uses a combined index. This would reduce measurement error and serve as a check on previous results.

Experimental research could be done where subjects are given a suicide ideation scale before and after viewing various types of suicide stories. This type of work would help to isolate which categories of suicide stories are most apt to promote audience identification. The ethical considerations revolving around the protection of human subjects may make this type of work difficult to complete.

Much of the current research involves the analysis of the impact of television news stories. A content analysis of the actual television news stories (tapes are available from the Joint University Libraries 1987) might uncover clues to the identification process that are simply not available in the printed abstracts of the television news stories. My review of tapes of the stories found that some stories never even showed a photograph of the victim. Other stories contained highly emotional footage of the crying relatives of the deceased. Work is needed to construct a taxonomy of the features of these stories that might be most apt to trigger identification and suicide.

There is essentially no work at the micro level of analysis. All previous work has been based on highly aggregated data. It is unclear, for example, whether or not the excess of suicides after a publicized suicide story involve people who read and subsequently imitated the suicides in the media. There are just a few scattered reports from journalists on individual cases where newspaper publicity did, in fact, contribute to a suicide (see Stack 1987j for a review). Field work is needed wherein the significant others of suicides clustering around the weeks after a publicized suicide are interviewed. This work will be very difficult to do. It requires almost immediate access to lists of suicide victims so that their relatives can be interviewed before they are apt to forget the details of the victim's knowledge of recent publicized suicides. Many of the usual problems faced by micro level research also apply. Many suicidal people are relatively high in social isolation. Such persons' contact with the media may be unobservable.

REFERENCES

Baron, J., and P. Reiss. 1985a. Same time next year: aggregate analysis of the mass media and violent behavior. *American Sociological Review* 50:364–71.

——1985b. Reply to Phillips and Bollen. *American Sociological Review* 50:372–76.

Berkowitz, L. 1984. Some effects of thoughts on anti- and prosocial media effects: A cognitive-neoassociation analysis. *Psychological Bulletin* 95:410–27.

Berman, A. 1987. Fictional suicide and imitation effects. Paper read at the annual meeting of the American Association of Suicidology, San Francisco, California.

Blumer, H. 1969. Suggestion for the study of mass media effects. In H. Blumer, Ed., *Symbolic Interactionism.* Englewood Cliffs, NJ: Prentice Hall, p. 183–194.

Breault, K.D. 1986. Suicide in america: A test of the durkheim's theory of religious and family integration. *American Journal of Sociology* 92:628–56.

Coleman, L. 1987. *Suicide Clusters.* Boston: Faber and Faber.

Durkheim, E. 1966. *Suicide.* New York: Free Press.

Dyer, R. 1979. *Stars.* London: British Film Institute.

Gibbs, J., and W.T. Martin. 1964. *Status Integration and Suicide.* Eugene, OR: University of Oregon Press.

Gould, M.S. and D. Shaffer. 1986. The impact of suicide in television films. *The New England Journal of Medicine* 315:690-93.

Gould, M.S. 1987. Suicide and the media. Paper read at the meeting of the American Association of Suicidology, San Francisco, California.

Joint University Libraries. 1987. Television News Archive. Nashville, TN: Joint University Libraries.

Kessler, R., and H. Stipp. 1984. The impact of fictional television suicide stories on U.S. fatalities: a replication. *American Journal of Sociology* 90:151-67.

Menninger, K. 1938. *Man Against Himself* New York: Harcourt Brace.

Phillips, D.P. 1974. The influence of suggestion on suicide. *American Sociological Review* 39:340-54.

———1982. The impact of fictional television stories on U.S. adult fatalities: new evidence on the effect of the mass media on violence. *American Journal of Sociology* 87:1340-59.

———1986. The found experiment: a new technique for assessing the impact of mass media violence on real world aggressive behavior. *Public Communication and Behavior* 1:259-307.

Phillips, D.P. and L.L. Carstensen. 1986. Clustering of teenage suicides after television news stories about suicide. *New England Journal of Medicine* 315:685-89.

Phillips, D.P. and D.J. Paight. 1987. The impact of televised films about suicide: a replicative study." *New England Journal of Medicine* 317:809-11.

Phillips D.P. and L.L. Carstensen. 1988. The effect of suicide stories on various demographic groups, 1968-1985. *Suicide and Life Threatening Behavior* 18:100-14.

Phillips, D.P., L.L. Carstensen and D. Paight. 1989. Effects of mass media news stories on suicide, with new evidence on the role of story content. In C. R. Pfeffer, ed., *Suicide Among Youth: Perspectives on Risk and Prevention.* Washington, D.C.: American Psychiatric Press, pp. 101-16.

Platt, S. 1984. Unemployment and suicidal behavior: a review of the literature. *Social Science and Medicine* 19:93-115.

———1987. The aftermath of angie's overdose: is soap (opera) damaging to your health? *British Medical Journal* 294:954-57

Schmidtke, A., and H. Hafner. 1986. Die vermittlung von selbstmordmotivation und selbstmord-motivation durch fiktive modelle. *Nervenarzt* 57:502-10.

Stack, S. 1982. Suicide: a decade review of the sociological literature. *Deviant Behavior* 4:41-66.

———1985. The effect of religious-family integration on suicide: 1954-1978. *Journal of Marriage and the Family* 47:431-37.

———1987a. Celebrities and suicide: A taxonomy and analysis: 1948-1983. *American Sociological Review* 52:401-413.

———1987b. The effect of status integration on suicide: New micro level data. Paper read at the annual meeting of the National Council on Family Relations, Atlanta, Georgia.

———1987c. The effect of publicized mass murders and murder-suicides on lethal violence, 1968-1980. Paper read at the annual meeting of the American Society for Criminology, Montreal, Canada.

———1987d. Divorce, suicide, and the mass media: An analysis of differential identification, 1948-1980. Paper read at the annual meeting of the National Council on Family Relations, Atlanta, Georgia.

———1987e. The media and suicide: a nonadditive model, 1968-1980. Paper read at the annual meeting of the American Association of Suicidology, San Francisco, California.

——1987f. Suicide impacts in war and peace, 1910–1920. Paper read at the annual meeting of the American Association of Suicidology, San Francisco, California.

———1987g. Audience receptiveness, the media, and aged suicide, 1968–1980. Paper read at the annual meeting of the American Public Health Association, New Orleans, Louisiana.

———1987h. The impact of the media on suicide in midlife. Paper read at the annual meeting of the American Public Health Association, New Orleans, Louisiana.

———1987i. Celebrities and suicide: another look. Paper read at the annual meeting of the American Sociological Association, Chicago, Illinois.

———1987j. The sociological study of suicide: Methodological issues. *Suicide and Life Threatening Behavior* 17:133–50.

———1988a. The impact of fictional television films on teenage suicide, 1984. Paper read at the annual meeting of the Society for the Study of Social Problems, Atlanta. Conditionally accepted for publication in *Social Science Quarterly*.

———1988b. The impact of the media on suicide in the context of the great depression. Paper read at the annual meeting of the American Association of Suicidology, Washington, DC.

———1989. The impact of divorce on suicide in Norway, 1950–1980. *Journal of Marriage and the Family* 51:229–38.

Stack, S., and J. Gundlach. 1988. The impact of hyper media coverage on suicide, New York City, 1910–1920. Paper read at the annual meeting of the American Association of Suicidology, Washington, D.C.

Stafford, M., and J. Gibbs. 1985. A major problem with the theory of status integration. *Social Forces* 63: 643–60.

Tarde, G. 1903. *The laws of imitation.* New York: Henry Holt and Company.

Trovato, F. 1986. The relationship between divorce and suicide: the Canadian case. *Journal of Marriage and the Family* 48:341–48.

Trovato, F. 1987. A longitudinal analysis of divorce and suicide in Canada. *Journal of Marriage and the Family* 49:193–203.

Wasserman, I. 1984. Imitation and suicide: a reexamination of the Werther effect. *American Sociological Review* 49:427–36.

8

Ecological Analysis of Suicide: Problems and Prospects

Ferenc Moksony

As even a cursory reading of literature shows, the term "ecological" is interpreted in a number of different ways. Sometimes it refers to the use of areal data as substitutes for their individual-level counterparts unavailable for some reason. For example, in the absence of information on how people who committed suicide are distributed in terms of employment status, one might look at the correlation between rates of suicide and unemployment in various areas to guess the corresponding microlevel relationship. In so doing one runs, of course, the risk of committing what is called the "ecological fallacy." In the ecological fallacy, results from correlational studies of regions are assumed (erroneously) to hold true for individuals. If we find, for example, that regions with high rates of illegitimate births have high rates of suicide, this does not imply that the parents of illegitimate children have high rates of suicide. Results of such analyses are, therefore, very often said to be suggestive but not conclusive; researchers must make serious efforts to uncover the conditions under which inferences from aggregate to individual data are still permissible.

The term ecology can also denote the study of the development of spatial differentiation from selective migration of individuals. A most important form of this process—the favorite subject of social ecology—is the emergence of segregated neighborhoods as a result of residential mobility. In the field of deviance, the spatial diffusion of drug abuse (Mariak 1986) or the selection of target areas by offenders and the resulting evolution of danger zones within the city (Brantingham and Brantingham 1982) are examples of that process.

In other cases, ecological analysis can refer to the study of the impact areas—local environments—and the influence they exert on the behavior of the individuals residing in them. In criminology, for instance, investigations of this kind abound; they include research on topics as diverse as the influence of neighborhood socioeconomic status on the reaction of police to young criminals (Sampson 1986) or the effect of the safety or dangerousness of place of residence on feelings about victimization (Maxfield 1984).

It is this third interpretation that I mean when I speak in this chapter of an ecology of suicide; in other words, the analysis of how certain residential areas can be the breeding ground of self-destructive motives and behavior. This is not to say that the other two meanings of the ecological approach mentioned above should not be considered: On the contrary, taking them into account greatly facilitates the recognition of some important problems associated with the study of environmental effects on suicide. As we shall see, these problems arise from the fact that investigators often confuse the various meanings attached to the term ecology and these different interpretations assume the presence of different processes that are alternative causes of the same spatial pattern. To be aware of all three approaches is necessary to a more perceptive and reflective method of research.

My aim in this chapter is to point out some major problems in the ecological analysis of suicide one has to face if the more reflective research practice mentioned above is to carry real validity and to develop as a sound perspective. I do this by focusing on one line of research within this broader field—the study of spatial differences in suicide in the city. The history of this branch of ecological analysis exemplifies the shortcomings characteristic of the entire field in an extremely clear manner. I begin with a survey of research on suicide and its relation to urban areas from its origins up to the present. I then subject that research to criticism, stressing mainly conceptual and methodological, not substantive, issues. From there, I proceed to show how the deficiencies identified in the critique could be removed, at least in part, by employing a method known as contextual or multilevel analysis.

RESEARCH ON SUICIDE AND URBAN AREAS: REVIEW AND CRITIQUE

Scientific interest in areal differences in suicide within the city dates back to the first decades of the twentieth century. At that time researchers at the University of Chicago developed a theory of sociospatial differentiation of the city. Stimulated by this theory, a number of studies were conducted on the distribution of various forms of deviance across urban areas and on the relation of this distribution to the characteristics of the local environment. Among these early investigations were those by Cavan (1965) and Schmid (1928) on suicide in Chicago and Seattle. These studies showed that the suicide rate was highest in the center of the city and declined gradually as one moved toward the periphery. The authors attributed this spatial pattern to the characteristics that inner city districts possessed as a consequence of their location in the ecological structure of the city. Due to their unique spatial position, the argument ran, these districts had a mixed composition of residents and an increased turnover of population.

These features, in turn, impeded the development of a coherent system of norms and values governing behavior and of stable social relationships that could provide people with support and a sense of belonging. As a result, individuals became isolated from their environment, and their behavior ceased to be controlled by the community—conditions favorable to suicide, especially when certain personality traits were also present.

After the early attempts presented above, the study of suicide and urban areas gained ground again in the 1950s, and interest in the topic has continued. When surveying literature from this period of thirty years or so, two forms of research design are discernible. The majority of investigators (Sainsbury 1955; Wendling and Polk 1958; Gronholm 1962; McCulloch et al. 1967; Maris 1969; McCulloch and Philip 1972; Lester 1970; Koller and Cotgrove 1976; Wenz 1977; Jarvis et al. 1982) use aggregate data derived mainly from official statistics to establish ecological relationships between various characteristics of areas and the suicide rate. These characteristics are usually interpreted as indicators of unmeasured theoretical constructs, e.g., anomie or social disorganization. The other form of design is of a less extensive and macrolevel nature and consists in selecting a few areas with highly different suicide rates and asking in each of them a sample of individuals about factors supposed to be related to suicide. Studies adopting this approach rely on two major theories of deviance—the subcultural or learning theory and the integration or control theory. Platt (1985), for instance, examines the hypothesis that people living in areas with high prevalence of self-destruction differ from those residing in other parts of the city in their general value orientation, their more permissive evaluation of various forms of deviance, and the more frequent occurrence of suicide among their acquaintances. Wenz (1974), on the other hand, raises the Durkheimian question of whether inhabitants of areas with high suicide rates are characterized by a low level of participation in the activities of social organizations, an increased sense of isolation, difficulties in establishing and maintaining interpersonal relationships—i.e., by a lack of social integration. He also tests if these same individuals feel their life has no meaning and is void of any goal—an indicator of anomie in the sense of normlessness.[1]

In general, the level of research on suicide and urban areas can be said to have declined in the course of time. To be sure, the early studies by Cavan (1965) and Schmid (1928) left much to be desired as to scientific rigor. Indicators were assigned to theoretical constructs in a fairly accidental manner, leaving the measurement model largely implicit. Also, the causal chain leading from ecological factors to self-destruction was, for the most part, assumed but not tested by proper statistical methods; nor could it have been, since only aggregate data were available. As to the conceptual framework developed to explain environmental effects on suicide, however, these studies certainly exceeded the more recent ones (and they were not superseded by them methodologically either). On closer inspection, three important features of this conceptual framework can be identified.

First, Cavan and Schmid made a clear distinction between the effects of areas as environments and the effects of the composition of the population of those areas and attributed spatial differences in suicide to the former. This distinction was of particular importance in the case of those variables that described the relative size of a subgroup in the population and that were potential sources of both kinds of influence. The proportion of migrants among the inhabitants of an area is a case in point. In an attempt to explain its influence on suicide rate, it would be obvious to refer to the corresponding individual-level relationship—migrants themselves, no matter where they live, are more vulnerable to suicide than are non-migrants. Given this areally constant relationship, territorial units with high percentages of newcomers can be expected to exhibit high suicide rates as well. This would amount to offering an explanation that is based on the effect of the composition of the population. Cavan and Schmid did not, however, proceed that way; in fact, they showed such an explanation to be insufficient. As an alternative, they treated the proportion of migrants as a characteristic of areas not of individuals, and argued that the high level of residential mobility impeded the development of a stable social life and this transiency of norms, values, and interactions led, in turn, to suicide among newcomers and old dwellers alike. That is, they accounted for the ecological relationship between migration and self-destruction in a manner that involved in a central way the effect of the local environment on individual behavior.[2]

Second, they not only traced observed differences in suicide rates back to the influence of the environment (as contrasted with the effect of the composition of the population), but also linked this influence to the process of urban development and the resulting position of areas in the ecological structure of the city. They treated, in other words, environmental forces as originating in the distinct spatial location of the environment.

Third, they made an attempt to spell out the causal processes leading from ecological factors to social and personal disorganization. To be sure, these processes were, as already noted, merely assumed, not established empirically. Nevertheless, in so doing they addressed, at least on a conceptual level, the central issue of ecological analysis as understood here—the issue of how the local community becomes causally relevant to the individual who lives in it.

Gradually, all the above features of earlier studies have disappeared. The most deleterious consequence for the quality of research is that the distinction between the effects of areas as environments and the effects of the composition of the population has become blurred. Indeed, more recent studies, while intending to find environmental forces sui generis, attribute the spatial patterns observed almost exclusively to differences in composition. The change is most apparent in the case of variables describing the relative size of various socio-demographic groups such as the proportion of migrants or of white-collar workers. For Cavan and Schmid, such variables were, as we have seen, indicators of the quality of community life. In contrast, from about the 1950s on, they are increasingly treated as owing their explanatory power only to the fact that their individual-level counterparts (e.g., being a migrant or a white-collar worker) are, independent of place of residence, related to suicide.

Maris' (1969) research in Chicago is a good example of the new attitude to the above kind of variables. He reports a positive association between suicide rate on the one hand and the amount of residential mobility, as well as the proportion of inhabitants with higher levels of education and white-collar occupations, on the other. In an effort to explain that relationship, he relies on the term "anomie," referring by it to disturbances in the normative regulation of behavior. That term is not, however, used to account for the impact of certain characteristics of the environment; it only serves for interpreting the effect of properties of individuals who constitute the majority of the population in a given area. This is clearly indicated by the fact that in discussing the influence of the proportion of white-collar residents in terms of anomie, Maris quotes Durkheim's assertion that higher status persons are less constrained by the society than are those lower in the social hierarchy and that it is this relative lack of constraints that makes them most vulnerable to suicide. Maris reduces, then, the observed macrolevel correlation to the corresponding individual-level relationship; he offers, in other words, an explanation that is based on composition effect. This is in sharp contrast with his stated intention to "use the community characteristics as a rough indicator of what Durkheim called the 'social *environment*' of the suicides" (p. 137—emphasis added).

The explanatory strategy Maris' research exemplifies is of limited value for at least two reasons. First, an inference from a macrolevel relationship to the microlevel process that has generated it (in this case, composition effect) is possible only if each such relationship underlies a single process at the level of individuals. Unfortunately, this is not the case; the same relationship between aggregate (in our case, areal) data may result from different microlevel processes only one of which is the effect of the composition of the population (e.g., Hummell 1972, p. 90–113). With aggregate data alone, it is, therefore, extremely difficult to figure out which of these processes, or which combination of them, has produced what we observe at the level of territorial units, since the macrolevel findings may well be consistent with each. By arbitrarily picking out one such process, Maris thus makes a fallaciuos inference to the degree that, instead of, or in addition to, the influence of differences in composition, other processes (including effects of the environment) have been at work.[3]

Second, by referring to composition effect as the source of some spatial pattern, we assume, in essence, that it is merely the number or proportion of people with different risks of suicide that varies across areas; the risks themselves for those with similar individual characteristics are the same in every geographical unit.[4] We assume, in other words, the absence of any impact of the local environment on self-destruction—a fairly disappointing fact from an ecological point of view (Valkonen 1974; p. 55-6). Even if it is not flawed methodologically, there is still not much substantive interest in this kind of explanation.

Surprisingly, even studies such as those by Platt (1985) and Wenz (1974) fail to separate composition and environmental effects. These investigations have been conducted in communities widely divergent as to the proportion of inhabitants belonging to various sociodemographic groups. This feature of the design has introduced a new source for the variation of the dependent variable: differences in norms and values, or in the level of social integration, across areas that may well have arisen—in addition to possible influences of the environment—from dissimilarities in the composition of the population. In fact, both Platt and Wenz account for their findings mainly by such dissimilarities.[5] Contrary to analyses based exclusively on aggregate data drawn from official statistics, in these studies it would be possible to assess the validity of this explanation, given the availability of both individual- and community-level characteristics. Still, except for a few tables Wenz (1974; p. 119-22) presents in the Appendix, leaving their interpretation to the reader, neither researcher uses information on individuals as independent variables. Rather, they average people's responses to various questions within each area and compare the spatial differences in these averages to those in the composition of the population. In so doing, they, in essence, constrain themselves in the same way that data availability constrains those relying on aggregate data alone.

In some cases, researchers move even further away from the original intentions of Cavan and Schmid to uncover real environmental effects. As do those mentioned above, they not only shift the focus to the influence of the composition of the population; they abandon interest in understanding territorial patterns altogether. For them, ecological analysis is but an indirect way of studying individuals—i.e., they adopt the first of the interpretations of the term ecology listed in the introduction. This is indicated, among other things, by the fact that investigators often describe their work as a preliminary or exploratory one, with the next step being a direct observation of individuals themselves (McCulloch and Philip 1972, p. 66; Jarvis et al. 1982; p. 100). Also, results obtained from aggregate analysis are sometimes checked subsequently by using a sample of individuals not broken down by place of residence—another sign of shifting attention to the microlevel (Sainsbury 1955; McCulloch and Philip 1972).

How this shift in interest has gradually taken place can best be seen in the study by Sainsbury (1955). On the one hand, he calls his work ecological and he means by that the investigation of the dependence of the behavior of individuals on the environment in which they are embedded. Also, in his major hypothesis, the amount of mobility and the degree of isolation in a district are linked to suicide rate in a way very similar to that found in the investigations by Cavan and Schmid. Specifically, these variables are said to contribute to a community life that is "unstable, without order and purpose" (p. 30); they do not merely determine the relative size of an area of inhabitants vulnerable to suicide because of their own personal characteristics. On the other hand, Sainsbury repeats his computations on increasingly lower levels of aggregation to see if his ecological correlations truly indicate causal relationships. "True" relationships are in this case apparently areal constant associations among properties of the same individual. This, in turn, amounts to giving up any real interest in the functioning of the local environment.

The use of areal data to study individuals and the explanation of territorial patterns by composition effect are not unrelated. For example, the assumption that the impact of being divorced on the probability of committing suicide can safely be inferred from the influence of divorce rates on suicide rates as measured across areas is equivalent to the assumption that the latter macrolevel relationship is entirely due to spatial differences in the composition of the population (Valkonen 1974; Duncan et al. 1961). And both assumptions imply the same about the local community—namely, that it is of no causal importance to the behavior of individuals living in it. (For a detailed discussion of the role of environmental effects in ecological or cross-level inference, see Iversen 1973; Hammond 1973; Firebaugh 1978; Boyd and Iversen 1979.)

During the last decades, not only the crucial distinction between compositional and environmental sources of territorial patterns has become blurred, but also the effort to link these sources with the distinct spatial location of areas has disappeared. In literature on suicide, it is Douglas (1967) who most criticizes this departure from the original intentions of Cavan and Schmid. The neglect of the spatial dimension has also been observed in other branches of ecological research on deviance. In reviewing more recent studies on urban crime, for instance, Bley (1987) notes a similar lack of interest in the sociospatial differentiation of the city and in the resulting ecological position of high crime areas. However, neither author clearly distinguishes this issue from the more fundamental problem of confounding composition and environmental effects, an important omission in my view.[6] It is one thing to treat the local community as an environment of the same kind as a school or a workshop, leaving out of consideration that communities (but not schools or workshops) also exhibit a distinct territorial arrangement or configuration; and it is another not to treat it as an environment at all but as an aggregate of individuals unrelated to each other.

A possible reason for not fully recognizing the above difference is that in earlier studies two relatively independent issues were entwined. Cavan and Schmid raised simultaneously the question of how the local community influenced individual behavior and the question of how that community depended for its origin on the processes of urban development. Of these two questions, the first seems to be related to the dichotomy of environment vs. aggregate, whereas the second has probably more to do with the dichotomy of spatial vs. nonspatial environment. Moreover, the first question appears to reflect the adoption of an interpretation of ecology that regards as its subject the reaction of people to the characteristics of the community they live in—the last of the meanings of ecology listed in the introduction. In contrast, the second question displays a view of ecology that takes it as the study of sociospatial differentiation—the next to the last of the meanings enumerated at the beginning of this chapter. Given the way ecological analysis is understood here, it seems to make more sense to focus on the first of the twin issues dealt with in earlier investigations and concentrate accordingly on the distinction between environment and aggregate, leaving the explicit treatment of the spatial dimension to those committed to the other interpretation of ecology. What I am actually suggesting here is something of a division of labor between those interested in effects of the social environment and those interested in territorial processes.

A third feature of the development of research from about the 1950s on, is the decline in attention paid to the causal processes linking characteristics of the local community with individual behavior. In keeping with the shift in the focus of interest from real environmental effects to either composition effects or the study of individuals with aggregate data, assumptions on how the community becomes causally relevant to the people living in it have gradually been replaced by assumptions on how properties of individuals constituting the majority of the population in an area relate to self-destruction. One-level micro theories (i.e., theories about relationships between attributes of the same person) have thus gained ground at the expense of cross-level theories (i.e., theories connecting characteristics of objects belonging to different levels of aggregation).

CONTEXTUAL ANALYSIS: A POSSIBLE SOLUTION

The previous critique has identified a number of shortcomings, both conceptual and technical, in more recent ecological studies of suicide. It has also revealed what may be termed as a methodological lag in investigations of the 1920s and 1930s: the analytical tools used to test the theoretical ideas about how the community becomes an important determinant of behavior fell behind the ideas themselves.

During the last several decades, a method known as contextual analysis has emerged as a means of examining the ways the social environment influences the behavior of those living in it. I believe the use of this method in ecological research could help to eliminate most of the deficiencies found in studies of today and link the conceptual framework developed by Cavan and Schmid with appropriate research procedures.

Empirical sociology is dominated by two forms of inquiry: sample surveys and the analysis of aggregate (time-series or areal) data. While diverging in many respects, they do have something in common—both are confined to a single level of aggregation, either the individual or the social. Contextual analysis breaks with this onesidedness: it combines different levels and explains people's behavior by two sets of characteristics—one describing people themselves (the microlevel) and one describing their environment (the macrolevel). The two sets of variables may be independent of one another in affecting behavior; in this additive case, properties of the environment influence individuals in the same way no matter what characteristics people themselves possess. Or, they may be interdependent; in this interactive case, the impact of the environment varies with the attributes of individuals. Researchers use a number of techniques to study these different kinds of effects; these techniques are, in essence, common statistical procedures slightly modified to capture the multilevel nature of analysis. One of the most simple of them is cross-tabulation in which the microlevel relationship between the behavior under investigation and its individual-level determinant is stratified by the kind of environment; influences arising from the social setting are then ascertained by comparing the corresponding cells (or differences between cells) across environments. One of the most advanced of the procedures employed is multiple regression, which treats characteristics pertaining to different levels of aggregation (and possible interactions among them) as distinct independent variables and allows an inspection of their explanatory power by looking at the corresponding regression coefficients (Boyd and Iversen 1979).

Applications of contextual analysis in ecological research on suicide are relatively rare. Durkheim's pioneering monograph at the end of the last century contained an example of multilevel relationship; it fact, it is often referred to as the very first appearance of the contextual approach in sociology. Durkheim (1967) showed that among men the relative protection of married individuals with respect to suicide was negatively related to the frequency of divorce in the country these individuals lived in. This finding is, no doubt, a nice example of interactive environmental effect, i.e., of the situation in which the influence of some characteristic of the social setting (frequency of divorce) on behavior (self-destruction) depends on whether or not people themselves possess a certain attribute (being married). Still, it would be misleading to say Durkheim discovered and first applied contextual analysis. For, in discovery, as Kuhn (1984) points out, observation and conceptualization, the empirical fact and its building in a theory, are inseparably tied together. In the case of Durkheim, it was just the conceptualization, the theoretical generalization of what he observed that was lacking.[7] It was only about half a century later that a more conscious and reflective approach to the impact of the environment emerged.

It was still later that the technique of contextual or multilevel analysis first appeared in ecological studies on urban suicide. In Appendix A of his paper already mentioned, Wenz (1974) looked at how individual and neighborhood social status combined to affect various personal characteristics that the author assumed to be of causal relevance to self-destruction (isolation, negative self-evaluation, etc.). In the form of simple cross-tabulation he stratified the individual-level relationship between those characteristics and personal social status by the social status of place of residence and showed, for instance, that low status individuals were more likey to have a positive self-evaluation if they resided in a high status area than if they lived in a low status neighborhood. Unfortunately, Wenz made no attempt to interpret his findings; rather, he left this task to the reader.

While Wenz used the hypothesized psychological antecedents of suicide, not suicide itself, as dependent variables, a study by Welz (1979) examined how the risk of self-destruction for different sociodemographic subgroups depended on the relative sizes of those subgroups in the population of areas. The author found, among other things, that the relationship between age and suicide at the level of individuals varied inversely with the age structure of the community. That is, in areas with a great proportion of elderly inhabitants, it was young, not old, people who had the highest suicide rate and vice versa.

Although not strictly belonging with the literature on areal differences in suicide, the book by Farber (1968) is still worth mentioning, since it contains a most interesting example of possible environmental effects on self-destruction. The author addresses the question of how a high proportion of "individuals wounded in their sense of competence and therefore psychologically dependent" in a society might be related to an increased frequency of self-destruction in that society. An obvious answer would be that these individuals are, because of their personality traits, more vulnerable to suicide—an explanation that reduces the macrolevel correlation to its microlevel counterpart. Farber says this reasoning tells only part of the story. People with psychological disturbances do not live in isolation but constitute the environment for each other. Personality factors play a *dual* role: they function both as characteristics of individuals and as characteristics of the social setting. A person's negative self-evaluation may precipitate not only their own death but also the deaths of others for whom they are unable to provide support in crisis just because they themselves are wounded in their sense of competence. It is this latter environmental effect, i.e., the great likelihood of encountering someone who cannot help when searching for assistance, that explains why "a given increase in the number of vulnerable personalities in a society (may result) in *disproportionately* large numbers of suicides" (p. 78—emphasis mine).

The above examples demonstrate the new prospect that the use of contextual analysis opens up to the ecological study of suicide. Still, a somewhat more systematic treatment of how this method contributes to the solution of the problems discussed earlier seems to be in order.

Let us begin with the issue of confounding composition and environmental effects and confine our attention to the case in which a single variable underlies both kinds of influence. As we have seen, it is this situation where the gap between earlier and more recent studies is the most apparent. Let us take the example of the proportion of migrants again. An explanation of the composition effect type traces the impact of this aggregate variable on self-destruction back to the individual-level influence of being a migrant on committing suicide. Such an explanation implies that if we controlled this latter influence by statistical means, the macrolevel characteristic (proportion of migrants) would have no effect any longer. In contrast, an explanation of the environmental effect type assumes that the role of that characteristic is not confined to the impact of its microlevel counterpart so the proportion of migrants does influence suicide even after that impact has been taken into account.

By focusing simultaneously on different levels of aggregation, contextual analysis tests just the above assumptions. It controls for relevant properties of individuals and displays the net influence of macrolevel characteristics. In simple cross-tabulation, for instance, we compare cells that contain the values of the dependent variable for people having identical personal attributes but living in different areas. In multiple regression, the coefficients attached to aggregate characteristics reflect the impact of those characteristics, with microlevel determinants of behavior held constant. If that impact is significantly different from zero, the hypothesis of composition effect only must be rejected in favor of the alternative hypothesis that also permits the environmental effect to operate.

Contextual analysis is not, of course, confined to the case in which the same variable is responsible for influences of both the composition and the social setting. Separating these two kinds of impacts is just as important when different characteristics underly them and the method presented works in that situation as well. Nevertheless, for some reasons[8], the use of contextual analysis is very often reduced to the former case, with deleterious consequences for both theory and methodology.

As to the second problem mentioned in the critique, the neglect of the territorial dimension, the possible contribution of contextual or multilevel analysis can best be assessed by referring back to the difference between the dichotomy environment vs. aggregate and the dichotomy spatial vs. nonspatial environment. This kind of analysis treats areas simply as environments (along with schools, workshops, etc.), not as a special sort of environment—namely, spatial environments. By separating the effects of community-level variables from those of personal characteristics, it does, however, contrast real environments with mere aggregates of individuals unrelated to each other. It is thus a useful analytical tool for those interested in how the local community affects the behavior of its inhabitants, but not for those interested in how the community emerges from the processes of territorial differentiation. This concentration on the influence of the environment (as against its historical roots relating to urban development) is, in turn, in full agreement with the way ecological research is understood in this chapter.

Finally, the method presented renders a useful service in reviving interest in the causal processes that mediate between characteristics of areas and suicidal behavior. Contextual analysis is far more than merely a research technique; in fact, the selection and interpretation of the variables that appear in the statistical model must always underly a theory about the way the environment becomes causally relevant to the behavior of individuals. Some important variants have already been identified in the literature; they include phenomena as diverse as social comparison, imitation of behavior, or conformity to majority norms (for a review of the various substantive forms of environmental effect, see Valkonen 1974; Van den Eeden and Huettner 1982). While the correspondence between formal and substantive aspects is far from perfect Erbring and Young 1979), there is a growing demand to base the specification of the mathematical model on theoretical considerations. Researchers using contextual analysis are increasingly bound to spell out their assumptions about the role of the social setting in shaping behavior and make their choices in technical matters accordingly.

When applying contextual analysis to the ecological study of suicide, there are problems as well as benefits. An exhaustive list is, of course, well beyond the scope of this chapter so I will discuss only two issues of fairly different sorts to indicate the wide range of the difficulties involved (for a more detailed treatment of the problems of contextual analysis see Boyd and Iversen 1979).

One problem relates to the ruling out of competing explanations. By introducing relevant properties of individuals as separate independent variables into the model, the method presented controls for the composition effect as an alternative to the true impact of the environment. However, before concluding that the local community causes self-destructive motives and behavior, the role of some other factors has also to be considered.

First, areas may not produce suicide but may attract persons who contemplate it. The result of such selective migration (the very process that researchers adopting the second of the three interpretations of the term ecology listed in the introduction focus on) is the same as that of a real causal impact of the environment—an association between community-level characteristics and self-destruction—not of the influence of the properties of individuals. No control for microlevel determinants of suicide could, then, prevent one from finding an environmental effect in this case, even though no such effect is present at all in the proper sense of the word. What is needed to eliminate such spurious influences is to introduce the value of the dependent variable prior to entering the community (e.g., the presence or absence of suicidal ideas) into the model. When such longitudinal information is not available, more remote indicators of selective migration have to be used.[9]

Second, even when the observed impact of the environment is of a causal nature, it may still consist in processes other than the community giving rise to self-destructive motives and behavior. As Lowman (1986) has pointed out in his critique of areal studies on crime, researchers with an interest in the impacts of the territorial context are highly selective in their use of theories of deviance when explaining their findings. In particular, they rely on traditional ideas that focus on factors due to which one is inclined to take one's life or commit a crime, rather than on more radical theories that stress the role that the behavior of those surrounding deviants plays in labeling a given act as suicide or crime. A possible result of such a bias in the choice of the explanatory framework is the failure to control for factors affecting the classification of behavior (as contrasted with factors influencing the occurrence of that behavior). This, in turn, may result in overestimating the impact of the community on committing suicide if the two kinds of environmental effect (producing vs. labeling deviance) are positively correlated. In literature on ecological analysis of suicide within the city, the dangers of this overestimation are stressed most by Douglas (1967). He argues that a low level of social integration in certain areas may well be associated with a high suicide rate not because loneliness and isolation induce people to take their life, but because individuals not embedded in a stable community cannot avoid being labelled, after their death, as suicides, since they have no friends or relatives who could exert pressure on those making the decision about cause of death. An empirical test of a hypothesis of this sort would require the simultaneous use of indicators of both kinds of environmental effect in a single research; analyses of this type are, unfortunately, almost nonexistent. An exception is the study of Pescosolido and Mendelsohn (1986) which shows that biases in official statistics, though present, have little impact on the relationship between suicide and the traditionally presumed underlying causes.

In addition to the issue of ruling out competing explanations, problems of a more technical nature emerge as well. One such problem relates to the separation of composition and environmental effects in those frequent cases in which the two kinds of influence have a common source. Not even the simultaneous use of micro- and macro-level characteristics can relieve us entirely of methodological difficulties in that situation. Our troubles arise from the fact that aggregate variables (e.g., proportion of migrants) are defined as perfect mathematical functions of the distribution of their microlevel counterparts (e.g., being a migrant). In models containing both micro- and macro-level properties, we encounter the problem of collinearity. This collinearity is the greater the more social settings differ from each other with respect to the aggregate variable (Tannenbaum and Bachman 1964; Hummel 1972) A researcher thus finds herself in a strange situation: as the research case becomes more interesting substantively (i.e., as environments become more different), it becomes more hopeless methodologically. An important consequence of collinearity is that the effects of the micro- and macro-level characteristics depend largely on which of them appears first in the model (Boyd and Iversen 1979). Fortunately, some procedures have already been proposed in the literature on contextual analysis that can help cope with the problem of correlated independent variables.[10]

CONCLUSIONS

The major message I have tried to convey is that the ecological analysis of suicide, as practiced today, calls for a fundamental renewal, both conceptual and methodological. As to conceptual reorientation, attention has to be turned again to the impact of areas as real environments on the suicides of those residing there—as contrasted with interest in the composition effect or inference from aggregate to individual relationships. Moreover, influences stemming from the local community have not only to be established; they have to be explained as well by developing causal theories about how the environment sets limits to the individuals living in it, how people perceive those constraints, and how they respond to them. Future research has to return to the program of studies of the 1920s and the 1930s—with a higher level of scientific rigor, of course.

For this return on a higher level of sophistication to occur, a methodological renewal is also required. Specifically, reliance on aggregate data alone has to be replaced by the combined use of information pertaining to different levels of aggregation. A suitable framework for this is provided by contextual analysis.

In keeping with existing differences in the meanings attached to the term ecological, a distinction should be made between the analysis of the effect the local community has on the behavior of its inhabitants and the analysis of the dependence of that community in its origin on the processes of territorial differentiation. Something of a division of labor should develop along the two aspects of areas—environmental and spatial. In this respect, the program of early investigations should be somewhat constrained.

Throughout this chapter, I have placed emphasis on conceptual and methodological, not substantive, issues. That is, I did not deal with the logical and empirical adequacy of the different theories proposed to explain why suicide is more frequent in some areas than in others. This bias in the choice of focus reflects my conviction that what the future level of ecological analysis of suicide depends on is not so much the kind or content of the explanatory theory applied but rather the way that theory is used and the correctness of the methods employed to test it. Sometimes, the invention of ecological theories sui generis, as against the borrowing of nonecological explanations developed without any interest in the local environment, is believed to be of crucial importance for the quality of ecological research on deviance (Bley 1987). I doubt whether it is so. Given that the aim of social sciences is to find behavioral regularities as general as possible, seeking special laws for the spatial patterns of behavior does not seem to make much sense. What does make sense, in fact what is necessary, is rather to strive to use theories, ecological or not, in a way that assigns a separate causal role to areas as environments. It is in this, not in any uniqueness in the content of explanation, that lies the distinct nature of ecological analysis.

NOTES

(1) In literature on deviance, two relatively distinct meanings have been attached to the term "anomie." Often, it is interpreted as referring to the lack or breakdown of the normative regulation of behavior, to the estrangement of the individual from the society—not in terms of interpersonal relationships but rather in terms of goals, values, or meanings. Srole's well-known scale, for instance, rests on this interpretation. In other cases, the term is meant to refer to a sense or situation of relative deprivation arising from the discrepancy between culturally prescribed goals or aspirations and socially determined means or opportunities. This is the interpretation offered by Merton, among others. On reviewing ecological research on suicide, the reader is struck by the degree to which the first of the two meanings mentioned above is emphasized at the expense of the second. This is in contrast with what can be observed in ecological studies on crime, for instance. As part of a deeper interest in the social-structural sources of deviance, in that branch of research the relative deprivation conception of anomie appears, often by the name of strain theory, much more frequently (Friedrich 1985; Blau and Blau 1982).

(2) For a helpful discussion of the difference between the two ways variables such as proportion of migrants, of blacks, or of white-collar workers may be related to another macrolevel phenomenon, see the restatement of Boudon's distinction by Hannan (1971); see also Blau (1960) and Firebaugh (1978).

(3) Needless to say, the inference that a macrolevel relationship underlies an individual-level process in which behavior is affected by the environment may be, if it is based on aggregate data alone, just as erroneous as the inference that the macrolevel outcome is the result of composition effect. That is, in so far as it relies solely on aggregate data, the explanatory strategy the studies by Cavan and Schmid exemplify is subject to the same dangers as the one Maris' research is an example of.

(4) This feature of explanations based on composition effect can best be seen by looking at the procedure called standardization. This method has been developed to separate compositional and behavioral sources of variation in phenomena such as death or birth rates across areas, time periods, or other kinds of groupings. It rests on the analytical identity that the relative frequency of deaths, births, etc. in a population (the so-called crude rate) is the weighted average of the relative frequencies of those events in different subgroups of the population (the so-called group-specific rates), with the weights being the relative sizes of the subgroups (i.e., the composition of the population). On the basis of this identity, differences in crude rates can be described as arising from two distinct sources—from differences in the weights (i.e., in the composition), with the weighted values (the group-specific rates) being constant, and from differences in the weighted values, with the weights being invariant. Explanations based on composition effect assume areal, temporal, or other differences to stem exclusively from the first of the two sources.

(5) Platt, for instance, though starting from the observation of earlier studies that a great part of differences in suicide across areas cannot be due to composition effect (p. 258), attributes the (hypothetical) existence of a distinct subculture in areas with high suicide rates to the social class composition of those areas. He writes, "The geographical location of the subculture of parasuicide follows from the epidemiological finding that all three extremely high-rate parasuicide areas in Edinburgh are overwhelmingly working class in social composition." (p. 260)

(6) In criticizing Sainsbury's research, Douglas (1967), for instance, treats the author's failure to show what the characteristics of the communities used as explanatory variables have to do with (1) the interdependencies existing among the individuals living in the community and (2) the distinct spatial location of the community as one and the same shortcoming. In so doing, Douglas confounds the neglect of what he calls "environmental or neighborhood factors" and the neglect of what he terms as "geographical references."

(7) Durkheim did, of course, generalize his findings in terms of a substantive theory, i.e., a theory about why people kill themselves. What he failed to do was to generalize his observations in terms of what may be called a methodological theory, i.e., a theory about how to combine different levels of aggregation in a single research. A good example of a generalization of this latter kind is a paper by Kendall and Lazarsfeld (1950) where the idea of contextual analysis emerges from an examination of the formal structure of several observations made by Stouffer and his associates in their study on American soldiers.

(8) One reason is that in the course of its development, contextual analysis was strongly influenced by the related issue of ecological or cross-level inference. This influence manifested itself in at least two ways and both turned attention to contextual models in which individuals and areas were described by the same variable. First, environmental effects exerted by the macrolevel counterparts of the individual characteristics—the impacts of which researchers were ultimately interested in—proved to be important sources of bias in ecological inference (Hammond 1973; Iversen 1973; Firebaugh 1978). Second, by using a macro-level variable while controlling for its namesake at the micro-level, investigators tried to respond to the assertion made by Robinson (one of the first authors who warned against cross-level inference), that aggregate data merely serve as substitutes for their individual-level counterparts that cannot be observed directly. Another reason is that contextual analysis emerged in part out of the effort to show that society as a whole affects behavior in a way that is independent of, or cannot be reduced to, the impacts of the characteristics actors themselves possess. The proof of this required letting norms, values, etc. characterizing a group as a whole change while controlling for the corresponding norms, values, etc. held by the individual members of the group (see first of all Blau 1960).

(9) Among the more indirect approaches to selective migration is the comparison of the spatial distribution of deviants with different lengths of deviant career. The implicit assumption here is that career length is positively related to drift or selective migration and that the latter gives rise to

a high degree of spatial concentration of deviants. For instance, in their study on mental disorders, Levy and Rowitz (1970) compared the areal distribution of first admissions with that of all patients and found the latter to be more uneven than the former—a finding supporting the drift hypothesis. Similarly, Faris and Dunham (cited in Clausen and Kohn 1954) contrasted the degree of spatial concentration of younger and older mental patients and found essentially no difference between the two—a finding inconsistent with the drift hypothesis.

(10) One procedure suggested is the artificial orthogonalization of the micro- and macro-level variables (Hummell 1972; Boyd & Iversen 1979). Another is the estimation of the macro-level counterpart of the individual characteristics that appears in the model by using a data source that is definitionally, though not usually empirically, independent of the distribution of the micro-level characteristic (Sewell and Armer 1966; Sampson 1986).

REFERENCES

Blau, P.M. 1960. Structural effects. *American Sociological Review* 25:178–93.

Blau, J.R. and P.M. Blau. 1982. The cost of inequality: metropolitan structure and violent crime. *American Sociological Review* 47:114–29.

Bley, K. 1987. Kriminalitaet in der Stadt. Systematisierung und Vergleich oekologischer Studien staedtischer Kriminalitaet im deutschsprachigen Raum. Trierer Beitraege zur Stadt- und Regionalplanung, Band 13. Trier.

Boyd. L.H. and G.R. Iversen. 1979. *Contextual analysis: concepts and statistical techniques.* Belmont, Calif.

Brantingham, P.L. and P.J. Brantingham. 1982. Mobility, notoriety, and crime: a study in the crime patterns of urban nodal points. *Journal of Environmental Systems* 11:89–99.

Cavan, R. 1965. *Suicide.* New York: Russell and Russell.

Clausen, J.A. and M.L. Kohn. 1954. The ecological approach in social psychiatry. *American Journal of Sociology* 60:140–49.

Douglas, J.D. 1967. *The social meanings of suicide.* Princeton: Princeton University Press.

Duncan, O.D., R.P. Cuzzort and B. Duncan. 1961. *Statistical geography. Problems in analyzing areal data.* Glencoe, Ill.: Free Press.

Durkheim, E. 1967. *Az ongyilkossag (Suicide).* Budapest (in Hungarian).

Erbring, L. and A.A. Young. 1979. Individuals and social structure: contextual effects as endogeneous feedback. *Sociological Methods and Research* 7:396–430.

Farber, M.L. 1968. *Theory of suicide.* New York: Funk and Wagnalls.

Firebaugh, G. 1978. A rule for inferring individual-level relationships from aggregate data. *American Sociological Review* 43:552–72.

Friedrichs, J. 1985. Kriminalitaet und sozio-oekonomische Struktur von Grosstaedten. *Zeitschrift für Soziologie* 14:50–63.

Gronholm, L. 1962. The ecology of social disorganization in Helsinki. *Acta Sociologica* 5:31–41.

Hammond, J.L. 1973. Two sources of error in ecological correlations. *American Sociological Review* 38:764–77.

Hannan, M.T. 1971. *Aggregation and disaggregation in sociology.* Lexington, Mass. Lexington Books.

Hummell, H.J. 1972. *Probleme der Mehrebenenanalyse.* Stuttgart: Teubner.

Iversen, G.R. 1973. Recovering individual data in the presence of group and individual effects. *American Journal of Sociology* 79:420–34.

Jarvis, G.K. et al. 1982. The ecology of self-injury: a multivariate approach. *Suicide and Life-Threatening Behavior* 14:187–200.

Kendall, P.L. and P.F. Lazarsfeld. 1950. Problems of survey analysis. In R.K. Merton and P.F. Lazarsfeld, eds., *Continuities in social research.* Glencoe, Ill.: Free Press, P. 133–90.

Koller, K.M. and R.C.M. Cotgrove. 1976. Social geography of suicidal behaviour in Hobart. *Australian and New Zealand Journal of Psychiatry* 10:237–42.

Kuhn, Th. 1984. *A tudomanyos forradalmak szerkezete (The structure of scientific revolutions)*. Budapest (in Hungarian).

Lester, D. 1970. Social disorganization and completed suicide. *Social Psychiatry* 5:175–76.

Levy, L. and L. Rowitz. 1970. The spatial distribution of treated mental disorders in Chicago. *Social Psychiatry* 5:1–11.

Lowman, J. 1986. Conceptual issues in the geography of crime: toward a geography of social control. *Annals of the Association of American Geographers* 76:81–94.

Mariak, V. 1986. Raum-zeitdynamische Prozesse. Die Anwendung von STARIMA-Modellen zur Beschreibung und Bewertung sozialer Entwicklungsmuster, dargestellt am Beispiel der Ausbreitung der Drogenabhaengigkeit im Geibiet der Hansestadt Hamburg. New York: Lang.

Maris, R.W. 1969. *Social forces in urban suicide*. Homewood, Ill.: Dorsey.

Maxfield, M.G. 1984. The limits of vulnerability in explaining fear of crime: a comparative neighborhood analysis. *Journal of Research in Crime and Delinquency* 21:233–50.

McCulloch, J.W. and A.E. Philip. 1972. *Suicidal behaviour*. New York: Pergamon.

McCulloch, J.W. et al. 1967. The ecology of suicidal behaviour. *British Journal of Psychiatry* 113:313–19.

Pescosolido, B.A. and R. Mendelsohn. 1986. Social causation or social construction of suicide? An investigation into the social organization of official rates. *American Sociological Review* 51:80–101.

Platt, S.D. 1985. A subculture of parasuicide? *Human Relations* 38:257–97.

Sainsbury, P. 1955. *Suicide in London: An ecological study*. London: Chapman and Hall.

Sampson, R.J. 1986. Effects of socio-economic context on official reaction to juvenile delinquency. *American Sociological Review* 51:876–85.

Schmid, C.F. 1928. *Suicide in Seattle, 1914 to 1925: an ecological and behavioristic study*. Seattle, Wash: University of Washington.

Sewell, W.H. and J.M. Armer. 1966. Neighborhood context and college plans. *American Sociological Review* 31:159–68.

Tannenbaum, A.S. and G.G. Bachman. 1964. Structural versus individual effects. *American Journal of Sociology* 69:585–95.

Valkonen, T. 1974. Individual and structural effects in ecological analysis. In M. Dogan and S. Rokkan, eds., *Social ecology*. Cambridge, Mass.: M.I.T. Press.

Van den Eeden, P. and H. Huettner. 1982. Multi-level research. *Current Sociology* 30 (Winter).

Welz, R. 1979. Selbstmordversuche in staedtischen Lebensumwelten. Eine epidemiologische und oekologische Untersuchung über Ursachen und Haeufigkeit. Weinheim, Basel: Beltz.

Wendling, A. and K. Polk. 1958. Suicide and social areas. *Pacific Sociological Review* 1:50–3.

Wenz, F.V. 1974. Completed suicide, attempted suicide and urban social structure: a sociological and social psychological study of anomie, egoism and self-evaluation. Ph.D. Dissertation, Wayne State University, Detroit, MI.

Wenz, F.V. 1977. Ecological variation in self-injury behavior. *Suicide and Life-Threatening Behavior* 7:92–9.

9

Psychotherapy of Suicide: Individual, Group, and Family Approaches

Joseph Richman and James R. Eyman

Suicide is the only form of death whose classification is determined by a psychological variable, that of the motivation or intent of the deceased. It therefore seems fitting to use psychological forms of treatment with suicidal patients. This chapter presents the three major psychotherapy modalities used with suicidal patients: individual, group, and family approaches. The authors have written about the approaches they know best. Dr. Eyman covers individual psychotherapy, with special emphasis on the ego vulnerability model developed at Menninger, while Dr. Richman focuses on group and family therapy.

Effective psychotherapy is necessarily flexible and embraces any and all potentially helpful approaches. However, psychotherapy does not eliminate other methods. Quite the contrary. In practice, our treatment of suicidal individuals is multifocused. When necessary, we use medication and other physical methods, environmental changes (including short- and long-term hospitalization), and collaboration with schools, social agencies, and other health and social service providers. One frequent result of treatment is the development of a more accepting attitude by the patient toward the available resources.

INDIVIDUAL PSYCHOTHERAPY WITH ADULTS

A model for understanding why a person chooses to commit suicide (Eyman 1987; Smith 1985; Smith and Eyman 1988) has been developed as part of the Suicide Research Project at Menninger. The theory outlines psychological factors that might make someone vulnerable to committing suicide and suggests certain modifications for psychotherapy. This model posits three conditions for suicide: (1) a narrowly defined, unrealistic, and fragile identity; (2) an event that jeopardizes the individual's identity; and (3) deficits in the management of affect and difficulties in problem solving.

The Fragile Identity

Eric Erikson comes most readily to mind when considering the concept of identity. Erikson did not provide a single definition of identity because he believed that a person's identity continually evolves and changes over time. Erikson posited, however, that common to the identity of all healthy adults is a sense of who they are and a continuity of the way they experience the self. This cohesive and solid sense of self allows us to flexibly adapt to current and future realities while feeling reasonably competent and capable of meeting life's tasks (Erikson 1980).

Our research shows that the identity of the suicidally vulnerable patient is fragmented; a solid, cohesive sense of self is lacking. This lack of a cohesive self is most likely due in large part to various ego deficits that thwart an individual's development. Certainly this lack of a cohesive sense of self is not unique to suicidal individuals. However, the way that suicidally vulnerable persons attempt to manage this internal fragmentation seems unique to these individuals and is what makes them vulnerable to resorting to suicide. Two narrow and specific self and other ideals—conflicted high self-expectations and an ambivalent yearning to have others totally nurture and gratify—are typically found in suicide-prone people. They desperately cling to these ideals to provide a sense, albeit false, of self-definition, cohesion, and continuity. The search for the fruition of these ideals gives meaning and purpose to their life and is a central organizing principle of their identity. These ideals are so central to a suicidally vulnerable individual's existence that they dominate existence regardless of reality constraints and often without any appreciation of the needs and desires of others.

When suicidally vulnerable persons try to flexibly adjust their self-ideal and their hopes and expectations of others in relation to their self, it jeopardizes their fragile sense of self. Unable to be flexible about their expectations for themselves and the world, they feel increasingly hopeless and desperate about maintaining their sense of self. Suicide becomes an attempt to prevent further insult to their hopes for themselves and their expectations of the world, and to avoid self-disintegration by preserving the self-defining and integrating function of these ideals.

There are two common ideals that suicidally vulnerable individuals typically possess: (1) conflicted, unrealistic self-expectations; and (2) conflicted expectations of others. These characteristics can be modified in individual psychotherapy; the psychotherapist must investigate and bring to awareness these ideals as they relate to the patient's suicidal state.

Conflicted, Unrealistic Self-Expectations: Many of the individuals in our studies who committed suicide had a conflicted, unrealistic self-ideal. Typically, their personal goals far exceeded their actual capabilities, and their self-ideal often involved attaining some type of perfection. Although these patients had quite low self-esteem, many were driven; they always expected more from themselves and were rarely satisfied. Not only was there a gulf between the dismal way that they experienced themselves in reality and in how they wished to be, but their hopes and dreams for themselves were also likely to be extremely unrealistic and unattainable. Experiences that shattered their self-esteem and fragile identity were inevitable, and they were often left feeling bitter, empty, frustrated, and full of rage (Smith and Eyman 1988). Not only was the self-ideal of these suicidal patients unrealistic and unattainable; they felt guilty and unconsciously believed that they did not have a right to a better life and that their success meant that other people would be robbed, depleted, or destroyed. Because they were left conflicted about achieving their ego ideal, they often sabotaged success (Colson, Lewis and Horwitz 1985).

> A woman in her mid-thirties entered psychotherapy soon after completing her doctorate in chemistry. Despite her long history of vocational and academic excellence, she had always felt like an imposter with a hidden incompetence and basic inadequacy. She had expected that obtaining her degree would be rewarded by giving her a feeling of being totally competent and in control, of being perceived as the best chemist in her corporation, and of being started on a meteoric rise up the career ladder. She became suicidal when she continued to feel unsure of herself and to have the same interpersonal and professional struggles she had had prior to her matriculation.

During a suicidal crisis, these patients are most aware of their failure to achieve their hopes and dreams. The psychotherapist helped this patient gently explore her unrealistically high self-expectations by making her aware of the discrepancy between how she saw herself in reality and how she wished to be. Since this patient tended to feel successful and content only when she perceived herself as perfect, the psychotherapist helped her expand her view of herself and provided her with a model for more self-acceptance. The psychotherapist conveyed an acceptance of what the patient perceived to be her imperfections, as well as a recognition and acceptance of the therapist's own flaws. The acceptance by the psychotherapist of what the patient perceived to be hideous defects, coupled with the psychotherapist pointing out the patient's inevitable bitter dissatisfaction because of the inability to achieve perfection, eventually brought the patient to an awareness of the toll exacted by her unrealistically high expectations, and she was able to modify her harsh and unaccepting superego. A major focus of the psychotherapy was the humanness of feeling unsure and the unrealistic nature of seeking to always be "the best" and "perfect in every respect." The patient also eventually realized that her fear of "being found out" as incompetent prevented her from turning to others for much-needed support.

Patients who masochistically sabotage themselves, must be encouraged to become aware of their underlying belief that they do not deserve success and happiness, a belief that is at the root of their wish to be punished and to destroy any good that might come their way. The psychotherapy itself often provides an arena in which the patient can play out this masochism by viewing the therapist as critical and unhelping and by attempting to sabotage the therapist's treatment efforts (Eyman 1987).

Conflicted Expectations of Others: Many of the seriously suicidal patients in our studies had an ideal that entailed an unconscious and desperate desire to be passively nurtured, taken care of, and totally fulfilled and gratified by others. They expected people to magically meet their every need without any demands being placed on them. These individuals seemed to be searching for an all-powerful, perfectly attuned mother who would supply them with endless comfort and gratification, and who could help them recapture the pleasures of infancy and the feelings of completeness and oneness. However, these patients were also seriously conflicted about their strong dependency wishes, so they often acted in counterdependent ways. On the one hand, they desperately wanted nurturance but, because of problematic early depriving or traumatic childhood experiences, they feared that expressing their dependency desires would leave them vulnerable to a depriving and critical bad mother (Eyman 1987; Eyman and Conroy 1988; Litman and Tabachnick 1968; Richman 1986; Smith and Eyman 1988). These patients often related to others by trying to entice them into symbiotic-like unions and then raging at them when they did not satisfy the patients.

Paradoxically, these patients also employed a variety of maneuvers to distance people and to avoid true intimacy, because they feared that others would somehow harm them. They oscillated between yearning for fusion yet fearing that this fusion would bring loss of identity and self-disintegration. Not only were their unrealistic hopes for a perfectly attuned mother never fulfilled, but their counterdependency also often meant that they could not take advantage of and obtain whatever nurturance and support was available. The high self-expectations mentioned previously can be seen not only as a compensation for the unusually low self-esteem of these patients but also as a reaction formation against their strong conflicted dependency wishes.

In psychotherapy, there is often rapid development of an ambivalent symbiotic transference in which suicidal patients quickly come to hope and believe that all possible gratification will now come from the therapist (Eyman and Conroy 1988; Eyman 1987; Stone and Shein 1968). They hope that the therapist is perfectly good, caring, and understanding, and that the therapist has an unlimited ability to soothe and gratify. A patient's effort to create this relationship paradigm is also an attempt to enter into an alliance with the psychotherapist (Peebles 1986; Smith 1977). Some theorists (Lesse 1975; Shneidman 1985) suggest that by fostering, gratifying, and taking full advantage of the seriously suicidal individual's childlike magical expectations, the psychotherapist can facilitate a positive therapeutic alliance and instill hope in the patient. From this position, the psychotherapist might encourage the patient's belief in the psychotherapist's omnipotence with repeated reassurances that the patient will eventually feel better and that life will be less problematic if only the patient will follow the psychotherapist's direction and advice.

During crisis intervention, with the short-term goal of overcoming a suicidal crisis, the therapist can foster whatever expectations the patient has, including infantile ones, in order to engage and help the patient through the crisis. Even in psychotherapy the therapeutic alliance initially can be developed by letting some idealization go untouched, in particular the patient's idealization of the psychotherapist as all-caring and consumed with helping the patient. However, it can be disadvantageous and even dangerous in psychotherapy for the therapist to present himself as perfect and omnipotent and by so doing thus gratify the patient's childlike wishes (Eyman 1987; Eyman and Conroy 1988; Smith and Conroy 1984). Since suicidal patients are often conflicted about their search for an all-powerful and good mother, they often sabotage therapeutic efforts at providing nurturance and leave the psychotherapist in the position of feeling that whatever is done is not good enough. In addition, therapists can easily fall into the trap of trying to be an ideal mother, supplying the patient with immediate gratification and nurturance while avoiding analyzing and understanding the reasons for the patient's suicidal urges (Hendin 1981). It is misleading for psychotherapists to foster and gratify the suicidally vulnerable patient's fantasy that someone can actually meet the patient's every desire and need, and can totally take care of the patient. Such patients may begin by believing that they have finally found the lost ideal mother but will eventually realize that the psychotherapist does not fit the bill. The suicidally vulnerable patient can then become more bitter, more disillusioned, and increasingly suicidal.

A distinction should be made at this point between the therapist accepting and empathizing with the patient's childlike fantasies and the therapist attempting to foster and gratify those fantasies. The psychotherapist's accessibility, warmth, and efforts to accept and understand the patient may eventually provide a realistic gratification of the patient's childlike wishes. Thus, therapists should not directly confront the fantasies of their patients but rather should empathize with their strivings and allow them to elaborate on their hopes that someone can gratify their every need. Quickly confronting a patient's fantasies could easily be interpreted as an attack that leaves the patient with a stark and ungratifying reality. By exploring these fantasies, the therapist can make the patient aware that these expectations are never fulfilled and that the patient will inevitably be disappointed in others. Such exploration enables the patient to eventually realize that continual disappointment in others is fueled by unrealistic expectations and maintained by a hesitancy to engage others and to take advantage of the available nurturance. Empathizing with, and exploring, the patient's childlike fantasies is quite different than attempting to foster and gratify those fantasies.

> Mr. C. was aware that he had felt suicidal ever since he was a young boy. He had had many suicidal crises but had made only one attempt, albeit a serious one. During psychotherapy, Mr. C.'s ex-wife remarried and left on vacation with her new husband and the patient's children. Prior to the wedding, much time had been devoted in psychotherapy to discussing the patient's jealousy and anger about his ex-wife's marriage and his concern that the marriage would affect his relationship with his children and his competition with their soon-to-be stepfather. Nevertheless, Mr. C. became extremely suicidal the day after the wedding. He progressively withdrew into himself and isolated himself from friends.
>
> Although he was aware of being angry about "not feeling a part of my children's life," Mr. C.'s suicidal crisis did not begin to abate until he was able to articulate his desperate yearning for "always wanting more attention and time with my children." Even when he was with his children, he was painfully aware of feeling dissatisfied. When Mr. C. explored his relationships with other important people, he quickly became aware that he felt this way with "a lot of people." Gradually, it became clear that as a little boy he had experienced his parents as depriving, unavailable, and inaccessible. He was left yearning for more comfort, nurturance, and attention. Feeling unwanted, he typically withdrew into his loneliness, seeking reassurance and comfort from his pet dog. As a child and an adolescent, he remembered saying to himself many times "that if I can't have my parents total love, life is not worth living." He eventually realized that his ex-wife's wedding was reactivating his feelings about these early traumatic experiences and fueling his suicidal despair.

Seriously suicidal patients come to psychotherapy with at least two motives: (1) a wish to alleviate their despair (Shneidman 1985); and (2) a wish for the psychotherapist to make them more able to realize their unrealistic ideals. In psychotherapy, therapists should focus on the unrealistic components of the patient's identity and any reluctance to relinquish those unrealistic hopes. These patients' ideals come to light through a careful exploration of their hopes for themselves and their expectations of others, as well as their hopes and expectations of the therapist. As therapists gain greater understanding of their patients, they also can identify their sources of self-esteem, satisfaction, and hopes for nurturance (Smith 1983).

Once a patient's ideals are understood and articulated, the psychotherapist must help the patient give up the unrealistic fantasies and appropriately grieve and mourn the loss. In contrast to many psychotherapists whose work with suicidal patients focuses on overcoming their hopelessness, I believe that the psychotherapist must help patients acknowledge their hopelessness about achieving their unrealistic goals so that mourning can proceed. Patients need to be allowed, carefully and gradually, to feel realistically hopeless about never realizing the unattainable aspects of their ideals. This gradual process of realigning the patient's hopes must be very careful, controlled, and titrated, so that the patient does not feel more overwhelmed and despondent. To recapture a sense of hope, patients must be helped to substitute more realistic goals and desires. At that point, they can experience hopelessness as an attitude about a specific set of expectations about themselves and others, and not as a pervasive attitude about life (Smith 1983).

Difficulty Expressing Emotion: The adults in our studies who committed suicide or made serious suicide attempts tended to have great difficulty expressing emotion, particularly anger. These individuals were characteristically constricted, repressed, and inhibited. They typically directed their anger inward rather than outward. Although their anger was often apparent to others, they tended to repress it to such a degree that they were often shocked when others experienced them as angry. As with many emotionally constricted and repressed individuals, these suicidal persons had impulsive, angry outbursts, with subsequent feelings of overwhelming guilt. The more psychotic patients occasionally erupted with aggressive or violent behavior, as though their rage suddenly overwhelmed their diminished capacity to control their effect. When patients were organized at higher levels of ego functioning, their aggression would more typically surface in passive-aggressive fashion or in temporary and circumscribed angry outbursts (Smith 1985; Smith and Eyman 1988).

The deficits that suicidally vulnerable individuals have in integrating and containing strong affect results in their avoiding the intimacy of interpersonal relations, which can generate overwhelming and potentially disorganizing emotions. These individuals must dampen affect, and by so doing, lessen their emotional ties to others. Psychotherapeutic work with such patients should therefore aim at strengthening the ego's capacity to handle affect. The psychotherapist must serve as an auxiliary ego to the patient, emphasizing acceptance of anger, conveying its adaptive value, exploring situations in which anger is to be expected and contrasting overt and covert and adaptive and maladaptive ways to express anger (Stone and Shein 1968). The suicidal patient's anger is often so intense and pressured that the expression of the anger in therapy in a controlled and titrated fashion is necessary and therapeutic. Psychotherapists should expect to be the recipients of intense anger from the suicidal individual; they must endure the anger and help the patient understand what the anger means. The patient must to learn to articulate the anger and thereby understand who is its actual target. Until the anger is brought to consciousness and the patient is able to react appropriately to anger-producing situations without experiencing guilt, the patient will remain vulnerable to depression and suicidal urges (Lesse 1975). As the patient's capacity to accept, acknowledge, and verbalize anger increases, and as distorting anger in a self-destructive way de-creases, reality testing and coping abilities become more effective.

Death as a Solution: Another common characteristic among the seriously sui-cidal patients in our studies was a serious attitude toward death. These individu-als did not take the thought of death lightly; they had thought about death both as a real possibility and as a solution. Although thoughts of death often preoccu-pied much of their time, they did not easily share either their feelings about death or their suicidal thoughts (Smith 1985; Smith and Eyman 1988). In addi-tion to the suggestion by Shneidman (1985) that death was frequently seen as an escape from intolerable pain, the patients in our studies also fantasized that death was a total escape from pain into an idealized blissful, nirvana-like state—a wish akin to a longing to return to the protection and soothing of the ideal mother. Seriously suicidal patients are often obsessed with the prospect of death, they often have intense and ambivalent feelings about death, and they ultimately view death as a way to preserve their disintegrating identity.

At the height of a suicidal crisis, seriously suicidal individuals view their life and their struggles in either/or terms. This polarized, constricted, and dichoto-mous view of the world does not allow for an array of options or alternatives in a crisis but leads instead to an exclusive focus on suicide as the solution. One goal of psychotherapy is to help patients begin to see other options and alternatives, perhaps by encouraging them to identify with the more realistic views of the psychotherapist. Again, the psychotherapist serves as an auxiliary ego, lending the patient the ego strengths that are available at the moment, such as an ability to assess situations objectively, a sense of realistic hope and stabil-ity, and problem-solving skills. Once the psychotherapist is able to help the patient consider alternatives other than dying, they can then both begin to strug-gle with the real, everyday problems of living.

> One elderly man frequently commented that he had to struggle painfully just to get through each day. He often felt that death was preferable to life. In coping with even minor problems of living, he usually quickly resorted to some self-destructive behavior. His suicide attempts kept getting more serious and his perceived options more limited. One thrust of the psychotherapy was to expand this patient's sphere of alternatives by focusing concretely on problem-solving skills. The patient eventually began to respond positively to the praise and encouragement he earned through his increased ability to develop effective strategies for managing various situations and his suicidal behavior decreased.

The Atmosphere of the Psychotherapy

Usually by the time suicidal patients enter psychotherapy, they are already experiencing some degree of panic and despair about the impossibility of main-taining their brittle identity and living out their ideals. It can be painful and frightening for them to address the panic, disappointments, and psychological characteristics that fuel their suicidal motivation. The psychotherapist should attempt to create a safe environment where patients can feel understood, listened to, and positively regarded, and where resources are bolstered and previously unbearable thoughts and feelings can be expressed and contained. Winnicott (1965) addressed this need in his concept of the "holding environment," a term for the positive, nurturing, and protective behavior of the mother toward the child. While the mother supports and comforts the child, and metabolizes the child's angry feelings, she also sets realistic limits about acceptable and nonacceptable behavior and achievements. In psychotherapy, the holding environment provides a corrective version of the parenting function that apparently was far less than optimal when the patient was a child. The safe environment of the therapy allows patients to eventually let their "self" emerge and encourages them to develop the capacity for internalization and more mature identification (Peebles 1986).

In creating a holding environment, the therapist provides a consistent environment and empathizes with the patient's struggles by trying to establish what Smith (1983) has termed an empathic bridge. Forming an empathic bridge entails fully understanding the emotional perspective of these patients and the nature of their problems. By appreciating that patients feel hopeless and helpless, the therapist communicates to them a sense of being heard, respected, and contained.

The perspective such patients have about why they are suicidal may seem nonsensical to the psychotherapist. However, quickly contradicting a patient's perspective could easily make that patient feel misunderstood and could cast the psychotherapist in the role of critic. Premature interpretations, made before the patient's motivations for suicide are fully elaborated and understood, can worsen the patient's sense of isolation, persecution, and alienation; they can also increase the risk of suicide.

GROUP THERAPY WITH SUICIDAL PATIENTS

Group psychotherapy has found an accepted and even honored place in the treatment of suicidal patients, but such was not always the case. When therapy first began to be used with these patients, group methods were often lightly regarded and sometimes even considered counterindicated. Several reports of group therapy members who committed suicide while in treatment gave therapists the message to preclude patients with similar problems. Bowers, Mullan, and Berkowitz (1959), for example, emphasized the ever-present possibility of suicide in a therapy group and its potentially traumatic effect on other group members. Likewise, McCourtney (1961) speculated that the group process "may activate the death wish and encourage the group member to commit suicide.'' Responding to such reports, Strickler and Allgeyer (1967), in a pioneering work on crisis-oriented group therapy, specifically excluded those patients who were suicidal.

The earliest groups to include suicidal patients were composed of just those patients. In 1966, Indin started a group with eight suicidal women on a closed psychiatric ward. The results were positive, although Indin had to deal with the anxiety and resistance of other staff members. About the same time, Reiss (1968) observed similar dynamics in an informal group of six psychotic individuals on a psychiatric ward, all with a history of suicidal behavior. The patients in this group, which had formed spontaneously, had previously tended to form self-destructive dyads, in which each would instigate the other into committing suicidal acts. However, after the "Suicide Six" formed their own group, which was somewhat like a clique, none of them committed any further suicidal acts. The hospital staff finally intervened to dissolve the group, apparently unable to tolerate its organization by patients and its lack of control by staff members.

The implication from the Reiss article was that when two suicidal people get together they may stimulate each other's self-destructive behavior. A gathering of three or more suicidal people, however, may arouse caring, rescuing, and life-enhancing forces. These positive effects may be due to dynamics similar to those found in homogeneous groups of paraplegics, cancer patients, and other seriously ill or disabled persons.

The value of homogeneous groups of suicidal persons has been particularly recognized in California and Texas, where several investigators have organized such groups (Billings et al. 1974; Comstock and McDermott 1975; Farberow 1968). The success of these efforts has stimulated the formation of additional groups throughout the country, including are for geriatric patients formed by myself. As might be expected, there was much resistance to these homogeneous group therapy programs (Hackel and Asimos 1981), because they introduced a new procedure to an existing stable system.

Some clinics have accepted and even welcomed such innovative approaches; my group for depressed and suicidal geriatric patients was certainly greeted with interested interest and encouragement. With this elderly suicidal population, the group therapy was only part of a comprehensive treatment plan and program.

In my group work with suicidal geriatric patients, I have identified two distinct types of group members: (1) the more chronically depressed or suicidal person; and (2) the acutely depressed or suicidal patient whose condition is usually reactive to the loss of a spouse or some other major life crisis. The chronically depressed patients often cling to suicidal thoughts or possibilities, and resist efforts by the group or the leader to consider alternatives or to look at life more positively. The acutely depressed patients may be experiencing a depressive or suicidal episode that will resolve quickly. Several of the geriatric patients in this category have chosen, however, to remain in the group. As more than one member explained, "It's like insurance, in case I get depressed again."

The male members of these groups are usually more seriously suicidal than the female members. In addition, their marital status differs markedly. In the current geriatric group of eight members (four men and four women), all the women are widowed or single, three of the four men are married, and one man is a widower. The widower (whose group therapy process I will discuss later) has been the most suicidal member of the group.

The group as a whole, especially the male members, is representative of a high-risk group for suicide. Several of these patients have had to be hospitalized at psychiatric facilities sometime during their treatment for exacerbated depression or suicidal impulses. One patient was ultimately placed in a nursing home after a series of strokes and a heart attack. None of the patients has committed suicide.

For therapists who work with suicidally prone individuals, homogeneous group therapy is actually less strenuous than seeing the patients individually. When the patients in such a group are slow to voice suicidal ideation, the therapist can encourage its expression, then put the situation before the group—which usually does a fine job of interpreting. In my situation, I also see the group members individually and in family sessions, especially during periods of escalating suicidal tension. Most of my geriatric patients are taking antidepressants or psychotropic medication. Most also have some medical condition or physical illness, such as cardiac disease, pulmonary disorders, Parkinson's or other neurological conditions, and malignancies. The group members have developed a team spirit and are pleased to allow visits by trainees or interns. They are usually eager to tell trainees their life stories. I consider myself fortunate to be the leader of such a group.

To illustrate the benefits of group therapy, let us consider the case of Mr. V. Our association began with a call from a social worker at a nearby nursing home. One resident there was an 82-year-old woman who was terminally ill with a malignant brain tumor, but it was the woman's husband the social worker was concerned about. This 83-year-old man was walking around with a suicide note in his jacket pocket, addressed to the police. I asked the social worker to ask the husband, Mr. V., to call me. He did so immediately, in itself a positive prognostic sign.

"The social worker said I should call you," he said.

"She told me you are going through a very hard time," I replied.

"I've been through too much to live any more," he said. "My wife . . ." He broke into bitter and uncontrollable sobs (which I did not hear from him again with such intensity until over a year of continued therapy). Mr. V. was unable to continue talking, so we made an appointment for the next day. My tentative plan was to see him, establish further rapport, obtain some further information, and then hold the next meeting at his wife's bedside. Fate often determines our plans, however, more than ourselves. Unknown to us, his wife was expiring during our call, so our appointment was postponed.

We made another appointment, but Mr. V. phoned back once again to postpone that meeting because he was ill with a virus. "I'm so sick, I feel I'm going to die," he said.

"Don't die until you see me," I said, humorously, which was a covert message, *Don't die, I want you to live.*

"That's funny," he responded, and I thought, *This man is going to get better.*

I rarely use humor at initial contacts, especially with a patient I have not yet seen, and most especially with someone in deep mourning, but at the time I felt that it was appropriate.

Therapy was eventually initiated, and Mr. V. was seen as part of a comprehensive treatment program that included medication, the use of social resources, medical treatment, individual therapy, and group therapy. He was actually seen in two groups at first: a bereavement group run by another member of the clinic, and the suicidal group run by myself. His simultaneous membership in two groups at the same clinic was not a good idea, with a major complication being an enormous amount of splitting of the two therapists. We do not recommend such a procedure.

In group therapy, Mr. V. was quite emotional and tearful. He was sometimes drunk, usually difficult, and persistently suicidal, but always involved with the group and its members. He also demonstrated at least the rudiments of the sense of humor indicated in our first contact. For example, one member of the group complained about always arguing with her brother, who lives with her.

"Why don't you have an argument with me," Mr. V. suggested. "Then I'll get into a big temper and feel better."

Mr. V.'s multitude of medical as well as psychiatric symptoms required me (as well as other staff members and health professionals) to spend more time with him than with any other patient. Many of his complaints did not always ring true; and the group, which is usually solicitous of actively suicidal members, did not take Mr. V.'s suicidal ideation and threats seriously, although I did.

At one session, for example, Mr. V. said, "And no matter what you say, I'm going to commit suicide by jumping out the window." The group responded with silence, except for one woman, who said, "So why are you coming to therapy?" Mr. V. had no response. I believe that the group was in tune with him because they had all known despair and the suicidal impulse. However, I made an appointment to see him individually. He tearfully told me that he had opened his window and almost jumped, but at the last moment could not do so. He then burst into the convulsive sobs that I had first heard during our initial telephone contact.

This incident marked a turning point in Mr. V.'s treatment. It came as a result of the cathartic effect of his outburst, the cumulative effect of group cohesion and one-to-one intimacy, and the nonverbal drama of opening the window and then closing it. He had said No to suicide, at least at that point. Now, after two and one-half years of therapy, he is doing well; he is significantly less suicidal, more socially active, and less depressed and agitated.

The case of Mr. V.. illustrates how members of a group can empathize with and thereby help contain each other's suicidal impulses. The very fact that each patient in the group has experienced similar pressures enables them to create an atmosphere of understanding. By and large, the suicidal persons with a sense of humor get well, or at least get better. Those without humor are less likely to improve. Most of the members of the geriatric group have a good sense of humor. The sessions are often lively—even more so before I arrive. It is then that the group members confide in each other about ailments or family relationships that they do not tell me. One day, as their laughter rang down the hall, a colleague said to me, "I see that your suicide group is here."

FAMILY THERAPY

Scarcely a working day has gone by for the past 23 years without my treating at least one family with a suicidal person. The work has become so familiar that it is easier to do than to describe. I therefore welcome this opportunity to tell others about this valuable, trying, and most rewarding of all therapies. My family work with suicidal people has been an outstanding intellectual adventure as well as a memorable personal experience. That may be true of all psychotherapy; for me, it has applied doubly to the more encompassing family work. The major influences in the literature have ranged far and wide, including the great figures in psychoanalysis (Freud 1957a, 1957b), sociology, suicidology (Durkheim 1951), and, of course, family therapy (Ackerman 1958, 1966; Bowen 1978; Bowlby 1982, 1973).

There are two basic features of my approach. The first is that family therapy for the suicidal individual is most effective in the context of a multidisciplinary approach. Family therapy is not a separate or unique method; it is part of the century-long development of modern psychiatry and psychology. But those who personally helped me at a most fundamental level were my mentors and guides, especially Ian Alger and the late Stephen Kempster. Second, family therapy is the treatment method that most quickly reduces the immediate risk of suicide, while resulting in the most enduring long-term effects. By helping members of both the younger and older generations, family therapy most effectively saves lives in the future.

Stress and the Family

The central tasks of family therapy are the elimination of destructive forces and the potentiation of positive forces in the family. These destructive forces are not intrinsic, but have evolved as a means of dealing with extraordinarily high stress, the presence of multiple problems among various family members, and intense family conflicts. These features are not unique to the families of suicidal people, but are particularly intense in such families. They can be considered exaggerations of problems that are present at various stress points in everyone's family life cycle.

Efforts to deal with the strains and conflicts of life eventuate in ten specific characteristics of suicidally vulnerable families: (1) separation and loss; (2) symbiosis; (3) primary attachments; (4) mourning; (5) a closed family structure; (6) role conflicts; (7) maladaptive interpersonal relationships; (8) affective disturbances; (9) communication disturbances, and (10) proneness to crises. These are not necessarily present at all times, but they are prominent at the height of the suicidal episode.

1) Suicidally vulnerable families have great difficulty dealing with separation and loss. Separation is perceived as a threat to the survival of the family system and its traditions. Therefore, the first goal of therapy (after preventing an imminent suicide or death), is to reduce separation anxiety.

2) The problem within the family also may involve the symbiotic familial relationship and the family's desperate response to its actual or threatened loss. Consequently, a later goal of family therapy is to increase individuation and personal autonomy.

3) The suicidally vulnerable family clings to primary attachments (i.e., to parents and siblings), to the detriment of later or secondary relationships. The potentially suicidal person symbolizes to other family members these primary figures in the family. To understand these "fixations," therapists will find that the concept of "the myth of exclusiveness" is particularly valuable. The family may believe that new relationships threaten rather than enrich older relationships, so they are therefore not permissible.

4) A disturbance in the mourning process and in the family's ability to grieve together is also characteristic of suicide-prone families. Mourning is inseparable from the first or primary attachments. To acknowledge their loss is unbearable. The lost loved ones are therefore kept artificially alive through introjection, projection, and projective identification—all designed to prevent mourning. The suicidal person plays a central role in this process.

5) In the closed family system, the family seals itself off from an outside world considered dangerous to the integrity of the family. Features of the closed family include prohibitions against intimacy outside the family, combined with an isolation of the potentially suicidal person within the family, especially from supportive relationships. When a family is identified as a closed system, the patient is best treated by including the entire family in the therapy.

6) Suicidally vulnerable families have many role conflicts that lead to strain and failure. Role obligations that are necessary in society may arouse separation anxiety and lead to further isolation of the family. But the family's inevitable interactions with school, work, and other institutions outside the family usually result in the development of maladaptive patterns and severe role strain.

7) Maladaptive interpersonal relationships are also characteristic of these families. From a family perspective, role difficulties and interpersonal disturbances are two aspects of the same problem. Role conflicts take the form of failures or strain in meeting various social obligations. Interpersonal conflicts allow role difficulties to surface through the psychological mechanisms of selective scapegoating, double binds, ambivalence, and sadomasochistic behaviors. Both the role disturbances and interpersonal conflicts are based on a loyalty to the family system and the preservation of earlier attachments.

8) The affective disturbances that are common to family members can be seen in their interpersonal relations. Without denying the possible biological components, the expression and discharge of affect in suicidal persons are considered here as based on rules governed by maladaptive responses. These include a one-sided pattern of the expression of aggression, in which the potentially suicidal person is much more often the recipient than the giver of aggression. Included, too, are an association of the expression of aggression with death or the disintegration of a relationship, and a prohibition against the free or spontaneous expression of affect.

9) Communication disturbances, with indirect, devious, selective, and destructive messages are often found in suicidally vulnerable families.

10) These families are also prone to frequent and unresolved crises, each one piling on further stress. Therapists should avoid prematurely resolving a crisis. Since a crisis takes the form of a negative therapeutic reaction, its slow introduction to the therapy will be more effective, especially as the treatment starts to succeed.

These ten characteristics of suicidally prone families are based on the interrelationship between the dynamics of separation and the measures taken by the family to deal with an actual or threatened loss. Because of the family history of traumatic losses, the potentially suicidal person is born into a milieu where separation anxiety is in the air and death is a familiar theme. Thus the family is preoccupied with death, a theme that Eyman noted earlier in this paper. The family's obsession with death and suicide is an effort to cope with and to master anxiety about death.

Initiating and Maintaining the Family Health Process

The optimal treatment of suicidal patients necessitates a coalition of the dynamic and family system approaches. How the family deals with separation within the family and in therapy forms the material for the therapeutic work. Separation becomes a major life-and-death issue when it involves someone the suicidal person is attached to symbiotically. However, the entire family will rally to ward off any threat to its symbiosis (Richman 1986).

On the one hand, these families have been described as being "enmeshed" (Minuchin 1974), as having an "undifferentiated family ego mass" (Bowen 1978), and as carving everlasting togetherness (Boszermenyi-Nagy and Spark 1973). On the other, their proneness to suicide has been linked (Litman and Tabachnick 1968) to a regression to the separation-individuation phase of development described by Mahler, Pine, and Bergman (1975). The first theory, which is systems oriented, deals with families, while the second theory, which is psychodynamically oriented, deals with individuals. Despite such differences in these theories of family process, the descriptions of the families all bear a close resemblance to each other.

Thus the individual psychotherapist and the family therapist can work fruitfully together by integrating and unifying their different approaches to understanding and treating the suicidal patient. Therapy, in fact, is more effective when the dynamic and systemic approaches are used interactively rather than when the therapist relies exclusively on one method.

Determining which assessment and therapy procedures to use with suicidal persons is influenced by the training and personality of the therapist, and by the particular problems associated with suicide. Both the individual therapist and the family therapist should be familiar with the basic principles of suicidology, as well as psychotherapy in general, and crisis intervention in particular. All treatment of suicidal patients begins with crisis intervention. The first order of business is to pinpoint the major crisis and to determine whether hospitalization or outpatient treatment is called for. Then the initial tasks of therapy include lowering the patient's separation anxiety and stress by beginning a process of stress reduction and stress management. Later goals include improving social and personal functioning, increasing individuation and competence, and widening the areas of social cohesion outside the immediate family.

I favor a multidisciplinary approach to the assessment, therapy, and stress management of the suicidal person and family. This method requires brief individual interviews with each family member during the initial assessment session, followed by a family interview, all of which form the basis for the treatment plan and further intervention. During this entire procedure, which takes about one and one-half hours, I try to identify the basic sources of stress; the problems, conflicts, and major crisis of the moment; and the developmental tasks and blocks against growth and competence. I also systematically evaluate depression, suicidal risk, and the presence of death wishes, both in the patient and in other family members, and then decide whether to hospitalize the suicidal person. By identifying the key figure in a family and getting that person to support the treatment, the therapist can facilitate improvement in the suicidal family member and reduce the family's resistance to treatment.

Although the goals of interventions are to reduce separation anxiety and resolve stress in the suicidal person and family, much of the family's tension and turmoil are brought into the therapy, which can place extreme stress on the therapist. Therapists may find themselves in a no-win situation.

> One 40-year-old, divorced, unemployed patient went to his mother's house with a gun and said he was going to kill himself. The patient's mother phoned her son's therapist, who spoke to him.
>
> When the therapist said that she would come to the house, the patient said, "If you do, I'll shoot myself."
>
> Then when the therapist said she would call the police, the patient replied, "If the police come, I'll certainly shoot myself."
>
> "And if they don't come?" asked the therapist.
>
> "I will shoot myself anyhow," the patient replied.
>
> The therapist did call the police, who went to the house. The man calmly told them that he was all right and that they should leave, which they did. The man continued in therapy, began to work again, and is now completing a degree needed to advance him in his field. He is no longer in therapy and he is not now suicidal.

Suicidal persons can skillfully place their therapist in a double bind. Such situations reflect a crisis in the therapy, but the therapist who does nothing gives a message of not caring. Because such stressful encounters are not unusual, therapists must strive to reduce the anxiety and turmoil that are frequently generated by them. In general, therapists must deal with their countertransference, which may require entering or returning to a personal psychotherapy. Above all, therapists who work with suicidal persons require a good support system, both professionally and personally.

To conclude, a stress model of suicide and the family contains several implications for reducing tension, solving problems, decreasing conflicts, and resolving crises. To bring these developments about first requires therapists to become more tolerant to stress. They must also skillfully use therapeutic methods in general and family therapy in particular, they must develop a special ability for establishing relationships with individuals involved in conflict, and they must emphasize the positive. If therapists can also use humor, then so much the better, but equally important is their ability to pinpoint the positive aspects of whatever the suicidal person and family members communicate and to convey that perception back to them.

CONCLUSION

In this chapter we have emphasized the multifaceted nature of self-destructive behavior. Suicide is based on individual stress, family components, and social factors, which are all associated with neurochemical changes. At one point in a vulnerable person's life, the psychological, biological, familial, and social components coalesce. The serious and potentially fatal suicidal urge then gains impetus, until the suicidal process runs its course. Nevertheless, ambivalence is ever present. At the same time that suicidal persons are determined to end their life, one part of them is also asking to be stopped and helped to live.

Other approaches to the treatment of suicidal individuals, such as cognitive behavior therapy (Beck et al. 1979) and brief interpersonal therapy of depression (Klerman et al. 1984) also contain many insights. We have concentrated here on those modalities we know best, but it is evident that psychotherapy covers a great deal of territory.

On the face of it, different treatment modalities perform different functions. In addition, the situation of the patient may call for a change of approach at different stages of therapy. Although the results of all the therapies overlap, individual therapy encourages individuation, ego strengthening, and personal growth; group and family methods strengthen cohesion and social integration. Most often, multiple approaches are needed simultaneously, and various combinations of individual, group, family, and biological therapies may be the treatment of choice.

It is evident, too, that there are commonalties as well as differences in all these approaches. The clinical value of all psychotherapy lies in a combination of factors: forming a positive relationship, providing a corrective emotional experience, helping the patient develop self-understanding and empathy toward others, reducing stress and feelings of hopelessness, and increasing well-being and satisfaction in living.

The nature of the transference and countertransference is central to all these goals. So, too, is the presence of a hopeful and positive attitude in the therapist, a commitment to the therapeutic task, and a refusal to give up on the patient or the family and its potential for improving social cohesion and increasing self-esteem.

In conclusion, if this chapter can stimulate readers to a greater interest in the task of understanding and treating the suicidal patient, whatever the theoretical approach, then our efforts will have been worthwhile. Therapists should keep in mind that, whatever the treatment method, it is the patient, the group, and the family who must do the actual healing. Therapists are only the catalysts who have found that living well is the best role model. We therefore provide a positive approach and know-how, and we sometimes serve as a guide.

REFERENCES

Ackerman, N.W. 1958. *The Psychodynamics of family life: Diagnosis and treatment of family relationships.* New York: Basic Books.

——1966. *Treating the troubled family.* New York: Basic Books.

Beck, A.T., A.J. Rush, R.R. Shaw and G. Emery. 1979. *Cognitive therapy of depression.* New York: Guilford.

Billings, J.H., D.H. Rosen, C. Asimos and J. A. Motto. 1974. Observations on long-term group therapy with suicidal and depressed persons. *Life-Threatening Behavior* 4:160–70.

Boszormenyi-Nagy, I. and G. M. Spark. 1973. *Invisible loyalties: Reciprocity in intergenerational family therapy.* New York: Harper & Row.

Bowen, M. 1978. *Family therapy in clinical practice.* New York: Jason Aronson.

Bowers, M.K., H. Mullan and B. Berkowitz. 1959. Observations on suicide occurring during group psychotherapy. *American Journal of Psychotherapy* 13:93–106.

Bowlby, J. 1982. *Attachment.* Vol I. of *Attachment and loss.* 2d ed. New York: Basic Books. (Original work published 1969).

——1973. *Separation: Anxiety and anger.* Vol. II of *Attachment and loss.* 2d ed. New York: Basic Books.

Colson, D., L. Lewis and L. Horwitz. 1985. Negative outcome in psychotherapy and psychoanalysis. In D.T. Mays and C.M. Franks, eds., *Negative outcome in psychotherapy and what to do about it.* New York: Springer, pp. 59–75.

Comstock, B. S. and M. McDermott. 1975. Group therapy for patients who attempt suicide. *International Journal of Group Psychotherapy* 25:44–49.

Durkheim, E. 1951. *Suicide: A study in sociology.* Translated by J.A. Spaulding and G. Simpson. New York: Free Press.

Erikson, E. 1980. *Identity and the life cycle.* New York: W. W. Norton. (Original work published in 1959).

Eyman, J. 1987. Unsuccessful psychotherapy with seriously suicidal borderline patients. Paper presented at the joint meeting of the American Association of Suicidology and the International Association of Suicidology, May, San Francisco, California.

Eyman, J. and R. Conroy. 1988. Suicide: The loss of a fantasy. Paper presented at the meeting of the American Association of Suicidology, April, Washington, D.C.

Farberow, N.L. 1968. Group psychotherapy with suicidal persons. In H. L.P. Resnik, ed., *Suicidal behaviors: Diagnosis and management.* Boston: Little, Brown, pp. 328–40.

Freud, S. 1957a. Five lectures on psycho-analysis. In Vol. II of *Standard edition.* London: Hogarth Press, pp. 1–56. (Original work published 1910).

——1957b. Mourning and melancholia. In Vol. 14 of *Standard edition.* London: Hogarth Press, pp. 237–58. (Original work published 1917).

Hackel, J. and C.T. Asimos. 1981. Resistances encountered in starting a group therapy program for suicide attempters in varied administrative settings. *Suicide and Life-Threatening Behavior* 11:93–98.

Haley, J. 1980. *Leaving home: The therapy of disturbed young people.* New York: McGraw-Hill.

Hendin, H. 1981. Psychotherapy and suicide. *American Journal of Psychotherapy* 35:469–80.

Indin, B.M. 1966. The crisis club: A group experience for suicidal patients. *Mental Hygiene* 50:280–90.

Jacobs, J. 1971. *Adolescent suicide.* New York: Wiley-Interscience.

Jacobs, J. and J.D. Teicher. 1967. Broken homes and social isolation in attempted suicides of adolescents. *International Journal of Social Psychiatry* 13:138–49.

Klerman, G. L., M.M. Weissman, B.J. Rounsaville and E.S. Chevron. 1984. *Interpersonal psychotherapy of depression.* New York: Basic Books.

Langsley, D.G. and D.M. Kaplan. 1968. *The treatment of families in crisis.* New York: Grune & Stratton.

Lesse, S. 1975. The range of therapies in the treatment of severely depressed suicidal patients. *American Journal of Psychotherapy* 29:308–26.

Litman, R.E. and N.D. Tabachnick. 1968. Psychoanalytic theories of suicide. In H. L.P. Resnik, ed., *Suicidal Behaviors, Diagnosis and management.* Boston: Little, Brown, pp. 73–81.

Mahler, M.S., F. Pine and A. Bergman. 1975. *The psychological birth of the human infant: Symbiosis and individuation.* New York: Basic Books.

McCourtney, J.L. 1961. Suicide as a complication to group psychotherapy. *Military Medicine* 126:895–98.

Minuchin, S. 1974. *Families and family therapy.* Cambridge, MA: Harvard University Press.

Neill, J.R. and D.P. Kniskern eds. 1982. *From psyche to system: The evolving therapy of Carl Whitaker.* New York: Guilford.

Peebles, M.J. 1986. The adaptive aspects of the golden fantasy. *Psychoanalytic Psychology* 3:217–35.

Reiss, D. 1968. The suicide six: Observations on suicidal behavior and group function. *International Journal of Social Psychiatry* 14:201–12.

Richman, J. 1986. *Family therapy for suicidal people.* New York: Springer.

Shneidman, E. 1985. *Definition of suicide.* New York: John Wiley and Sons.

Shneidman, E.S., N.L. Farberow and R.E. Litman., eds. 1970. *The psychology of suicide.* New York: Science House.

Smith, K. 1983. *Treating the seriously suicidal person within a psychotherapy.* Unpublished manuscript.

——1985. Suicide assessment: An ego vulnerabilities approach. *Bulletin of the Menninger Clinic* 49:489–99.

Smith, K. and R. Conroy. 1984. Towards an integrated assessment and treatment model for suicidal inpatients. Unpublished manuscript.

Smith, K. and J. Eyman. 1988. Ego structure and object differentiation in suicidal patients. In H. D. Lerner and P. M. Lerner, eds., *Primitive mental states and the Rorschach.* Madison, CT: International Universities Press, pp. 175–202.

Smith, S. 1977. The golden fantasy: A regressive reaction to separation anxiety. *International Journal of Psychoanalysis* 58:311–24.

Stone, A.A. and H.M. Shein. 1968. Psychotherapy of the hospitalized suicidal patient. *American Journal of Psychotherapy* 22:15–25.

Strickler, M. and J. Allgeyer. 1967. The crisis group: A new application of crisis theory. *Social work* 12:28–32.

Winnicott, D.W. 1965. The theory of the parent-infant relationship. In *The maturational processes and the facilitating environment: Studies in the theory of emotional development.* New York: International Universities Press, pp. 37–55. (Original work published 1960).

10

Psychological Perspectives on Suicide

Antoon A. Leenaars

No one really knows why human beings commit suicide. One of the most frequent questions asked about suicide is, "Why do people kill themselves?" or more specifically, "Why did that individual commit suicide?" People are perplexed, bewildered, confused, and even overwhelmed when they are confronted with suicide. Understanding suicide—like understanding any complicated human act—is a complex endeavor, involving knowledge and insight drawn from many points of view.

The modern era of the psychological study of suicide began around the turn of the twentieth century with the investigations of Sigmund Freud (1901, 1909, 1917a & b, 1920, 1921, 1923, 1933, 1940). Freud's clinical research suggested to him that the root cause of suicide—within a developmental context—was the experience of loss or rejection of a significant, highly cathected object (i.e., a person). In 1920, Freud further developed what he termed a "deeper interpretation" of what leads someone to kill himself after such a loss or rejection. He stated:

> Probably no one finds the mental energy to kill himself unless, in the first place, in doing so he is at the same time killing an object with whom he has identified himself and, in the second place, is turning against himself a death wish which had been directed against someone else (p.162).

Freud—eschewing the two popular notions about suicide at the turn of the twentieth century, sin and crime—placed the focus of blame on man; specifically, in man's unconscious. An excellent summary of Freud's perspective has been presented by Litman (1967). However, since around 1900, there have been a host of psychological theories besides Freud's that have attempted to define suicide. Indeed, a—if not the—major advance in the psychology of suicide in our century is the development of various models beyond Freud's that have attempted to understand this complicated human act. Elsewhere (Leenaars 1988a), I have outlined the perspectives of ten suicidologists: Alfred Adler, Ludwig Binswanger, Sigmund Freud, Carl G. Jung, Karl Menninger, George Kelly, Henry A. Murray, Edwin Shneidman, Harry Stack Sullivan, and Gregory Zilboorg. Although my space here is more limited, one of my major points in that volume will be argued here anew—suicide is open to various psychological constructions.

In his famous experiment on volume where the experimenter pours fluid from a short, fat beaker into a tall, thin one, Piaget (1970) has demonstrated that the young child will say there is more fluid in either the first or second beaker. The child is centered on only one dimension to the exclusion of others. Later in human development, the child can take into account both dimensions simultaneously and use multiple perspective on the same event. To be decentered in general, is to be able to take an abstract view of things, rather than to be influenced totally by the characteristics of concrete particulars ("stimulus bound"). To view suicide only from Freud's original view is perhaps to be too concrete and stimulus bound. To introject only Freud's or any other specific view may be seen as acting like the young preconservative child, i.e., centered. Although Freud provided a sound basis in the very early years of suicidology, what we have discovered thus far about suicide is that it may be best to define suicide from multiple perspectives; not being concrete but also not being overinclusive. In this sense, it may be wise to follow Kelly's (1955) dictate of constructive alternativism:

> We take the stand that there are always some alternative constructions available to choose among in dealing with the world. No one needs to paint himself into a corner; no one needs to be completely hemmed in by circumstances; no one needs to be the victim of his biography (p.15).

For this chapter, I have decided to present four points of view: psychoanalytic (Freud); cognitive-behavioral (Beck); social learning (Lester); and multidimensional (Shneidman). I hope to in some way clarify the central issue—knowing why human beings commit suicide.

The four perspectives will be presented in the form of protocol sentences or what might be construed to be aphorisms. Protocol sentences are testable hypotheses. In that sense, they are like aphorisms. An aphorism is a short statement stating a truth. It is a principle expressed tersely in a few telling words. In the Western world the best known set of aphorisms are in Pascal's Pensees. Recently, Shneidman (1984) presented a set of aphorisms about suicide. A major difference between protocol sentences and aphorisms is that the latter tend to be general. Although protocol sentences may be general, they must be testable (although some form of specificity is implied for the sentence to be testable). One must be able to determine the truth or falsity of the statement. Aphorisms, if they are true, should also be subject to the possibility of verification (falsifiability). The protocol procedure was first introduced by Carnap (1931/1959) and applied in my own research in suicide for the last ten years (Leenaars 1979, 1985, 1986, 1987, 1988a, b and c, 1989; Leenaars and Balance 1981, 1984a, b and c; Leenaars, Balance, Wenckstern and Rudzinski 1985).

Protocol sentences (or aphorisms) are one means of defining an event. It is obvious, as Shneidman (1984) noted, that one way to discuss suicide is to do so aphoristically.

PSYCHOANALYTIC

As I have already mentioned, the psychoanalytic perspective was first formulated by Sigmund Freud early in the twentieth century. Other noteworthy suicidologists in this tradition are Karl Menninger, Henry A. Murray, and Gregory Zilboorg. Elsewhere (Leenaars 1988a), I have presented a complete discussion of these views. Here are some protocol sentences (or aphorisms) derived from Freud's work.

1. Suicide is motivated by unconscious intentions. Even if the person communicates that he has consciously planned to kill himself, the focus of the action is in the unconscious.
2. The root cause of suicide is the experience of loss and rejection of a significant highly cathected object (i.e., a person)—the person, in fact, is singly preoccupied with this loss/rejection.
3. The suicidal person feels quite ambivalent. He is both affectionate and hostile toward a loss/rejecting person.
4. The suicidal person is, in some direct or indirect fashion, identifying with a rejecting or lost person. Attachment, based upon an important emotional tie, is the meaning of identification.
5. The suicidal person exhibits an overly regressive attachment—"narcissistic identification"—with the object. He treats himself as if he were reacting to another person.
6. The suicidal person is angry at the object although the feelings and/or ideas of vengefulness and aggression are directed toward himself.
7. The suicidal person turns back upon himself murderous wishes/impulses/needs that had been directed against the object.
8. Suicide is a fulfillment of punishment; i.e., self-punishment.
9. The suicidal person experiences a sense of guilt or self-criticism. The person develops prohibitions of extraordinary harshness and severity towards himself.
10. The suicidal person's organization of experiences is impaired. He is no longer capable of any coherent synthesis of his experience.

COGNITIVE BEHAVIORAL

The cognitive behavioral perspective is most widely associated with Aaron T. Beck and his colleagues (1963, 1967, 1971, 1975a and b, 1976, 1978, 1979).

Ellis and Meichenbaum are also associated with this view. Here are ten protocol sentences deduced from Beck's writings.

1. Suicide is associated with depression. The critical link between depression and suicidal intent is hopelessness.
2. Hopelessness, defined operationally in terms of negative expectations, appears to be the critical factor in the suicide. The suicidal person views suicide as the only possible solution to her desperate and hopeless, unsolvable problem (situation).
3. The suicidal person views the future as negative, often unrealistically. She anticipates more suffering, more hardship, more frustration, more deprivation, etc.
4. The suicidal person's view of herself is negative, often unrealistically. She views herself as incurable, incompetent, and helpless, often with self-criticism, self-blame, and reproaches against the self (with expressions of guilt and regret) accompanying this low self-evaluation.
5. The suicidal person views herself as deprived, often unrealistically. Thoughts of being alone, unwanted, unloved, and perhaps materially deprived are possible examples of such deprivation.
6. Although the suicidal person's thoughts (interpretations) are arbitrary, she considers no alternative, accepting the validity (accuracy) of the cognitions.
7. The suicidal person's thoughts which are often automatic and involuntary, are characterized by a number of possible errors, some so gross as to constitute distortion; e.g., preservation, overgeneralization, magnification/minimization, inexact labeling, selective abstraction, negative bias.
8. The suicidal person's affective reaction is proportional to the labeling of the traumatic situation, regardless of the actual intensity of the event.
9. Irrespective of whether the affect is sadness, anger, anxiety, or euphoria, the more intense the affect the greater the perceived plausibility of the associated cognitions.
10. The suicidal person, being hopeless and not wanting to tolerate the pain (suffering), desires to escape. Death is thought of as more desirable than life.

SOCIAL LEARNING

The social learning view has recently been summarized by Lester (1987): Bandura and psychologists in the classical (Pavlov) and operant (Skinner) traditions are the best known theorists in this view. The ten aphorisms of this paradigm are as follows:

1. Suicide is a learned behavior. Childhood experiences and forces in the environment shape the suicidal person and precipitate the act.
2. Child-rearing practices are critical, especially the child's experiences of punishment. Specifically, the suicidal person has learned to inhibit the expression of aggression outward and simultaneously learned to turn it inward upon oneself.
3. The suicide can be predicted on the basic laws of learning. Suicide is shaped behavior—the behavior was and is reinforced in his environment.
4. The suicidal person's thoughts provide the stimuli; suicide (response) is imagined. Cognitions (such as self-praise) can be reinforcers for the act.
5. The suicidal person's expectancies play a critical role in the suicide— he expects reinforcement (reward) by the act.
6. Depression, especially the cognitive components, is strongly associated with the suicide. Depression goes far toward explaining suicide. For example, depression may be caused by a lack of reinforcement, learned helplessness, and/or rewarded.
7. Suicide can be a manipulative act. This is reinforced by others.
8. Suicide is not eliminated by means of punishment.
9. The suicidal person is nonsocialized. He has not been sufficiently socialized into traditional culture. The suicidal person has failed to learn the normal cultural values, especially toward life and death.
10. The suicide can be reinforced by a number of environmental factors, for example, subcultural norms, suggestions on television, gender preferences for specific methods, suicide in significant others (modeling), a network of family and friends, cultural patterns.

MULTIDIMENSIONAL

The psychologist who has consistently argued for a multidimensional view is Shneidman (1967, 1973, 1980, 1981, 1982, 1985, 1986, 1987). This chapter itself can be seen as a development from this tradition. Here is a brief summary, utilizing our previous procedure, of his work.

1. The suicidal person is in unbearable psychological pain. The person is focused almost entirely on this unbearable emotion (pain), and especially one specific (an arbitrarily selected) way to escape from it.
2. The suicidal person experienced a situation that is traumatic (e.g.,

poor health, rejection by the spouse, being married to a nonsupportive spouse). What is implied is that some needs are unfilfilled, thwarted, or frustrated.

3. For the suicidal person, the idea of cessation (death, stopping, or eternal sleep) provides the solution. It permits her to resolve the unbearable state of self-destructiveness, disturbance, and isolation.

4. By the suicide, the person wishes to end all conscious experience. The goal of suicide is cessation of consciousness and the person behaves in order to achieve this end.

5. The suicidal person is in a state of heightened disturbance (perturbation), e.g., she feels boxed in, rejected, harassed, unsuccessful, and especially hopeless and helpless.

6. The suicidal person's internal attitude is ambivalence. The suicidal person experiences complications, concomitant contradictory feelings, attitudes and/or thrusts (not only toward herself and other people but toward the act itself).

7. The suicidal person's cognitive state is constriction (tunnel vision, a narrowing of the mind's eye). She is figuratively intoxicated or drugged by her overpowering emotions and constricted logic and perception.

8. The suicidal person needs or wishes to egress. She wants to leave (the scene), to exit, to get out, to get away, to be gone, not to be around, to be "elsewhere" . . . not to be.

9. There is a serial pattern to the suicide. The suicidal person exhibits patterns of behavior that diminish or truncate her life, which subtract from its length or reduce its scope.

10. The person's suicide has unconscious psychodynamic implications.

CONCLUDING REMARKS

Suicide is best understood as a multidimensional human malaise. What we have discovered so far in our century is that suicide can be defined differently from various psychological points of view. I do not mean to suggest that all these views are mutually exclusive or equally accurate or helpful—we do not have to follow the cognitive processes of the suicidal person. Nor do I believe that my protocol (aphorism) method is the only way to outline a point of view; indeed, it may well lose some of the complexity in the theories themselves. It is, however, one way to understand the event.

The real importance of protocol sentences is that they must be verifiable. In that regard, what aphorisms of Freud or Beck or Lester or Shneidman are true? Which are empirical? Suicidology's future endeavor, in general, will be the need to develop some form of empirical verification of the various constructions of the event. Research will be an important aspect of such efforts. I do not mean to suggest only the controlled experiment. But, following Allport (1942) and Maslow (1966), we must be open-minded, utilizing both ideographic and nomothetic approaches. Suicide is plagued by the difficulty of obtaining data (Maris 1981). In my own research, I have utilized suicide notes as my data base. Despite their limitations (Leenaars 1988a), suicide notes have been historically useful in describing the suicide since the individual is at the final throes of the life vs. death decision. Other documents as well as statistics, third-party interviews, and the study of nonfatal suicide attempters have a place in understanding suicidal phenomena—if the data is put in the context of broad theoretical formulations about suicide and personality functioning in general.

Although misuse of psychological theory(ies) is possible (e.g., finding support only for one's view and, thus, acting like the suicidal person himself), theoretical formulations have an important place in the use of personal documents (e.g., suicide notes) and in any form of research. Research must be embedded in theory. To avoid our constriction, I would argue that we must critically evaluate alternative explanations and interpretations. We must no longer look at suicide from Freud's perspective alone but from Beck's, Lester's Shneideman's, etc.

Theory, explicit and implicit, plays some role in research whether solving a specific problem, testing an existing theory, developing new theories, or expanding existing theories. The problem is that frequently the theory is not articulated. Regretably, much of the research on suicide is atheoretical. Equally regretable, often remediators have no stated conceptualization or, more accurately, the conceptualization is characterized, if I can use Beck's descriptions, by a number of cognitive errors, some so gross to constitute distortion; e.g., perservation, overgeneralization, magnification/minimization, inexact labeling, selective abstraction, bias. One is simply too centered. I do not mean to suggest this chapter solves the problem, but I hope to have clarified the issue—psychologically, suicide is best understood from different points of view.

An understanding of suicide can be used to assist us in preventing the event. Remediation follows empirically verified definition. When understanding is centered and based not on any sound empiricism, remediation (i.e., prevention, intervention, and postvention) is likely to be ineffective. Hopefully, the definition of suicide derived from the four points of view, once empirically verified in our adult years, will assist a needful individual in some way.

As a final comment, I do not mean to suggest that psychology alone has a role in defining suicide. It is not sufficient to define all of the event. Suicide is a multidimensional human malaise. It would seem most accurate to define suicide as an event with biological (including biochemical, neuropsychological), sociocultural, interpersonal, philosophical/existential, psychological, and other aspects. All such empirical definitions may assist a suicidal person in some way.

REFERENCES

Allport, G. 1942. *The use of personal documents in psychological science.* New York: Social Science Research Council.

Beck, A. 1963. Thinking and depression I. Idiosyncratic content and cognitive distortions. *Archives of General Psychiatry* 9:324–35.

———1967. *Depression.* New York: Harper and Row.

———1976. *Cognitive therapy and the emotional disorders.* New York: International Universities Press.

Beck, A., R. Beck and M. Kovacs. 1975a. Classification of suicidal behaviors: I. Quantifying intent and medical lethality. *American Journal of Psychiatry* 132:285–87.

Beck, A. and R. Greenberg. 1971. The nosology of suicidal phenomena: past and future perspectives. *Bulletin of Suicidology* 8:10–17.

Beck, A., M. Kovacs and A. Weissman. 1975. Hopelessness and suicidal behavior: An overview. *Journal of the American Medical Association* 234:1146–49.

Beck, A., and A. Rush. 1978. Cognitive approaches to depression and suicide. In G. Serban, ed., *Cognitive defects in the development of mental illness.* New York: Burnner/Mazel.

Beck, A., A. Rush, B. Shaw and C. Emery. 1979. *Cognitive theory of depression.* New York: Guilford.

Carnap, R. 1959. Psychology in physical language. In A. Ayer, ed., *Logical positivism.* New York: Free Press (original published in 1931).

Freud, S. 1901. Psychopathology of everyday life. In Vol. 6 of *The standard edition of the complete psychological works of sigmund freud.* Ed. and Trans. by J. Strachey. London: Hogarth Press 1974.

———1909. A case of obsessional neurosis. In Vol. 10 of *The standard edition.*

———1917. Mourning and melancholia. In Vol. 14 of *The standard edition.*

———1917. General theory of neurosis. In Vol. 16 of *The standard edition.*

———1920. A case of homosexuality in a woman. In Vol. 18 of *The standard edition.*

———1921. Group psychology and the analysis of the ego. In Vol. 18 of *The standard edition.*

———1923. The ego and the id. In Vol. 19 of *The standard edition.*

———1933. New introductory lectures. In Vol. 22 of *The standard edition.*

———1940. An outline of psycho-analysis. In Vol. 23 of *The standard edition.*

Kelly, G. 1955. *The Psychology of Personal Constructs.* 2 vols. New York: Norton.

Leenaars, A. 1979. *A study of the manifest content of suicide notes from three different theoretical perspectives: L. Binswanger, S. Freud, and G. Kelly.* PhD diss., University of Windsor, Canada.

Leenaars, A. 1985. Freud's and Shneidman's formulations of suicide investigated through suicide notes. In E. Shneidman, chair, *Suicide notes and other personal documents in psychological science.* Symposium conducted at the meeting of the American Psychological Association, Los Angeles, California.

———1986. A brief note on the latent content in suicide notes. *Psychological Reports* 59:640–42.

———1987a. An empirical investigation of Shneidman's formulations regarding suicide: age & sex. *Suicide and Life-Threatening Behavior* 17:233–50.

———1988a. *Suicide notes.* New York: Human Sciences Press.

———1988b. The suicide notes of women. In D. Lester, ed., *Suicide in women.* Springfield, IL: Thomas.

————1988c. Are women's suicides really different from men's? *Women & Health* 14:17–33.

————1989. Suicide across the adult life-span: An archival study. *Crisis* 10:132–51.

Leenaars, A. and W. Balance. 1981. A predictive approach to the study of manifest content in suicide notes. *Journal of Clinical Psychology* 37:50–52, 1981.

————1984a. A logical empirical approach to the study of the manifest content in suicide notes. *Canadian Journal of Behavioral Science* 16:248–56.

————1984b. A predictive approach to Freud's formulations regarding suicide. *Suicide and Life-Threatening Behavior* 14:275–83.

————1984c. A predictive approach to suicide notes of young and old people from Freud's formulations regarding suicide. *Journal of Clinical Psychology* 40:1362–64.

Leenaars, A., W. Balance, S. Wenckstern and D. Rudzinski. 1985. An empirical investigation of Shneidman's formulations regarding suicide. *Suicide and Life-Threatening Behavior* 15:184–95.

Lester, D. 1987. *Suicide as a learned behavior.* Springfield, IL: Thomas.

Litman, R. 1967. Sigmund Freud and suicide. In E. Shneidman, ed., *Essays in self-destruction.* New York: Jason Aronson.

Maslow, A. 1966. *The psychology of science.* New York: Harper & Row.

Maris, R. 1981. *Pathways to suicide.* Baltimore, MD: John Hopkins University Press.

Piaget, J. 1970. *Structuralism.* Trans, by C. Maschler. New York: Harper & Row.

Shneidman, E. 1967. Sleep and self-destruction: a phenomenological approach. In E. Shneidman, ed., *Essays in self-destruction.* New York: Science House.

————1973. Suicide. *Encyclopedia britannica.* Chicago: William Benton.

————1980. *Voices of death.* New York: Harper & Row.

————1981. *Suicide thoughts and reflections: 1960–1980.* New York: Human Science Press.

————1982. The suicidal logic of Cesare Pavese. *Journal of the American Academy of Psychoanalysis* 10:547–63.

————1984. Aphorisms of suicide and some implications for psychotherapy. *American Journal of Psychotherapy* 38:319–28.

————1985. *Definition of suicide.* New York: John Wiley and Sons.

————1986. Melville's cognitive style: The logic of Moby-Dick. In I. Bryant, ed., *A companion to Melville studies.* Westport, CT: Greenwood Press.

————1987. A psychological approach to suicide. In G. VandenBos and B. Bryant, ed., *Cataclysms, crisis, and catastrophes: Psychology in action.* Washington, DC: American Psychological Association.

11

Suicide Risk and Treatment Problems in Patients Who Have Attempted Suicide

H. J. Möller

From studies concerning the possible means by which to predict suicidal behavior, it is known that those individuals who have already attempted suicide are especially at risk for further suicidal behavior. In other words: the descriptor "previous suicide attempt" can be considered the best predictor of further suicidal behavior (Bürk and Möller 1985). One medically relevant conclusion to be drawn from this is that patients who have attempted suicide must receive sufficient after-care to reduce not only the immediate but also the long-term risk of further suicidal behavior (Möller et al 1987). Apart from this task, it is of course the general purpose of the psychiatric/psychotherapeutic after-care to implement appropriate therapeutic measures for the treatment of the psychopathologic findings and of the disturbances in social adaption that are to be found in many of these patients (Möller and Lauter 1986).

The after-care of patients who have attempted suicide is usually composed of both an inpatient and an outpatient phase. During the inpatient phase, besides the somatically oriented management by the medical or surgical team there is an initial psychiatric/psychotherapeutic intervention. The latter has several goals:

1. Evaluation for further suicidality
2. Diagnosis of possible psychiatric illness
3. Crisis intervention through problem-oriented sessions with the patient and including relevant significant others.

In smaller general hospital, the initial psychiatric/psychotherapeutic intervention will be conducted by the treating internist or surgeon; in larger facilities this intervention will usually come from a consulting psychiatrist or from the team of a special psychiatric crisis-intervention station (Böhme 1980; Möller et al. 1982). Depending on the specific type of management required, the amount of staff and time available, and the psychiatric/psychotherapeutic qualifications of the staff involved, there will be significant differences in after-care regimens with respect to duration, effort, and quality.

When there is adequate psychiatric/psychotherapeutic crisis intervention within the setting of a general hospital, only about 12 percent of patients who have attempted suicide must be transferred to a psychiatric hospital for further treatment (Möller et al. 1983). In such cases the patients will usually have an endogenous psychosis or a major depression of another origin. By far the largest portion of these patients can be discharged within a few days; the duration of the inpatient stay depends both on the somatic complications of the suicide attempt and on the severity of the psychiatric disorders. A large portion of these patients will be judged by their managing physicians as requiring outpatient after-care, although the indication will vary according to the specific circumstances of each case.

In the course of the work performed by the Psychiatric Liaison Service in the Toxicology Department of the hospital of the Technical University of Munich (Klinikum rechts der Isar), the indication for after-care following intensive inpatient crisis intervention is very liberally defined. Seen as a group, those patients who are not referred to outpatient treatment programs differ from those who are referred to such programs in the following ways:

—higher percentage of female patients
—no current unemployment
—less frequent previous history of unemployment
—less marked neurotic symptomatology during childhood and adolescence
—fewer previous suicide attempts
—no previous substance dependence
—no previous psychiatric treatment
—fewer suicidal thoughts and intentions
—active help-seeking at the time of index suicide attempt
—less life-threatening suicide attempt

A basic question is whether the selection thus determined, which is based on the clinically intuitive decisions of the managing physicians, is actually a meaningful selection. If the above selection is compared with the predictors of suicidal behavior summarized in Bürk's literature review (Bürk et al. 1985), it appears that the essential risk factors have indeed been accounted for. The literature review in question formulates the following predictors of suicidal behavior:

—previous suicide attempts
—previous psychiatric treatment

—substance dependence
—personality disorder
—advanced age
—male sex

In a prospective one year follow-up study, approximately 500 individuals who had attempted suicide were evaluated using, among other tools, a standardized procedure for recording psychopathological findings (Torhorst et al. 1984). Applying modern univariate and multivariate statistical analyses to these data, we were able to derive a series of further predictors (Table 1), which, however, still require replication by cross-validation. As the table illustrates, the predictor characteristics are dependent upon both the method of analysis and the variable being predicted. Also interesting in this context are the cluster-analytic groupings in the sense of types encompassing specific combinations of characteristics; however, this topic has been the subject of another paper (Kürz et al. 1986) and will not be further discussed here.

Numerous attempts have been made to employ the precise prediction of the risk of suicidal behavior as a means of determining more clearly the indication for inpatient versus outpatient after-care. Unfortunately, on the basis of the single predictors enumerated above, no sufficient means of establishing prognosis could be developed, and, in particular, no adequate basis for a decision regarding individual prognosis could be derived. Other attempts were then made to improve this situation by grouping relevant characteristics together in prognosis scales that were supposed to offer a better prediction of potential suicide risk. A number of such suicide risk scales have been described in the literature, among them several that are specialized to evaluate suicide risk in patients who have just attempted suicide (Table 2). A critical review of these scales has been published by Bürk and Möller (1985). Without going too deeply into the details, it can be said that the prediction of suicide risk afforded by such scales is superior to the predictions based on single predictors, and that these scales lead to a meaningful differentiation of various groups. However, if judged with respect to sensitivity and specificity (Table 3), one can not but draw the conclusion that suicide risk scales do not offer a satisfactory prediction of behavior in the individual case (Kürz et al. 1988.)

The outpatient management of patients following attempted suicide cannot be described as comprising a uniform procedure. Depending on who is managing a specific case, different aspects will be emphasized and different treatment methods preferred. A physician without comprehensive training in psychotherapy, for example, will tend more toward using a supportive, problem-oriented approach and possibly toward concomitant prescription of psychoactive medication; a more psychodynamically oriented physician will tend more toward brief

Table 1: Predictors of suicidal behavior (A one-year follow-up study involving 500 patients who had attempted suicide by intoxication)

Predictor Variable	OUTCOME CRITERIUM								
	Suicide			Attempted Suicide			Global Assessment Scale		
	Frequency and Means	Multiple Regression	Discriminance Analysis	Frequency and Means	Multiple Regression	Discriminance Analysis	Frequency and Means	Multiple Regression	Discriminance Analysis
Age							x	x	
Living Alone	x	x							
Unemployed			x				x	x	x
Previous Psychiatric Treatment		x	x	x	x		x	x	x
Previous Suicide Attempt				x	x		x	x	
Suicidal Thoughts				x	x		x		
Site of Suicide Attempt Hidden				x		x			
Measures to Prevent Discovery			x				x		
Stressful Life Events									
Intention to commit Suicide	x	x							
Non-Reactive Psychiatric Disorder	x		x	x		x	x	x	
Depressive-Apathetic Syndrome				x	x	x	x		

Table 2: Risk inventories for the estimation of suicide risk in patients who have attempted suicide

Cohen/Motto/Seiden 1966 14 Items	Tuckman/Youngman 1968 17 items	Buglass/McCulloch 1970 3 Items (men)	7 Items (women)	Buglass/Horton 1974 6 Items
previous suicide attempt	previous suicide attempt or gesture		previous suicide attempt	previous parasuicide (with hospitalization)
previous psychiatric hospitalization			previous psychiatr. treatment	previous inpatient psychiatric treatment previous outpatient psychiatric treatment
alcohol problem (current or previous)	neurologic or psychiatric illness, remarkable affect or behavior (including alcoholism)	alcoholism	substance-/drug dependence	alcohol problem
previous substance dependence		physical abuse of significant others	psychopathy	sociopathy
antisocial behavior				
45 years and older	45 years and older			
male	male			
Caucasian	Caucasian		4 or more changes in domicile within past 5 years	

Separated, divorced, widowed	separated, divorced, widowed	not living together with relatives
domicile in area around an urban center	unemployed, retired	
poor physical condition during past 6 months	poor physical condition during past 6 months	
Suicide means: oral application, fire arms, jump	in physician's care within last 6 months	
unconscious or confused following attempt	Suicide Means: hanging, shooting, jumping, drowning	
loss(es) during past 6 months (real, imminent, imagined)	Months: April—September	Separation from mother (6 months or more before age 10)
under influence of alcohol at the time of attempt	Time of day: 6 AM—6 PM	
	Site: at home or in home of someone else	
	When discovered: soon	separation from father
	Suicidal intention denied	
	Suicide note	

Table 3: Sensitivität und Spezifität der Prädiktion auf der Basis von Suizid-Risiko-Skalen

Study	Sensitivity [1]	Specifity [2]
Cohen et al., 1966	0,96	0,32
Dean et al., 1967	0,75	0,93
Tuckman and Youngman, 1968	insufficient data	
Pöldinger, 1968	insufficient data	
Miskimins and Wilson, 1969	insufficient data	
Buglass and McCulloch, 1970	0,87	0,37
Van de Loo & Diekstra, 1970	0,77	0,79
Buglas and Horton, 1974	0,88	0,44
Lettieri, 1974	insufficient data	
Zung, 1974	insufficient data	
Farberow & MacKinnon, 1974 (11-Item-Scale)	0,85	0,84
Motto und Heilbronn, 1976 m.	0,61	0,58
Motto und Heilbronn, 1976 w.	0,31	0,84
Pallis et al, 1982, 1984 (short scale)	0,92	0,81
Henseler et al., 1983	insufficient data	
Patterson et al., 1983	non-empirical study	

1 $\dfrac{\text{correctly predicted positives}}{\text{all positives}}$

2 $\dfrac{\text{correctly predicted negatives}}{\text{all negatives}}$

psychotherapy. Of course, the entire process depends to a great degree on the condition of the patient, whereby the referral procedures within the health-care system will probably result in sending those patients who require medication to the first type and all others to the second type of care provider. The rational use of psychoactive medication at the time of crisis intervention or in the management of suicide attempters must be emphasized here (Winter and Möller 1986), especially in cases where the patient is severely depressed or anxious. Beyond this, more recent studies have shown that for patients with a history of multiple suicide attempts—usually patients with severe personality disorders, who for the most part do not fulfill the requirements for psychotherapy—the use of medication (neuroleptics and benzodiazepines) may also serve as effective prophylaxis against recurrence (Möller 1985). There is no need to emphasize here the fact that patients with endogenous psychosis require medication.

It is difficult to establish rules for psychotherapeutic after-care since here, as elsewhere in the realm of psychotherapy, the only rule that might apply is that the therapist should use the method that he learned. Psychodynamically oriented approaches are very frequently employed, a state of affairs that is surely a reflection of the training possibilities presently available (Wächtler 1982). It should also be emphasized that in the after-care of patients who have attempted suicide, the psychoanalytic protocol has to be extensively modified—the most apparent reason being to avoid patient frustration. The therapist must be more supportive and generally more active than is customarily the case in analytic therapy (Kürz and Möller (1984b). Individual therapy is definitely to be preferred over group therapy, since these patients seem to an especially great degree to be seeking the trust and the close relationship implicit in the one-on-one setting (Torhorst and Möller 1983).

A particular problem in the postdischarge after-care of patients who have recently attempted suicide is the poor rate of follow-up. Under usual management conditions, only 30 to 40 percent of patients will make use of the after-care opportunities offered them (Möller et al. 1978; Kürz and Möller 1984a). One of the reasons appears to be that these patients are often very anxious, insecure, overly sensitive, and withdrawn, and can accept only with great difficulty the referral from one therapist (inpatient treatment) to another (outpatient treatment). Besides this, the peculiar dynamics of the suicidal crisis often leads to a momentary improvement in the critical situation (e.g., through a temporary "giving in" of the conflict partner who has responded to the patient's call for help), an improvement that is, however, no real solution, but only a pseudosolution. This apparent improvement takes the pressure of suffering away from the patient—and thus his motivation for therapy, too. If one wants to achieve patient acceptance of after-care, one could at least try the simple strategy of making a definite appointment for the patient with the after-care provider. Our studies in this area have shown that a definite arrangement for the commencement of after-care increases the rate of acceptance significantly (Möller and Geiger 1981, 1982). The acceptance of outpatient after-care is best ensured when the after-care arrangements are made by the psychiatrist who treated the patient during the inpatient phase. In a relevant management oriented study involving over 200 patients who had attempted suicide, we could show that by this method the primary rate of after-care acceptance could be raised to 70 percent (Möller et al. 1984; Kürz et al. 1984). The decisive point is that the increase in the primary acceptance rate, i.e., the percentage of patients who actually keep the first appointment, was not offset by an increase in the drop-out rate subsequent to the initial session, so that the treatment model under discussion proved to be effective, for the full course of treatment.

Whether other simple and temporally limited methods aiming at improving motivation have an effect on the acceptance rate is a question that has yet to be answered. In another of our studies we arranged for a period of "motivation work" during the outpatient session. The motivation work was limited to a maximum of 30 minutes, during which time the motivational deficits that had been revealed by a self-evaluation questionnaire were addressed by the patient and therapist. In addition, those patients who had missed an appointment were recontacted by mail. The result of these efforts to improve motivation was a statistically insignificant increase in the acceptance rate from 40 percent to 50 percent (Torhorst et al. 1986).

In this latter context, the question arises as to the extent to which the patient's motivation, as assessed by the psychiatrist during the inpatient phase, allows a prediction concerning the actual acceptance of subsequent outpatient treatment. One of our studies, in which the relationship between a global clinical assessment of motivation and acceptance of after-care was analyzed, produced a negative result (Möller and Geiger 1982). In a more recent study, the aforementioned questionnaire for the self-assessment of motivation was used in an attempt to reach more specific and more reliable conclusions regarding patient motivation, as well as a global objective assessment of patient motivation by the psychiatrist. Neither the very complicated self-assessment of motivation by the patient nor the more global assessment by the psychiatrist showed a statistically significant correlation with the actual acceptance (Torhorst et al. 1986; Möller and Lauter 1986). The conclusion to be drawn from these results is that, at least for the present, neither the treating psychiatrist nor the patient himself can make a statement during the inpatient stay as to whether sufficient motivation for the acceptance of outpatient after-care exists. Thus, the clinician should, without regard for the assessment of motivation, refer every patient for whom he feels the indication for after-care is justified to an appropriate pro-

Table 4: Temporal distribution of recurrent suicidal behavior in 247 patients

	1.	2.	3.	4.	5.	6.	7.	8.	9.	10.	11.
SUICIDE ATTEMPTS	*****	**		**	**	**	***	***	*	*	*
SUICIDES	+		++	+	+	+					

Month after index suicide attempt

vider, so that the patient, regardless of his motivation at the time of referral, may have the option of accepting qualified after-care.

Considering the results of relevant epidemiologic and controlled studies, it appears controversial as to whether psychotherapeutically oriented outpatient after-care programs are actually efficacious with regard to preventing suicidal behavior (Kurz and Moeller 1982). This uncertainty is by no means an excuse for resignation, but rather should serve as stimulation for the development of better after-care models and more effective therapy methods. Seen on the whole, however, research efforts in this area have not been particularly active, especially in the Federal Republic of Germany. Even in the extensive management oriented study mentioned above—which was basically conceived as an analysis of acceptance problems and not as an efficacy study per se—we were not able to gather evidence indicative of the efficacy of psychotherapeutic after-care in preventing suicide attempts. In a one-year follow-up investigation, it could not be shown that the higher after-care acceptance rate of the experimentally evaluated management cases relative to the control group correlated with a reduced rate of recurrent suicidal behavior (Moeller et al. 1984; Moeller and Lauter 1986). However, there was indication of a temporal shift of recurrent suicidal behavior to the time subsequent to the three-month period of outpatient after-care at least for the experimental group with the higher acceptance rate. The temporal distribution of recurrent suicidal behavior for all the patients involved in this study is illustrated in Table 4, whereby only the first suicide reattempt is counted in those cases where multiple instances of suicidal behavior following after-care occurred. Eleven percent of the patients again attempted suicide within a year after the index attempt, and three patients died by suicide.

Of particular interest was the question of the extent to which recurrences of suicidal behavior during the follow-up period related to stressful life events and the patient's mood state. Using the "life-event" list of Holmes and Rahe (1967), at the time of the one year follow-up session the patients were asked to retrospectively indicate stressful life events. For every positive answer, the month in which the event had occurred was documented. These life-events were weighted

Table 5: Life event stress (weighted) as related to recurrent suicidal behavior

	patients with attempts n = 22	patients without reattempts n = 214
mean	225	217
standard deviation	137	142

t = 0,26, no significant difference

by employing the numerical factors defined by Holmes and Rahe (1980). Table 5 contains a comparison of patients who did and did not attempt suicide during the period of follow-up with respect to the available information concerning the stress imposed by critical life events (mean of the weighted life events per patient). No differences in suicidal behavior are shown. This means that the patients who reattempted suicide during the follow-up period did not as a group experience more critical life events than the patients who did not demonstrate recurrent suicidal behavior. Furthermore, a more detailed analysis of the life events shows that the patients with suicide attempts did not more frequently identify severely stressful life events. The temporal relationship between stressful life events and suicidal behavior was examined case by case: in only 4 out of 22 cases did the peak of the stressful life event occur in the month directly before or in the month in which the suicide attempt occurred. This finding counters the assumption that a maximally stressful life event usually precedes a suicide attempt. However, it is conceivable that a suicide attempt was not necessarily related to a maximum of life event stress during the follow-up period, but rather that the suicide attempt was preceded merely by an increase of chronic stress over a limited period of time. Based on the 31 cases for which this hypothesis could be tested, the results show the contrary tendency, namely a drop in the level of stress in the month of or before a suicide attempt; this drop was relative to the level during the two preceding months.

In order to obtain comparable information about mood states during the time following discharge from inpatient care, the patients involved in the one year follow-up study were presented with a global mood scale, according to which they were requested to retrospectively estimate their mood for every month of the follow-up period. One hundred and seventy-eight patients were able to complete this form. The validity of this retrospective mood estimation could be ascertained by the comparison with the scores of the Mood Assessment Scale of von Zersson (1976), which the patients in the experimental group had completed during the three-month period of outpatient after-care. This comparison demon-

Table 6: Mood course characteristics as related to recurrent suicidal behavior

	Recurrent suicidal behavior	
course type	yes	no
favourable (n = 119)	5	105
unfavourable (n = 68)	10	58

$X^2 = 5.62$
1 df
P <0.01

strates satisfactory agreement, at least with regard to the general tendency. If one considers the global mood state during the first three months following the index suicide attempt, then from the data supplied by the patients concerning the postdischarge course one could also reach some conclusions regarding the duration of crisis situations. Thus, a short-term crisis was defined by the recording of low mood assessment scores (<2) during the first month after discharge; all other mood courses during the first three months were considered to represent longer-term crises. By this definition, about two thirds of the patients who had been judged by the referring physicians to be in need of outpatient aftercare reported short-term and about one third longer-term crisis situations.

We attempted two different approaches with regard to developing a typology of mood courses. A visual evaluation of the mood curves formed the basis of the first approach. Accordingly, 29 percent of the mood courses were classified as Type 1 (uniformly good mood); 35 percent were Type 2 (continuous improvement); 7 percent Type 3 (uniformly bad mood); 24 percent Type 4 (very variable mood); and 5 percent Type 5 (continuous worsening). If one takes the first two types to be favorable mood courses and the others to be unfavorable, then the outpatient mood course during the first year after discharge was favorable in 64 percent of patients and unfavorable in 36 percent. In the second approach, a favorable mood course was defined by the frequency of qualitatively negative extreme scores (at least three values <2). Applying this criterion, 62 percent of the patients described a favorable and 38 percent an unfavorable course, a result very similar to that of the first approach.

One might assume that an unfavorable mood course would be related to increased stress from critical life events. However, the mean (weighted) life-event score was not significantly higher in patients demonstrating unfavorable courses than in those having more favorable ones.

If one now compares the course characteristics of patients who reattempted suicide with those who exhibited no further suicidal behavior (Table 6), one sees that reattempts correlate significantly with unfavorable courses ($p < 0.05$). Comparing the course characteristics as defined by the second approach described above with the rate of recurrent suicidal behavior, there results an even clearer correlation between unfavorable courses and the frequency of repeated suicidal behavior ($p < 0.01$). All of these findings obviously require verification through prospective investigations, but for practical purposes one could perhaps now draw the conclusion that it might make sense to regularly evaluate patients who are at particular risk with such a mood assessment scale. If recognized, unfavorable mood states could serve as an aid in the timely diagnosis of imminent recurrent suicidal behavior.

REFERENCES

Böhme, K. 1980. Zur praktischen Versorgung von Suizidenten. *Nervenarzt* 51:152–58.

Bürk, F. and H.J. Möller. 1985. Prädiktoren für suizidales Verhalten bei nach einem Suizidversuch hospitalisierten Patienten. *Fortschritte der Psychiatrische und Neurologie* 53:259–70.

Bürk, F., A. Kurz and H.J. Möller. 1985. Suicide risk scales. *European Archives of Psychiatry and Neurological Sciences* 235:153–57.

Holmes, T.H. and R.H. Rahe. 1967. The social readjustment scale. *Journal of Psychosomatic Research* 11:213–18.

Holmes, T.H. and R.H. Rahe. 1980. Die "Social readjustment rating scale." In H. Katschnig, ed., *Sozialer Stress und psychische Erkrankung*. München: Urban & Schwarzenberg.

Kurz, A. and H.J. Möller. 1982. Ergebnisse der klinisch-experimentellen Evaluation von suizidprophylaktischen Versorgungsprogrammen *Archiv fur Psychiatrie und Nervenkrankheiten*. 232:97–118.

Kurz, A. and H.J. Möller. 1984a. Hilfesuchverhalten und Compliance von Suizidgefährdeten. *Psychiatrische Praxis* 11:6–13.

———1984b. Merkmale der psychotherapeutischen Kurzzeitbetreuung bei Patienten nach Suizidversuch. In M. Wolfersdorf and V. Faust, eds., *Aspekte der Suizidalität*. Weinheim: Belz.

Kurz, A., H.J. Möller, F. Bürk, A. Torhorst, C. Wächtler and H. Lauter. 1984. Ein Versuch zur Verbesserung der psychiatrischen Versorgung von Suizidpatienten am Allgemeinkrankenhaus. In R. Welz and H.J. Möller, eds., *Bestandsaufnahme der Suizidforschung: Epidemiologie, Pravention und Therapie*. Regensburg: Roderer.

Kurz, A., H.J. Möller, G. Baindl, F. Bürk, A. Torhorst, C. Wächtler C. and H. Lauter. 1986. Klassifikation von Suizidversuchen durch Cluster-analyse. In F. Specht and A. Schmidtke, eds., *Selbstmordhandlungen bei Kindern und Jungenlichen*. Regensburg: Roderer.

Kurz, A., H.J. Möller, A. Thorhorst and H. Lauter. 1988. Validation of six risk scales for suicide attempters. In H. J. Möller, A. Schmidtke and R. Welz, eds., *Current issues of suicidology*. New York: Springer-Verlag.

Möller, H.J. 1984. Biochemische Hypothese und medikamentöse Behandlungsmöglichkeiten suizidalen Verhaltens. In R. Welz and H. J. Möller, eds., *Bestandsaufnahme, der Suizidforschung*. Regensburg: Roderer.

Möller, H.J. and V. Geider. 1981. Möglichkeiten zur "Compliance". *Crisis* 2:122–29.

———1982. Inanspruchnahme von Nachbetreuungsmassnahmen durch Parasuizidenten. In H. Helmchen, M. Linden and U. Rüger, eds., *Psychotherapie in der Psychiatrische*. Berlin: Springer-Verlag.

Möller, H.J. and H. Lauter. 1986. Suizidversuch und Nachsorge. *Psychologie* 12:231–43, 433–40.

Möller, H.J., V. Werner and W. Feuerlein. 1978. Beschreibung von 150 Patienten mit Selbstmordversuch durch Tabletten. *Archiv fur Psychiatrische und Nervenkrankheiten* 226:113-35.

Möller, H.J., C. Torhorst and C. Wächtler. 1982. Versorgung von Patienten nach Selbstmordversuch. *Psychiatrische Praxis* 9:106-12.

Möller, H.J., F. Bürk, A. Kurz, A. Torhorst, C. Wächtler and H. Lauter. 1983. Empirische Untersuchungen zur poststationären Versorgung von Suizidpatienten im Rehmen eines psychiatrischen Laisondienstes. In H. Pohlmeier, A. Schmidtke and R. Welz, eds., *Suizidales Verhalten*. Regensburg: Roderer.

Möller, H.J., F. Bürk, A. Kurz, A. Torhorst, C. Wächtler and H. Lauter. 1984. Stationäre und poststationäre psychiatrische Versorgung von Patienten nach Suizidversuch durch Intoxikation. In E. Deutsch, G. Kleinberger, R. Ritz and H.P. Schuster, eds., *Diagnose, Verlaufskontrolle und Therapie schwerer exogener Vergiftungen*. Stuttgart: Schattauer.

Torhorst, A. and H.J. Möller. 1983. Gruppenpsychotherapie mit Suizidalen. *Psychologie* 33:31-41.

Torhorst, A., H.J. Möller, F. Bürk, A. Kurz, C. Wächtler and H. Lauter. 1984. Ein-Jahres-Katamnese bei einer Stichprobe von 485 Patienten nach Suizidfersuch. In R. Welz and H. J. Möller, eds., *Bestandsaufnahme der Suizidforschung*. Regensburg: Roderer.

Torhorst, A., G. Baindl, F. Bürk, H. Hacker, A. Kurz, H.J. Möller and C. Wachtler. 1986. Motivation zur Inanspruchnahme psychotherapeutischer Nachbeteuung bei Patienten nach einem Suizidversuch. In F. Specht and A. Schmidtke, eds., *Selbstmordhandlungen bei Kindern und Jungendlichen*. Regensburg: Roderer.

Wächtler, C. 1982. Erfahrungen mit der einzeltherapeutischen Betreuung von Suizidgefährdeten. In P. A. Fiedler et al., eds., *Herausforderungen und Grenzen der klinischen Psychologie*. Tubingen: DGVT.

Winter, I. and H.J. Möller. 1986. Notfall: neurotische Depression mit Suizidalität. *Münchener Medizinische Wochenschift*. 128.

von Zerssen, D. 1976. *Klinische Selbstbeurteilungsskalen aus dem Münchener Psychiatrischen Informationssystem: Manual*. Weinheim: Belz.

12

The Prevention of Suicide: Public Health Approaches

David Lester

Suicide prevention is today one of the major goals of the Public Health Service of the United States government. Indeed, this has been a goal since the 1960s; the persistence of this goal attests to our failure to have any impact whatsoever upon the suicide rate in America.

The suicide rates during the past fifty years presented below indicate that suicide rates have not changed much at all since the Second World War.

	suicide rate per 100,000 per year
1933	15.9 (the first year all states reported)
1940	14.4
1950	11.4
1960	10.6
1970	11.6
1980	11.9
1985	12.3

In America in 1985, there were 29,543 suicides out of 2,086,440 deaths. It is easy to document that suicide rates are higher in men than in women, in whites than in blacks, and in native Americans than in others (Lester 1983).

However, two important features of suicide rates have called for special attention in the 1980s. First, suicide rates are highest in the elderly. For example, in 1985, the suicide rates by age were:

	men	women
10–14	2.3	0.9
15–19	16.0	3.7
20–24	26.2	4.9
25–29	25.3	5.6
30–34	23.5	6.3

35–39	22.2	6.5
40–44	22.3	7.8
45–49	23.0	8.4
50–54	24.0	8.1
55–59	26.8	8.2
60–64	26.8	7.2
65–69	29.0	6.7
70–74	38.9	7.2
75–79	48.4	7.4
80–84	61.9	6.0
85 +	55.4	4.6

Suicide is clearly a major problem for those concerned with the psychological health and social well-being of the elderly.

Second, there has been a tremendous increase in the suicide rates of young adults in recent years, especially among white males. The suicide rate of white males aged 15–19 has risen from 9.3 in 1970 to 15.0 in 1980 (Centers for Disease Control 1986). For white males aged 20–24, the rate has risen from 19.2 to 27.8 in the same period.

Members of the public, as well as those involved in mental health, are extremely concerned by the high rate of suicide in the young today and by the fact that the rate is increasing. Not only do the young have so much potential, but their improved material well-being makes their strong self-destructive tendencies hard to comprehend.

There have been two major strategies adopted in the past to prevent suicide. First, suicide prevention centers have been established in communities and, second, the psychiatric and counseling professions have sought effective treatments for depressed and suicidal patients. Let us examine these two approaches in detail.

Suicide Prevention Centers

Following the lead of the Los Angeles suicide prevention center that was established in the 1950s by Edwin Shneidman and Norman Farberow, and stimulated by a center for suicide prevention established at the National Institute of Mental Health, communities across America established suicide prevention centers in the following decades. In the United Kingdom, the Salvation Army started an early suicide prevention service in 1905, but more recently one central organization, the Samaritans, has organized suicide prevention centers throughout the country.

Suicide prevention centers are primarily oriented around a crisis model of the suicidal process (Lester 1989a). People who are suicidal are conceptualized as being in a time-limited crisis state. Immediate crisis counseling will help the suicidal individual through the suicidal crisis, whereupon a normal life may resume.

Suicide prevention centers typically operate a 24-hour telephone service that people in distress can call in order to talk to a counselor. Counselors are usually paraprofessionals (ordinary people who have graduated from a brief training program) who use crisis intervention as the mode of counseling (active listening, assessment of resources, and problem solving).

Some centers have walk-in clinics, while a few have also set up stores in the poorer sections of cities and operate crisis teams who can leave the center to visit people in distress in the community.

Suicide prevention centers are well equipped for secondary prevention (early intervention with persons who are on the verge of suicide), but these centers are essentially passive. The suicidal person has to contact the suicide prevention center. Active approaches, such as seeking out discharged psychiatric patients, elderly males living alone, and other high risk groups are rarely pursued. Community workers such as police officers, clergymen, physicians—and perhaps groups such as bartenders, prostitutes, and hair dressers, who also come into contact with the public—ought to be sensitized to the detection of depressed, disturbed, and suicidal people so that they can refer them to suicide prevention centers.

The American approach to the apparent failure of suicide prevention attempts in the 1970s was to focus upon the improvement of suicide prevention centers (Resnik and Hathorne 1973). The importance of identifying and locating high risk groups in the population and fashioning specific programs for them was stressed. On the whole, the focus was on better ways of intervening rather than on social action programs to change the social environment of the citizens and reduce those forces that lead to suicide.

One study in this vein was by Wold and Litman (1973) who had the excellent idea of following up on those who had killed themselves after calling a suicide prevention center. They found inadequate counseling on the part of some of the volunteers who handled the calls. More important, they found that the crisis counseling approach was not a suitable means of dealing with chronic, high suicide risk callers. On the other hand, alternative means of providing help to these callers were not available, except for referring the callers to other agencies, referrals that the callers typically did not follow up. Wold and Litman discussed the possibility of setting up a special out-reach program to deal effectively with such callers.

Are Suicide Prevention Centers Effective?

There have been several studies on whether suicide prevention centers actually prevent suicide. In the first of these, Bagley (1968) compared English cities and found that those with a suicide prevention center did experience a reduction in the suicide rate as compared to cities without such a center. However, Lester (1980) reanalysed Bagley's data and found errors in his analysis. Lester concluded that Bagley had been unable to demonstrate the preventive effect of suicide prevention centers that he claimed.

In a more carefully controlled study, Barraclough and his colleagues (1977) compared another group of English cities, matching them for ecological similarity, and found no effect from suicide prevention centers on the suicide rate.

Nor was much evidence of success found in a series of similar studies undertaken in the United States. Lester (1973a, 1973b, 1974a, 1974b) studied large samples of American cities, controlling for size of the city, and found no effect from suicide prevention centers on the suicide rate. For example, from 1960 to 1970, the suicide rate in cities without a suicide prevention center rose from 9.4 to 10.7 while the suicide rate in cities with suicide prevention centers rose from 12.1 to 13.6.

Bridge et al. (1977) examined 100 countries in North Carolina and explored correlates of their suicide rates. The presence of a suicide prevention center was not associated with the suicide rate, and the multiple regression confirmed this. However, Bridge did not examine changes in the suicide rate in the countries over time, and so his study is less than adequate.

In the most recent evaluation, Miller et al. (1984) have reported more favorable results. They compared a sample of counties in the United States with and without suicide prevention centers and found that the centers had a beneficial impact on the suicide rates for white females younger than 24 years of age (but for no other group). This result was replicated on a new sample of counties. Since young white females are among the more frequent callers to suicide prevention centers, this result makes sense.

Thus, at the present time it looks as if we must revise previously negative conclusions about the effectiveness of suicide prevention centers. If Miller's results are replicated in other locales, then we may conclude that suicide prevention centers do prevent suicide in the sociodemographic groups that they serve.

However, all of the evaluations of suicide prevention centers were severely criticized in a review by Auerbach and Kilmann (1977). They noted the impracticality of using suicide rates as a measure of effectiveness and stressed the importance of focusing on measures of treatment processes and of change in client behavior.

TREATMENT OF THE DEPRESSED AND SUICIDAL PERSON

The psychiatric/psychological approach to suicide prevention is to take individual clients and identify the most effective ways of medicating or counseling them so as to reduce the risk of suicide. Since depression is both the most common psychiatric syndrome and the most common mood accompanying increased potential for suicide, much of the focus of this approach has been on the treatment of depression.

Barraclough (1972) examined 100 cases of completed suicide and found that 64 had depressive illnesses. Of these, 44 had previous depressive episodes and 21 of these met a strict criteria for diagnosing recurrent affective illness. Barraclough felt that the suicide rate would have been reduced by 21 percent if these patients had been given lithium carbonate. Barraclough argued, therefore, for good diagnostic practices and the prescription of effective medication as a way of preventing suicide. For example, Montgomery and Montgomery (1984) have recently shown that flupenthixol (a depot neuroleptic) resulted in a significant decrease in suicide attempts in suicidal patients diagnosed as having a personality disorder. In contrast, neither a placebo nor Mianserin, a less toxic oral antidepressant, had a significant effect on suicidal behavior.

Ratcliffe (1962) noted that changing Dingleton mental hospital from a locked-ward to an open-door system of patient management was accompanied by a drop of about 60 percent in the number of suicides in the surrounding community during the following ten years (while the suicide rate in Scotland as a whole stayed constant). Ratcliffe suggested that the open-door policy had induced more of the psychiatrically disturbed citizens in the community to use the psychiatric facility. However, no such drop in the suicide rate was noted by Walk (1967) when a community mental health center was opened in Chichester, England.

Montgomery and Montgomery (1982) reviewed six previous studies on the effects of counseling on suicidal behavior and found that only three were adequately designed and only one of these showed that counseling had a significant impact on suicidal behavior. Some studies, however, have reported beneficial effects of psychotherapy. For example, Liberman and Eckman (1981) compared the effectiveness of behavior therapy and insight-oriented therapy for repeated suicide attempters. Each program included individual, group, and family therapy components. They found that the behavior therapy program had a more positive outcome than the insight-oriented program both after nine months and after two years. (The behavior therapy program included training in social skills, anxiety management, and family negotiation and contingency contracting.)

Thus, while medication certainly has a place in the treatment of the depressed suicidal patient we cannot be too optimistic about the effectiveness of other psychiatric/psychological approaches at the present time. Furthermore, these approaches are useful only for those individuals who seek out clinics and private psychotherapists for help with their personal problems.

REDUCING ACCESS TO THE MEANS FOR SUICIDE

One suggestion that has been made from time to time in the past has concerned the removal of the means for suicide from the environment of the suicidal person. Robin and Freeman-Browne (1968) noted that the majority of attempted suicides are released into a home environment where there exist lethal quantities of suicidal methods. Barraclough et al. (1971) recommended reductions in the size and number of prescriptions, wrapping the tablets in foil or plastic blisters, use of nonbarbiturates where available, recalling unused tablets, setting up procedures to prevent forging of prescriptions, and not prescribing for patients without seeing them. Cases have been reported where patients have forged prescriptions in order to obtain lethal quantities of drugs (Friedman 1966). Stoller (1969) noted that legislation to limit the prescribing of barbiturates in Australia was followed by a drop in the suicide rate.

The following is a typical case reported by Barraclough:

> A 45-year-old, single woman lived alone since the recent death of both parents. She was drawing sick benefits on psychiatric grounds but was actively looking for work. In the preceding seven years there had been four admissions for agitated depression, with reasonable response to treatment. At the time of death the drug treatment was amitriptyline 100 mg daily and Sodium Amytal 1 G (15gr.) daily. This prescribing was recorded for the previous six months but had probably been going on for twelve months. She had not seen the doctor for seven months and obtained prescriptions on request from his receptionist. There had been a recent occurrence of her depressive symptoms. (Barraclough et al. 1971, p. 652.)

The reduction in the suicide rate following the detoxification of domestic gas in the United Kingdom has been described by Kreitman (1976) and Brown (1979). The impact of the increased availability of firearms in the United States on the suicide rates, especially in the young, has been explored by Boor (1981), Boyd (1983), and others.

David Lester and Ronald Clarke have conducted a series of studies during the 1980s on this problem; the following sections will present the major results of their research.

Firearms

The Effect of Strict Handgun Control Laws   The United States consists of 50 states (48 continental plus Alaska and Hawaii), each of which is permitted to pass its own laws on the control of firearms. Bakal (1968) examined the handgun control laws of each state and coded them for the presence of various characteristics, such as whether a licence is required to sell handguns at retail stores, whether sales are reported to the police, and whether a permit is required to purchase a handgun.

Lester and Murrell (1980) created a Guttman scale of strictness for the 48 continental states from these codings and found that states with the strictest handgun control laws had the lowest firearm suicide rates—and the lowest overall suicide rates in 1960 and 1970. Those states with the stricter handgun control laws and the lower firearm suicide rates did not have higher suicide rates by poisons or hanging/strangulation, though the suicide rate by ''other'' methods was higher. Thus, Lester and Murrell concluded that switching to an alternative method for suicide did not occur in states in which the handgun control laws were stricter.

Further analysis of the data (Lester 1984) showed that the restrictions on the selling and purchasing of handguns were the most critical characteristics of the laws in the association with lower firearm suicide rates. Restrictions on carrying were unrelated to firearm suicide rates. Finally, controls for social variables (such as percent of blacks and percent of males in each state) did not eliminate these associations.

Lester (1987b) examined the power of the strictness of handgun control laws and the moral attitude toward suicide as predictors in explaining the suicide rates of the continental states. The strictness of the handgun control laws and the percentage of citizens attending church (the operational measure of moral attitudes toward suicide) were both highly correlated with the states' suicide rates, giving a multiple correlation of 0.68, thereby accounting for 46 percent of the variation in the states' suicide rates.

Attempting to Measure the Extent of Firearm Ownership in the States.   There are no measures of firearm ownership for each state. However, several indirect measures are available. Lester (1987c) examined the relationship of the accidental death rate from firearms in each state and the percent of homicides committed using firearms with the suicide rate.

The accident death rate using firearms was positively associated with the firearm suicide rate, but not with the overall suicide rate. Similar associations were found for the percent of homicides committed with firearms. (The strictness of handgun control laws was negatively associated with overall suicide rate.)

Lester (1989b) also explored the use of per capita subscriptions to three firearm magazines as measures of firearm ownership. Per capita subscription rates to the three magazines were positively correlated to the firearm suicide rate and to the overall suicide rate.

Actual Firearm Ownership   Measures of actual firearm ownership are available for the 9 major regions of the continental United States (though not for the 48 individual states). Lester (1988a) found that this measure was positively associated with the firearm suicide rate, but not to the overall suicide rate. Lester (1988b) compared these results for the United States with results from an analysis of data from Australian states. In Australia too the per capita ownership of firearms in the states was positively related to the firearm suicide rate but not the overall suicide rate.

A Time-Series Analysis of Firearm Ownership in the United States The previous studies were regional studies over the states and major regions of the United States and Australia. Clarke and Jones (1989) obtained data on the household ownership of firearms in the United States as a whole from 1959 to 1984 using data from national polls. Their time-series analysis identified that the ownership of handguns was associated with the firearm suicide rate and with the overall suicide rate.

Car Exhaust

Detoxifying Car Exhaust In 1968, America began to impose emission controls for motor vehicles in order to clean up the environment. The result was that the carbon monoxide content in car exhaust dropped from 8.5 percent to 0.05 percent by 1980. This has made it more difficult to commit suicide using car exhaust. Poisoning from carbon monoxide takes much longer, increasing the risk of intervention by others and changes of mind in the suicidal person. Death from simple suffocation (elimination of oxygen) also takes much longer than poisoning by carbon monoxide.

Clarke and Lester (1987) explored the effects of the reduced toxicity of car exhaust on the use of car exhaust for suicide in the United States; they compared this trend with the same period in England and Wales where emission controls have not been imposed on motor vehicles.

Clarke and Lester found that the use of car exhaust for suicide in America has leveled off and perhaps slightly declined since 1968. (It must remembered that older, more toxic cars are still in use and that the emission control system can be disconnected to permit gas richer in carbon monoxide to fill the car or garage.) In contrast, in England and Wales the use of car exhaust for suicide has risen dramatically since 1970.

Clarke and Lester saw their results as indicating the usefulness of reducing the lethality of a method for suicide in reducing the suicide rate or preventing dramatic increases in the rate.

A Regional Study of Car Ownership and Suicide Lester and Frank (1989) have explored the relation between a simple measure of overall car ownership in the states of America (regardless of the year in which the car was made) and the use of car exhaust for suicide.

Lester found that per capita ownership of cars was related to the suicide rate using car exhaust, but not to the overall suicide rate. Thus, the more cars are available in a state, the more they are used for suicide.

Domestic Gas

The Effects of Detoxification of Domestic Gas in England & Wales, Scotland, and the Netherlands   Clarke and Mayhew (1988) have documented accurately the gradual detoxification of domestic gas in England and Wales and the declining suicide rate using domestic gas and overall. They showed that the two curves follow each other extremely closely. In 1958, out of 5,298 suicides there were 2,637 suicide using domestic gas, comprising 49.8 percent of the total number of suicides. By 1977, there were 8 suicides using domestic gas out of 3,944, comprising only 0.2 percent of the suicides.

Clarke and Mayhew (1989) then explored why Scotland and the Netherlands did not experience an overall decline in their suicide rate as domestic gas was detoxified. They presented evidence to show that the suicide rates were rising in those two nations when domestic gas was detoxified and they argued that this rising suicide rate masked the effect of the detoxification of domestic gas on the overall suicide rate.

However, in this context, the data presented by Clarke and Lester (1987) become relevant. Their data show that the use of car exhaust is rising dramatically in England and Wales in recent years. It may be that those who might have used domestic gas if it were still toxic are now turning to car exhaust. Perhaps people will switch to a similar method to their preferred method if their preferred method is unavailable.

Implications for a Theory of Suicide

It is common to think of suicide as a desperate measure, chosen by seriously dysfunctional people who are at their wits' end. It seems unlikely that such people would be deterred by the effort needed to overcome the restrictions placed upon obtaining a lethal amount of their preferred method for suicide.

However, the present viewpoint suggests that suicide may be a logical decision made by people based upon rational issues such as the availability of different methods for suicide (Yeh and Lester 1987). Many people when asked say that they would consider one and only one method for suicide. If access to this method was restricted, then suicide may well be averted in these people. The necessity of switching to a less preferred method may introduce costs that were not originally present. For example, those who fear the pain of a bullet and the disfigurement of the wound would in all probably not switch to firearms were medication no longer available.

Will People Switch Methods for Suicide?

Although this is the critical question for this method of preventing suicide, very few studies are relevant to the issue. It remains a matter of opinion. However, one suggestion can be made.

Rich and Young (1988) documented that the imposition of strict gun control laws in Toronto resulted in a decrease in the use of guns for suicide and a corresponding increase in the use of jumping (primarily in front of subway trains). Thus, apparently, people switched methods for suicide. However, if the new method is less lethal than the former method, then there is a greater likelihood that suicidal attempters will survive and, therefore, completed suicide will have been prevented.

However, Lester (1988c) has argued that a failure to make lethal methods and venues for suicide less available may render people legally liable for civil damages. For example, all houseowners in the United States must fence in swimming pools in their backyards or face civil liability law suits should some stranger drown in their pool. Lester argued that the municipal government in the Bay Area in California might be held similarly liable by those whose relatives jump from the Golden Gate Bridge, a popular suicide venue that is not fenced in.

Lester argued that suicide prevention organizations should therefore agitate for stronger firearm control laws, the fencing in of suicide venues, smaller prescriptions of less lethal medications, prescriptions of suppositories rather than oral tablets, and related measures to reduce the availability of methods for suicide.

CONCLUSIONS

This chapter has reviewed a series of regional and time series studies on the effects of reducing the availability of firearms, toxic car exhaust, and toxic domestic gas on suicide. Though the data do not provide for a definitive conclusion, the results do indicate that reducing the availability of a method for suicide reduces its use for suicide and may also reduce the overall suicide rate if the method restricted is a commonly used and lethal method. In the latter case, people who switch methods for suicide are forced to switch to a less lethal method from which survival is more likely.

It is likely that more research on this important topic will appear in the next few years, thus permitting us to evaluate this method of suicide prevention more precisely.

REFERENCES

Auerbach, S. and P. Kilmann. 1977. Crisis intervention. *Psychological Bulletin* 84: 1189–1217.

Bagley, C. 1968. The evaluation of a suicide prevention scheme by an ecological method. *Social Science & Medicine* 2:1–14.

Bakal, C. 1968. *No right to bear arms.* New York: Paperback Library.

Barraclough, B.M. 1972. Suicide prevention, recurrent affective disorder and lithium. *British Journal of Psychiatry* 121:391–92.

Barraclough, B.M., C. Jennings, and J.R. Moss. 1977. Suicide prevention by the Samaritans. *Lancet* I:237–39.

Barraclough, B.M., B. Nelson, J. Bunch, and P. Sainsbury. 1971. Suicide and barbiturate prescribing. *Journal of the Royal College of General Practitioners* 21:645–53.

Boor, M. 1981. Methods of suicide and implications for suicide prevention. *Journal of Clinical Psychology* 37:70–75.

Boyd, J. 1983. The increasing rate of suicide by firearms. *New England Journal of Medicine* 308:872–74.

Bridge, T., S. Potkin, W. Zung, and B. Soldo. 1977. Suicide prevention centers. *Journal of Nervous & Mental Disease* 164:18–24.

Brown, J. 1979. Suicide in Britain. *Archives of General Psychiatry* 36:1119–24.

Centers for Disease Control. 1986. *Youth suicide, 1970–1980.* Atlanta: Centers for Disease Control.

Clarke, R. V. and P. R. Jones. 1989. Suicide and the increased availability of handguns. *Social Science & Medicine* 28:805–809.

Clarke, R.V. and D. Lester. 1987. Toxicity of car exhausts and opportunity for suicide. *Journal of Epidemiology & Community Health* 41:114–20.

Clarke, R.V. and P. Mayhew. 1988. The British gas suicide story and its criminological implications. *Crime & Justice* 10:79–116.

Clarke, R.V. and P. Mayhew. 1989. Crime as opportunity. *British Journal of Criminology* 29:35–46.

Friedman, G. 1966. Suicide and the altered prescription. *New York State Medical Journal* 66:3005–07.

Kreitman, N. 1976. The coal gas story. *British Journal of Preventive & Social Medicine* 30:86–93.

Lester, D. 1973a. Prevention of suicide. *Journal of the American Medical Association* 225:992.

———1973b. Suicide prevention centers and prevention of suicide. *New England Journal of Medicine* 289:380.

———1974a. Effect of suicide prevention centers on suicide rates in the United States. *Health Services Reports* 89:37–39.

———1974b. Suicide prevention centers. *Journal of the American Medical Association* 229:394.

———1980. Suicide prevention by the Samaritans. *Social Science & Medicine* 14A:85.

———1983. *Why people kill themselves.* Springfield: Thomas.

———1984. *Gun control.* Springfield: Thomas.

———1987a. Preventing suicide. In J. Morgan, ed., *Suicide.* London, Ont.: King's College, 69–78.

———1987b. An availability-acceptability theory of suicide. *Activitas Nervosa Superior* 19:164–66.

———1987c. Availability of guns and the likelihood of suicide. *Sociology & Social Research* 71:287–88.

———1988a. Gun control, gun ownership and suicide prevention. *Suicide & Life-Threatening Behavior* 18:176–80.

———1988b. Restricting the availability of guns as a strategy for suicide prevention. *Biology & Society* 5:127–29.

———1988c. The AAS and political activism. *AAS Newslink* 14(2):8.

———1989a *Can we prevent suicide?* New York: AMS.

———1989b. Gun ownership and suicide in the United States. *Psychological Medicine.* 19:519–21.

Lester, D. and M. L. Frank. 1989. The use of motor vehicle exhaust for suicide and the availability of cars. *Acta Psychiatrica Scandinavia* 79:238–40.

Lester, D. and M. E. Murrell. 1980. The influence of gun control laws on suicidal behavior. *American Journal of Psychiatry* 137:121–22.

Liberman, R. and T. Eckman. 1986. Behavior therapy versus insight-oriented therapy for repeated suicide attempters. *Archives of General Psychiatry* 38:1126–30.

Miller, H., D. Coombs, J. Leeper and S. Barton. 1984. An analysis of the effects of suicide prevention facilities on suicide rates in the US. *American Journal of Public Health* 74:340–43.

Montgomery, S. and D. Montgomery. 1982. Drug treatment of suicidal behavior. *Advances in Biochemical Psychopharmacology* 32:347–55.

———1984. The prevention of suicide acts in high-risk patients. *Advances in Biochemical Psychopharmacology* 39:315–17.

Ratcliffe, R.W. 1962. The open door. *Lancet* ii:188–90.

Resnik, H. and B. Hathorne. 1973. *Suicide prevention in the 70s.* Rockville: NIMH.

Rich, C.L. and J.G. Young. 1988. *Guns and suicide.* American Association of Suicidology, Washington, DC.

Robin, A. and D. Freeman-Browne. 1968. Drugs left at home by psychiatric patients. *British Medical Journal* 3:424–25.

Stoller, A. 1969. Suicides and attempted suicides in Australia. *Proceedings of the 5th International Congress on Suicide Prevention.* London: IASP.

Walk, D. 1967. Suicide and community care. *British Journal of Psychiatry* 113:1381–91.

Wold, C. and R.E. Litman. 1973. Suicide after contact with a suicide prevention center. *Archives of General Psychiatry.* 28:735 39.

Yeh, B.Y. and D. Lester. 1987. An economic model for suicide. In D. Lester *Suicide as a learned behavior.* Springfield: Thomas p. 51–57.

13

A Problem-Solving Approach to Treating Individuals At Risk for Suicide

George A. Clum and Miriam Lerner

Understanding why individuals attempt to kill themselves can serve as a basis for developing treatment programs that target suicidal behavior. Successful treatment of the precursors to suicide should result in a reduction of behaviors associated with suicide, especially hopelessness, suicide ideation, and suicide attempting. One model for understanding suicide behavior is a diathesis-stress model in which the diathesis is a deficit in problem-solving behavior and the stress is an event or series of events that require adaptation in the individual (Clum, Patsiokas and Luscomb 1979). In this chapter we will examine evidence supportive of the etiological underpinnings of our treatment model. We will then examine the treatment model itself and evidence for its efficacy.

STRESS AND SUICIDE BEHAVIOR

The connection between life stress and suicide behavior has been amply demonstrated (Cochrane and Robertson 1975; Luscomb, Clum and Patsiokas 1980; Paykel, Prusoff and Myers 1975; Schotte and Clum 1982, 1987). A common finding is that specific kinds of stressors are associated with suicide behavior, including events that are classified as negative and events that are classified as losses (Cochrane and Robertson 1975; Paykel, Prusoff and Myers 1975; Schotte and Clum 1982, 1987). An example of the former is financial difficulties, while an example of the latter is the death of a spouse.

An early controlled study of this relationship was conducted by Cochrane and Robinson (1975). These researchers found that 100 parasuicides, matched on age and occupational status, had more frequent negative life events in the years preceding the suicide attempt than did a matched control group. Paykel et al. (1975) reported that a group of parasuicides experience four times as many negative life events as did a group of normal controls and one and a half times as many negative events as did a group of depressed controls. Greater frequency of negative life events was found for a group of college students with reported suicide ideation when compared to another group of college students who reported no recent suicide ideation (Schotte and Clum 1982). Likewise, Schotte and Clum (1987) found negative life events to be significantly higher in a group of at risk patients hospitalized on an inpatient service when compared to a group of other psychiatric patients not at risk for suicide.

One question that has been inadequately addressed is whether personally relevant stressors are more important than life changes that do not have personal relevance as precursors to suicide behavior. This question was answered affirmatively in one study (Motto, Heilbron and Juster 1985) who found personally relevant stressors to be predictive of future suicide completion in a group of hospitalized depressed and suicidal patients. Apparently, the finding that negative life events precede suicide behavior is robust, being found in individuals of varying age groups with varying levels of suicide behavior.

MODERATORS OF THE STRESS-SUICIDE BEHAVIOR RELATIONSHIP

While evidence exists linking recent negative life events to suicide behavior, it is clear that not all individuals who experience such stress exhibit such behaviors. Other factors mitigate or enhance the likelihood that stress will lead to suicide behaviors.

One factor mitigating the stress-suicide relationship is social support (Braucht 1979). In a community-based study, Braucht was able to demonstrate that individuals at risk for suicide differed from their neighbors both demographically and in the kind of environmental stress to which they were subjected. These data indirectly supports the possibility that being different from one's neighbors leads to reduced social support and increased vulnerability to suicide.

Another factor that has been found to increase the impact stress has on suicidal behavior is a defect in problem solving (Levenson and Neuringer 1971; Schotte and Clum 1982, 1987). Since suicide can be conceptualized as a potential solution to a life problem, defects in this ability should increase the negative impact of life stressors. D'Zurrilla and Goldfried (1971) identified several stages of the problem-solving process. These stages include: 1) a general set toward life's problems in which the individual sees them as a normal part of life and as solvable; 2) problem identification, definition, and formulation; 3) generation of alternative solutions to the problem; 4) evaluation of the likely effectiveness and positive and negative consequences of each alternative; and 5) implementation and evaluation of solutions. Deficits in problem solving can occur at any or all stages of this process. Research into whether suicidal individuals have such deficits has examined problem solving as a general phenomenon as well as problem solving as a dysfunction in specific steps.

Levenson and Neuringer (1971) were among the first to examine whether suicidal individuals had a problem-solving deficit. They found that adolescent parasuicides scored lower on the WAIS Arithmetic subtest and on the Rokeach

Map Test than did a control group. This study, while supportive of the hypothesis, lacked a conceptual framework that linked the problem-solving measures to suicide behavior. In contrast, two studies by Schotte and Clum (1982, 1987) examined the effects of interpersonal problem-solving defects plus stress in the etiology of suicide behavior. In the first study, suicide ideation was linked with stress only in those individuals who also were relatively less adroit at identifying alternative solutions to a set of standard interpersonal problems. In the second study (Schotte and Clum 1987), hospitalized patients at risk for suicide were differentiated from other hospitalized patients not at risk for suicide on two problem-solving variables: 1) ability to generate alternative solutions to identified interpersonal problems—lower ability characterized at risk individuals, and 2) identifying reasons why alternatives generated wouldn't work—more negative reasons characterized at risk individuals.

What kinds of problems are suicidal individuals attempting to solve? There is some beginning evidence on this question which indicates that the answer varies depending on age, sex, and type of suicidal behavior. Leenaars (1987) has shown that young females who are suicidal are more likely to have interpersonal motives while young males are more likely to fear they cannot adjust to social demands. In later life, males are more likely to identify interpersonal motives for suicide than are females. Clum (1987) has reported that adolescent males and females who have attempted suicide are more likely to identify problematic family relationships as a motive than are adolescent suicide ideators of both sexes. Clearly, the identification of normative motives for suicide is a complex but important undertaking. Knowledge of specific motives would be an important ingredient in developing tailored treatment programs.

According to D'Zurrilla and Goldfried's (1971) model, the last step in the problem-solving process is implementation of identified solutions. Suicidal individuals have been shown in a variety of studies to be characterized by a passive problem-solving stance. Simon and Lumry (1968), for example, reported that suicidal physicians were more passive than nonsuicidal physicians. Indirect evidence for a passive stance in suicidal individuals comes from studies of locus of control and suicide. Since individuals with an internal locus of control would more likely deal with stress with an active problem-solving approach, suicidal individuals could be expected to have an external locus of control orientation. This in fact has been found by several researchers including Luscomb, Clum and Patsiokas (1980) and Topol and Reznikoff (1982). Finally, another group of researchers (Linehan, Camper, Chiles, Strosahl and Shearin 1987) who defined passivity in terms of the types of problem-solving strategy utilized found suicidals to identify more passive strategies.

HOPELESSNESS

The research reviewed above indicates that suicide is a product of several converging factors. Essentially, one is more likely to engage in suicidal behavior if one has experienced recent, severe, negative stressors. If there is a lack of social support and/or a paucity of problem-solving skills, the solution of suicide becomes a more likely alternative. Another variable is likely to mediate the effects of stress plus absence of social supports plus problem-solving defects on suicide—namely, hopelessness. Several researchers have demonstrated the contribution of hopelessness, as measured by the Hopelessness Scale (Beck et al. 1974), to suicide behavior. An early study by Wetzel (1976) showed that hopelessness was more important than depression in differentiating both suicide attempters and suicide ideators from a group of nonideating controls. Hopelessness has proven more important a predictor of suicide behavior than depression in at least one other study (Kovacs et al. 1975). The link between stress and problem-solving defects to hopelessness and hence to suicide behavior was examined by Schotte and Clum in two studies. In the first of these studies (Schotte and Clum 1982), hopelessness acted as a mediator between stress plus problem-solving defects and suicide ideation. In the second study (Schotte and Clum 1987), hopelessness contributed uniquely, along with stress and problem-solving defects, to a criterion of being at risk for suicide. It is unclear at this juncture if hopelessness is the end point of a failure of normal problem-solving avenues in the face of overwhelming stress that in turn leads to suicidal behavior, or whether it is one of several factors that simply increase the likelihood of suicidal behavior.

REMEDIABLE AND NONREMEDIABLE FACTORS

Traditionally, stress has been conceptualized as something that happens to a person, not something that a person does to herself. From this view, the stressor part of the suicide equation is nonremediable. Stressors will occur—often they will occur outside of one's control. Both social support and problem-solving defects, however, are remediable. Social support might be increased by providing information to significant others as to the importance of increased efforts at making positive contact with people identified as at risk for suicide. The very act of entering a supportive psychotherapeutic relationship likewise increases the amount of social support available to a suicidal individual. In addition, skills at solving interpersonal problems can be taught, with the possible effect of reducing the vulnerability of the suicidal person to future as well as past stressors. We will now examine such a treatment model and the evidence that bears on its currently demonstrated, as well as its potential, efficacy.

A PROBLEM-SOLVING APPROACH TO TREATMENT

There has been very little controlled research concerning the treatment of suicidal behavior. There are a number of reasons for the lack of controlled treatment studies, including potential risk, the rarity of the behavior, feasibility in institutional settings, and the lack of standardized assessments. Most important, however, may be the absence of a coherent theory from which to devise a treatment approach.

The diathesis-stress model is the first theoretical framework firmly based on past empirical research to provide a specific direction for the treatment of suicidal behavior. The research described previously indicates that suicidal individuals: (1) are poor problem solvers in general and poor interpersonal problem solvers in particular; (2) have recently experienced a high number of stressful life events; and (3) feel a high degree of hopelessness, relative to nonsuicidal individuals. The diathesis-stress model suggests that people with poor interpersonal problem-solving skills are vulnerable at times of high stress to hopelessness and suicidal behavior. Vulnerability to stress is also reducible with social support systems that attenuate the effects of stressors. Suicide may be perceived as a potential solution to the problems, especially when problem-solving skills are reduced and social support is lacking. Thus, one intervention to reduce suicidal behavior is to improve problem-solving, especially interpersonal problem-solving, skills. Another, of course, would be to improve social support systems. Improving problem-solving skills could provide a coping mechanism that suicidal individuals could use under stress.

Very few controlled studies of the treatment of suicidal behavior have been completed. One such study (Liberman and Eckman 1981) compared the effects of a broad-based behavioral treatment to an insight-oriented treatment with a hospitalized suicidal population. The behavioral treatment package included assertiveness training, anxiety management, and family contracting. The first two approaches may be considered similar to teaching problem-solving skills. Assertiveness training deals with a particular type of interpersonal deficit—unassertiveness—and teaches people ways of coping more effectively with interpersonal problems. Anxiety management is also a problem-solving skill that assists individuals in dealing with affect modulation. Family contracting has two components—teaching individuals to deal with family conflicts and improving the social support system. Both of these skills attenuate the effects of stressors.

Liberman and Eckman's study demonstrated the effectiveness of the behavioral treatment package compared to the insight-oriented approach. While both treatments were effective in reducing depression and fears and increasing assertiveness, the behavioral approach produced more marked improvement, a difference significant through a nine month follow-up period. Further, the behavioral treatment was more effective than the insight-oriented treatment in reducing suicidal ideations and attempts over a two year follow-up period. This study is significant in that it was the first controlled comparison of two different treatment modalities. It also provides indirect support for the problem-solving treatment approach broadly defined since it clearly showed the superiority of a skills approach to dealing with suicidal behavior.

Problems with the study do exist, however. It was conducted in an inpatient setting where patients were receiving a variety of other treatments. Further, the behavioral treatment package was a multicomponent approach. It is unclear, therefore, which of the components were most important or whether all were important. Finally, it suffers from a lack of conceptual grounding. There is no comprehensive framework linking a theory of suicide behavior to the chosen treatment approach.

Some of these problems were dealt with in a study by Patsiokas and Clum (1985). These researchers conducted a controlled treatment study to examine the effectiveness of interpersonal problem-solving therapy in reducing suicidal ideations and hopelessness. They used a hospitalized psychiatric population with a history of suicidal behavior leading to their current hospitalization. They compared interpersonal problem-solving therapy to cognitive therapy and supportive therapy. The interpersonal problem-solving treatment was grounded in the theoretical framework described above. Problem-solving therapy consisted of teaching five problem-solving steps. The first step was to accept that problems are a normal part of life and are solvable. The last four steps included problem formulation, generation of alternatives, generation of consequences, and evaluation of the solution. The treatment was conducted in two stages, each five sessions in duration. The first five sessions were aimed at teaching the basic problem-solving approach to life's problems. The last five sessions were devoted to applying this approach to one of the specific problems leading to the suicide attempt and hospitalization. The problem-solving therapy resulted in significantly larger improvements in interpersonal problem-solving skills relative to the other two therapies, and significantly larger reductions in hopelessness relative to the supportive therapy. All three of the treatments reduced suicidal ideations, but were not significantly different from one another. Patsiokas and Clum (1985) suggested that the lack of differences between the therapies in affecting suicidal ideation was a result of the low pretreatment level of suicidal ideation.

Thus, this study provided support for the hypothesis that improved interpersonal problem-solving skills would reduce the hopelessness and improve the problem-solving skills of suicidal patients, both of which have been empirically tied to suicidal ideation and attempts.

This study is the only one to empirically examine the problem-solving approach to suicidal behavior. It also has a number of deficits. First, it was conducted in an inpatient setting, thus, confounding the treatments with other approaches. Second, it was conducted on a small sample of patients with no long-term follow-up. Third, the results show effectiveness for the problem-solving treatment with regard to variables associated with suicidal behavior but not with regard to suicidal behavior itself.

At present, the above two studies represent the only controlled treatment studies targeting suicidal behavior. In keeping with the model presented above, however, several studies have indirectly examined social support approaches in reducing suicidal behaviors. This has been accomplished by targeting at-risk groups using aggressive outreach programs.

One set of studies investigated the effects of aggressive outreach to patients who had engaged in suicide attempts. Motto (1976) found that those patients who were contacted on a regular basis by letter or by telephone showed a lower rate of suicide over a four year period than those who did not receive this contact, although the differences were not significant. Welu (1977) implemented a similar treatment plan and found significant differences between the contact and no-contact group in the number of subsequent suicide attempts. In contrast, however, two studies showed no significant differences in suicidal behavior following aggressive outreach versus standard crisis intervention (Chowdury, Hicks and Kreitman 1973; Gibbons et al. 1978), although they did show improvements in the social conditions of the individuals in the treatment group.

The Current Situation

It is obvious from the above discussion that the etiological model proposed vis-a-vis suicide has more support that an intervention approach based on this model. Nevertheless, there are at present several treatment studies in progress that take aim at this vacuum and begin to address some of the problems in research design. Linehan and her colleagues at the University of Washington, for example, have targeted borderline patients with multiple suicide attempts using a Dialectical Behavioral Treatment (DBT) program in many respects similar to the problem-solving approach proposed here. Preliminary data (Linehan et al. 1987) indicates that DBT is superior, in terms of reducing parasuicide behavior, to "usual treatment," defined as the treatment multiple suicide attempters received when left to their own devices. Linehan was able to show significant differences in the two groups in spite of the fact that "usual treatment" typically involved as many therapist contact hours as did DBT.

A study currently underway in our laboratory targets chronic suicide ideators in the adolescent age range. This study is being conducted on an outpatient rather than an inpatient basis and is using a control group that emphasizes group discussion and support. It is the first controlled outpatient study to examine the problem-solving approach discussed here.

Where to from Here?

A number of research questions remain unanswered at the present time. Future research in this area needs to clarify a number of etiological as well as treatment issues. We will enumerate some areas that appear to us of special import at this time.

(1) Measurement of problem-solving deficits is a major issue. Previous work has utilized broad-stroke devices such as the Means/Ends Problem-solving (MEPS) test and Schotte and Clum's Modified MEPS that was developed for parasuicides in particular. These devices are inadequate for a number of reasons. One is that they rely on what the suicidal person is able to identify as a problem leading to suicidal behavior. Another problem is that the MEPS relies on generic problem-solving skills largely unrelated to those leading to parasuicide while the Modified MEPS, though tailored to the idiosyncratic problems of the suicidal, inadequately samples the range of problems of the suicidal person. Future assessment approaches should be (a) tailored to the problems of the suicidal; (b) broadly based, perhaps on a taxonomy of problems leading to suicide behavior; and (c) based on behavioral, cognitive, and emotional components of the problem-solving process.

(2) The question of whether the suicidal individual's problem-solving deficits represent a chronic problem or are a situational response to stress has yet to be resolved. To date, problem-solving deficits in suicide attempters and ideators have been demonstrated during times of suicidal behavior or shortly thereafter. It is possible that the stressors that commonly precede suicidal behavior produce a decrement in problem-solving behavior.

A second possibility, of course, is that individuals who become suicidal or attempt suicide have a cognitive personality trait broadly conceptualized as "problem-solving deficit." The clarification of this issue has implications for treatment.

(3) The most important research issues for the future surround the question of effective treatment. Suicide behavior per se has with few exceptions not been the target of psychological interventions. Which treatments are most effective and whether suicide behavior can be targeted independent of broader issues of psychopathology are important questions. Controlled studies are the sine qua non of science, and future research into this area must utilize appropriate control groups. Because of ethical issues, such control groups are likely to be composed of such things as usual treatment or treatments of demonstrated efficacy for other types of problems. Because suicide behavior is embedded within a variety of psychopathologies including depression, borderline disorder, alcoholism, and schizophrenia, comprehensive treatment approaches will be required to be flexible with no one approach likely to prove successful with all populations.

REFERENCES

Beck, A.T., A. Weissman, D. Lester and L. Trexler. 1974. The measure of pessimism: The Hopelessness Scale. *Journal of Consulting and Clinical Psychology* 42:861–65.

Braucht, G. 1979. International analysis of suicidal behavior. *Journal of Consulting and Clinical Psychology* 47:653–69.

Chowdury, N., R.C. Hicks and N. Kreitman. 1973. Evaluation of an after-care service for parasuicide patients. *Social Psychiatry* 8:67–81.

Clum, G.A. 1987. The role of the family in the suicide motives of adolescents. Paper Papers presented at the annual meeting of the American Psychological Association, August, New York, New York.

Clum, G.A., A.T. Patsiokas and R. L. Luscomb. 1979. Empirically-based comprehensive treatment program for parasuicides. *Journal of Consulting and Clinical Psychology* 47:937–45.

Cochrane, R. and A. Robinson. 1975. Stress in the lives of parasuicides. *Social Psychiatry* 10:161–72.

D'Zurrilla, T.J. and M.R. Goldfried. 1971. Problem solving and behavior modification. *Journal of Abnormal Psychology* 78:107–26.

Gibbons, J.S., J. Butler, P. Urwin and J.L. Gibbons. 1978. Evaluation of a social work service for self-poisoning patients. *British Journal of Psychiatry* 133:111–18.

Kovacs, M., A.T. Beck and A. Weissman. 1975. Hopelessness: An indicator of suicidal risk. *Suicide* 5:98–103.

Leenaars, A. 1987. An empirical investigation of Schneidman's formulations regarding suicide: Age and sex. *Suicide and Life-Threatening Behavior* 17:233–50.

Levenson, M. and G. Neuringer. 1971. Problem-solving behavior in suicidal adolescents. *Journal of Consulting and Clinical Psychology* 37:433–36.

Liberman, R.P. and T. Eckman. 1981. Behavior therapy vs. insight-oriented therapy for repeated suicide attempters. *Archives of General Psychiatry* 38:1126–30.

Linehan, M.M., P. Camper, J.A. Chiles, K. Strosahl and E. Shearin. 1987. Interpersonal problem-solving and parasuicide. *Cognitive Therapy and Research* 11:1–12.

Linehan, M.M., J.A. Chiles, K.J. Egan, R.H. Devine and J.A. Laffaw. 1986. Presenting problems of parasuicides versus suicide ideators and nonsuicidal psychiatric patients. *Journal of Consulting and Clinical Psychology* 54:880–81.

Luscomb, R., G.A. Clum and A.T. Patsiokas. 1980. Mediating factors in the relationship between stress and parasuicide. *Journal of Nervous and Mental Disease* 168:644–50.

Motto, J. 1976. Suicide prevention for high-risk persons who refuse treatment. *Suicide and Life-Threatening Behavior* 6:223–30.

Patsiokas, A.T., and G.A. Clum. 1985. Effects of psychotherapeutic strategies in the treatment of suicide attempters. *Psychotherapy* 22:281–90.

Paykel, E., B. Prusoff and J. Myers. 1975. Suicide attempts and recent life events. *Archives of General Psychiatry* 32:327–33.

Schotte, D.E. and G.A. Clum. 1982. Suicide ideation in a college population: A test of a model. *Journal of Consulting and Clinical Psychology* 50:690–96.

——1987. Problem-solving skills in suicidal psychiatric patients. *Journal of Consulting and Clinical Psychology* 55:49–55.

Simon, W. and G.K. Lumry. 1968. Suicide among physicians. *Journal of Nervous and Mental Disease* 147:105–112.

Topol, P. and M. Reznikoff. 1982. Perceived peer and family relationships, hopelessness, and locus of control as factors in adolescent suicide attempts. *Suicide and Life- Threatening Behavior* 12:141–50.

Welu, T.C. 1977. A follow-up program for suicide attempters: Evaluation of effectiveness. *Suicide and Life-Threatening Behavior* 7:17–29.

Wetzel, R. 1976. Hopelessness, depression, and suicide intent. *Archives of General Psychiatry* 33:1069–73.

14

Survivors of Suicide: Research and Speculations

Kjell Erik Rudestam

My experience as a researcher in the area of suicide was marked by a rather inauspicious debut. In 1967 I traveled to Sweden, country of my birth, to conduct part of a cross-cultural study on the communication of suicidal intent. The study consisted of interviewing family members who had survived the recent death of a close relative through suicide and was one of the first of its kind (Rudestam 1971). Although I had the complete cooperation of the Office of the Medical Examiner in Stockholm, the medical community was apprehensive about having a young psychologist contact and invade the privacy of grieving parents and spouses. The study almost died a still birth after my first three written requests for subject cooperation resulted in two No's and one irate call to the police and hospital administration. Swedes, at least at that time, were not used to the daily deluge of surveys, studies, and door-to-door salespeople that we take for granted in the United States. I quickly revised my strategy by making the introductory letter more benign and relying on a follow-up telephone call. Fortunately, this made a significant difference and I was able to conduct a rather comprehensive study on suicide.

While my focus at that time was on the decedents and their lifestyles and personalities, perhaps the greatest contribution of the study was the therapeutic impact I was able to have on the survivors. They were clearly a beleaguered group, suffering from the bewilderment, anguish, sadness, anger, fear, and guilt that we now commonly associate with all forms of deep personal loss, but most especially with loss through suicide. Many of them had tightly wrapped their emotions under the control of pride and stoicism and had nowhere to turn to share their thoughts and feelings prior to this single two to three hour interview.

Since those early days I have engaged in other research studies which bear on the impact of suicide on surviving family members (Rudestam 1977). Most of what we know about survivors comes from clinic populations, those surviving family members who seek professional or paraprofessional support to help them deal with the effects of loss. There is obviously a host of people who do not make use of such resources, due to lack of knowledge, lack of availability, lack of need, or personal preference. We know much less about the struggles of these people.

SURVIVOR STUDIES

Recent reviews of the survivor literature have been conducted by Calhoun, Selby, and Selby (1982), Foglia (1984), and Henley (1984). Most studies fall short of the kind of methodological rigor one would demand in order to draw definitive conclusions. For instance, many have relied on very small samples of subjects (Hatton and Valente 1981; Herzog and Resnik 1969; Wallace 1973). Of the few studies of the aftermath of suicide to employ a control group, Sheskin and Wallace (1976) compared Wallace's (1973) sample of 12 widows of suicide with a totally different sample of 49 widows of nonsuicidal death interviewed by Glick, Weiss, and Parkes (1974). The authors reported more lack of social support for survivors in the case of suicide.

Even studies using larger samples of subjects have typically not employed control groups. Cain and Fast (1972) focused on the parents of 45 clinically disturbed children by looking at clinical materials after the death of the parent by suicide. Shepherd and Barraclough (1974) used a more generalized sample of 17 men and 27 women whose spouses had committed suicide 54 to 83 months earlier. I conducted intensive interviews from 39 cases of completed suicide taken from 82 consecutively occurring cases in Montgomery County, Ohio (Rudestam 1977). More recently, Solomon (1982–83) interviewed 90 subjects who had been bereaved by the suicide of a relative or close friend. These subjects were drawn from those who responded to advertisements in newspapers and other media, so it is impossible to gauge how representative of the general population they might be.

In spite of methodological shortcomings, there are certain conclusions that seem apparent from these studies. One is that survivors of suicide tend to suffer from a number of psychosomatic and medical dysfunctions as a component of the grief process. In addition to fears of being alone, sleeping problems, crying spells, and anxieties, I found numerous cases of ulcers, migraines, hypertension, and exhaustion that had either developed or become exacerbated after the event. Many survivors were on medication, which often meant tranquilizers for the women and alcohol for the men. Thirty-four of the 39 survivors in the Ohio study had visited their family doctors since the death, but only three had visited a therapist. This statistic reinforces the importance of family physicians serving as resource persons for emotional difficulties beyond prescribing tranquilizers or antidepressants.

Since so few studies have directly compared death through suicide with other modes of death, it is difficult to differentiate suicidal grief from other grief. Moreover, it is evident that the similarities outweigh the differences. Hauser (1987) has eloquently listed a number of reasons why grief is more apt to be unresolved in the case of death by suicide. One is that suicidal death is usually sudden and unexpected, both factors associated with more difficult resolutions. Secondly, death by suicide is often violent, in turn eliciting strong affective reactions, including anger, from survivors. Third, suicide engenders guilt in the survivors—guilt that may persist for long periods (44 percent of the Ohio sample experienced considerable guilt more than six months after the death). Fourth, suicide often occurs in systems already experiencing stress, meaning that multiple stressors lead to more difficult beareavement outcomes. Fifth, death by suicide can compromise usual mourning rituals, such as normal funeral rites and religious ceremonies that help facilitate the movement from grief to recovery. Sixth, suicide may engender harmful expressions of blame and anger and distorted communication patterns, in that survivors may deal with their own loss and rage by projecting blame onto others, avoiding discomfort and confrontation, and so on. Finally, usual social supports may be withdrawn following a suicide.

The conclusions reached by Calhoun et al. (1982) from their critical review of the literature overlap with Hauser's explanations. Calhoun and his colleagues maintain that suicide survivors engage in lengthier searching for an understanding of the death, experience more guilt, and experience less social support than other survivors. These themes deserve elaboration and comment.

Stages of Bereavement

We are beginning to challenge the notion that bereavement takes place in predictable stages; there is a growing body of literature suggesting that bereavement patterns are not nearly as predictable as we have believed. John Bowlby has been the most instrumental figure in linking the bereavement process to the dissolution of attachment bonds. Bowlby and Parkes (1970) described the phases of normal bereavement as beginning with shock and numbness, then moving to yearning and protest, disorganization, and finally reorganization. These stages help to explain in a broad sense the unsteady progress of the bereaved, but they operate at a purely descriptive level. My own data (Rudestam 1977) indicate that shock is by far the most common initial reaction to suicide, but there are certainly many survivors of suicide who have not negotiated these stages in a smooth nor predictable manner. Only some would fit Bowlby's (1980) description of unresolved bereavement: patterns of denial, chronic mourning, or euphoria.

Many of us in the field of suicidology have also operated from the assumption that there are universal responses to traumatic life events, whereas recent data are indicating a high degree of individual variability. One cornerstone of grief theory, for instance, has been that the experience (and discharge) of emotional distress is necessary for psychological resolution of the event. Yet studies of bereavement such as that by Vachon et al. (1982) have shown that those individuals who exhibit little overt grief shortly after the loss rarely experience a delayed grief reaction. There are times when we expect survivors to be more depressed than they really are, and I have noted occasions of great intolerance to survivors who choose to socialize, date, or remarry before a "proper" period of mourning has been observed. It is very important for health care providers not to be judgmental in reacting to the positive mood states and behaviors of suicide survivors. Data from an extensive study with surviving parents of children who died from Sudden Infant Death Syndrome suggest that some parents are never very depressed and it is they who have the best long-range outcomes (Silver and Wortman 1980). Since most studies of the suicidally bereaved use one-shot measures, we need to investigate which ways of coping in the early stages are predictive of better long-term outcomes.

Another fallacy is the assumption that a grief reaction "ought" to be over in a reasonable period of time. Certainly the search for an explanation to make sense of the suicide goes on and on. Only 7 (out of 39) of the survivors in the Ohio study had reached a stage of acceptance six to nine months after the event . It appears that the justifications people use to end their lives are never adequate or inadequate, right or wrong; they are simply compelling or not compelling, based on our understanding of their values. Furthermore, there is no good evidence to suggest that time itself is curative with most emotional problems; that is, that suicidal death becomes resolved merely as a function of time. Resolving the meaninglessness of the loss is essential. Long-term problems can persist even three years after a sudden death, yet by this time other family members, friends, and acquaintances can easily become drained and impatient for change. This is another side to the undesirability of maintaining strong expectations for how bereavement ought to be managed and resolve itself.

Social Support

The stress and coping model, initiated by Cannon and Selye, popularized by Holmes and Rahe, and currently central to the work of Lazarus and his colleagues, has suggested that the impact of a stressor is moderated by both personality variables and environmental variables. A personality variable that is commonly pointed to as a resource that helps mediate the negative effects of aversive events, and even influences the labeling of those events as aversive, is "hardiness." Hardiness has been defined as a combination of commitment, control, and challenge (Kobasa 1979). A key environmental variable that appears to moderate the impact of life stress is social support. Both of these variables emerge from the social psychological literature of the past decade and have been insufficiently noted by suicidologists.

With regard to social support, survivor groups in particular are providing a number of support services to help bereaved survivors. It is my sense that, on the whole, those survivors who feel the least relieved are those who never discuss the event with anyone. In support of this statement, there is a growing body of evidence that confiding one's thoughts and feelings about a traumatic event can lead to reduced health problems, while ruminating and inhibiting such openness leads to greater health problems (Pennebaker and O'Heeron 1984). My own research has suggested that friends and relatives are often experienced as helpful after a suicide, but that too often their social support consists of food, shelter, and concrete aid (what might be called tangible support) or clarification and information about resources (informational support), but less often emotional support (being listened to, cared for, and valued). In fact, there are relatively low correlations (.2–.3) among these three forms of social support (Dunkel-Schetter 1984).

Emotional support is not necessarily superior to other forms of support, but it is especially critical to the needs of suicide survivors. Participants in survivor support programs have indicated that they are more interested in feeling better about themselves, talking about their feelings, and getting the suicide in perspective than they are in getting practical advice and factual information (Rogers et al. 1982). Yet emotional support is probably least likely to be offered in circumstances such as suicide that elicit acute personal distress in the helper. The data suggest that friends and relatives will too often avoid the topics of death and suicide. It is very difficult for members of a support network not to be emotionally threatened by a friend or relative's bereavement around a suicidal death.

In the same way that stress is a transaction between a person and the environment in which one's adaptive resources are measured against external demands, so too is social support a transaction between a support network and an individual's coping methods. In other words, some people are better at eliciting and making use of support from the environment than others. There is evidence that people with a strong sense of personal control also possess beneficial support systems in the presence of stressful situations (Revicki and May 1984). On the other hand, we know that suicidal individuals are notoriously poor at maintaining positive social networks and view themselves as isolated and unsupported. It is my impression that many survivors of suicide not only lack social networks but also fail to see others as potential sources of support. Tolsdorf (1976) uses the term "network orientation" to describe beliefs, attitudes, and expectations concerning the potential usefulness of network members in helping them cope with their problems. We certainly need to know more about how to instill a network orientation in suicide survivors; that is, how to encourage them to take advantage of existing social resources and how to create others that are missing.

People ofen lack the skills to ask for help in ways that maximize their chances of receiving it. Individuals who cope with stress by withdrawing, maintaining self-control, or being aggressively confrontive have been shown to receive less support from others (Dunkel-Schetter 1984). One might predict that the signals sent by survivors, which reflect their appraisal of the event as well as their own needs, are apt to be a more important determinant of the support received than the amount of stress or grief being experienced. The true wizards of coping may be those who can effectively gather support without soliciting it.

Role of the Family

Most large scale studies of suicide survivors have addressed the impact of the death on surviving family members and it is clear that individually and as a unit, families suffer greatly in their efforts to manage their grief. Ironically, there is reason to believe that some families appear to emerge from the experience with seemingly improved functioning—better communication, fewer tensions, closer family bonds—at least six months down the line (Rudestam 1977). In the first place, suicidal members were often tremendous irritants in the family so that survivors experience considerable relief with their absence. Furthermore, many survivors conducted a reevaluation of personal values in a helpful direction. For example, one father of a teenage son who killed himself was amazed how much energy he had invested in fairly trivial concerns, such as the length of his son's hair. He was now much more tolerant and lenient with his other son. A study by Rohrbaugh and McGoldrick (1985) supports this observation. These authors compared 25 cases of suicide to 25 cases representing other modes of death and determined that 37 percent of the survivors of suicide reported that family functioning was better after the suicide, while no one claimed that family functioning improved after the other deaths.

These data do not detract from the conclusion that individual family members suffer greatly from the suicide of a close relative, but suggest that a systemic approach could aid us in understanding the impact of suicide on families. This perspective is different from the dominant, although useful, explanations of the role of the family in suicide (Richman 1986; Pfeffer 1981). Using a family systems theory approach we might speculate that suicide acts like other symptoms to maintain family stability and prevent the emergence of other family crises. It argues for examining family structures and interactional patterns to predict what kinds of problems, including the possible emergence of a new family scapegoat, might arise after the suicidal exit of a member. One would expect a family's structure and communication patterns to be fairly inflexible in order to necessitate the development of a dramatic and serious symptom such as suicidal behavior (Kronitz and Rudestam 1979). There are, of course, data to support the notion that youth often turn to suicide only after engaging in many other troublesome and self-destructive behaviors and after the family is viewed as unresponsive to demands for change.

An understanding of family structure and dynamics can help in elucidating the role of other family variables in cases of suicide. For example, Ken Adam and his colleagues (Adam, Bouckoms and Streiner 1982; Adam, Lohrenz, Harper and Streiner 1982) have conducted an informative, well-controlled group of studies that examine the role of early parental loss on suicidal behavior. They have concluded that family stability mediates the impact of parental loss on survivors. That is, while early loss might be conceptualized as a predisposing factor to suicide, suicidal behavior tends to emerge in families where loss leads to major disorganization and instability rather than in families that are able to restabilize and adapt to the loss. There is much to be learned about families that cope most effectively with suicide, and I would urge investigators to take a systemic perspective in this search, viewing the family as a functional unit with a set of developmental tasks to perform rather than as a collection of individuals who evidence varying degrees of pathology.

Relationship Between Survivor and Decedent

There is evidence as well that the relationship between the decedent and the survivor plays a role in the bereavement process. By engaging in suicidal behavior a person forces others to take control, to give attention or help, to care, to treat her in a particular way. In general, suicidal behavior functions to mobilize and to prompt others into defining the nature of the relationship with the identified patient (Kronitz and Rudestam 1979). It is possible, of course, for this tactic to fail. The other person may not respond in the desired fashion. Further suicidal or other problem behavior would then be likely to develop, unless underlying problems are resolved in some other fashion. The last move in the communication cycle belongs to the decedent, who leaves the survivor with a total sense of incompletion.

In a recent analogue study we looked at the effect of different kinds of suicide notes on the survivor's reactions (Rudestam and Agnelli 1984). Blame is an important variable. When survivors are blamed, their guilt, defensiveness, and anger are heightened. We know that guilt is related to feeling responsible for the death, to not having done enough to prevent it, and/or to regretting other relationship issues from the past (Henslin 1970). It is interesting to note that self-blaming suicide notes generated the most emotional discomfort other than guilt. And when self-blame was combined with forgiveness of the survivor, there was a potent effect. Self-blame can be very manipulative and forgiveness implies absolution from blame. But with a suicide note there is no opportunity for the survivor to respond and complete the communication loop, so the survivor is left with a tremendous emotional burden.

Public Perceptions of Suicide

An increasingly prolific research area concerns the public perception of suicide survivors. The primary question is to what extent the bereavement process of this vulnerable group is exacerbated or facilitated by the attitudes and reactions of others. In order to assess public reactions toward suicide survivors, a researcher can take one of two general courses of action. One general approach is to ask survivors of suicide how they have been treated by the public. This would include predictable contacts with police, coroners, and insurance agents, as well as relatives, friends, and strangers. Questions pertaining to these experiences have been part of a few large-scale studies of the aftermath of suicide. This literature has been reviewed elsewhere (Calhoun, Selby and Selby 1982; Rudestam 1987).

The second general approach is to survey members of the public, either directly or indirectly, and assess their attitudes. At a general level this investigatory approach would include content analyses of media reports of actual suicides (Gould and Shaffer 1986; Phillips and Carstensen 1986), as well as public opinion polls (Ginsburg 1971). Another strategy is to approach individual community members and obtain their responses either to survivors with whom they have had contact or with fictitious survivors. This method has produced a small, but growing number of interesting studies. The common methodology, devised by Calhoun, Selby, and Faulstich (1980) is to ask members of the community to respond to contrived newspaper accounts describing a person whose death was due to either suicide, accident, homicide, or natural causes, as a way of gauging public attitudes toward family members. The results of these studies, also reviewed in Rudestam (1987), typically find more blame and attribution of pathology in the case of suicide than other modes of death.

These studies give us a good sense of public attitudes toward various aspects of suicide in general (any variables can be built into and manipulated in the design by simply varying the newspaper article) as opposed to attitudes toward survivors of a known, actual case of suicide. The studies have also yielded knowledge about the "social rules" by which the public operates with regard to a social phenomenon such as suicide (Calhoun, Abernathy and Selby 1986). Calhoun and his colleagues, for instance, have found that the rules (norms) for interacting with persons bereaved by suicide are less clear and more restrictive than the rules for other types of death. In a study made particularly interesting because of its choice of subjects, Calhoun, Selby, and Steelman (1988–89) found that funeral directors have observed that the community reacts differently to survivors of suicide than to survivors of other types of death, reflecting more ignorance about what to do, more difficulty expressing sympathy, and more discomfort approaching the family members at the funeral.

I think the time is ripe to study the link between negative and ambivalent public attitudes toward survivors of suicide and the bereavement process itself. If it can be established that friends and family of suicide victims are exposed to and vulnerable to negative community attitudes, then we might infer that sanctions would follow that might complicate the bereavement process. Does being viewed as psychologically disturbed, for example, impact on one's coping with loss? Are supportive resources subsequently less available? While the media has recently worked hard to educate the public about suicide and present the mental health implications of this phenomenon, it is not clear to me that the public's increasing awareness of factors associated with suicide necessarily leads to helpful responses for the survivors. A frightening example of the public's attitude toward surviving family relatives of suicide victims is a recent case in Florida (cited in *The New York Times,* October 31, 1987), in which the mother of a 17-year-old girl faced criminal charges in her daughter's suicide. One might argue that the mother demonstrated clear evidence of psychological abuse in parenting her child, but in this case the guilty verdict seemed tied to the prosecution's contention, supported by expert witness, that she was directly responsible for the suicide. Is this really how we as a society wish to hold survivors of suicide in the public eye? Are we really so presumptuous as to believe that our data demonstrate that poor parenting "causes" suicide? One wonders about the likely impact of this kind of decision on surviving friends and family members who are left with a legacy of suicide.

REFERENCES

Adam, K.S., A. Bouckoms, and D. Streiner. 1982. Parental loss and family stability in attempted suicide. *Archives of General Psychiatry 39:*1081–1085.

Adam, K.S., J.G. Lohrenz, D. Harper, and D. Streiner. 1982. Early parental loss and suicidal ideation in university students. *Canadian Journal of Psychiatry 27:*275–81.

Bowlby, J. 1980. *Sadness and depression* (Vol. III). New York: Basic Books.

Bowlby, J. and C.M. Parkes. 1970. Separation and loss within the family. In E.J. Anthony and C. Koupernik, eds., *The child in his family* (Vol. 1). New York: Wiley Interscience.

Cain, A.C. and I. Fast. 1972. Children's disturbed reactions to parent suicide. Distortions of guilt, communication, and identification. In A.C. Cain, ed., *Survivors of suicide.* Springfield, Ill: Charles C. Thomas.

Calhoun, L.G., C.B. Abernathy and J.W. Selby. 1986. The rules of bereavement: Are suicidal deaths different? *Journal of Community Psychology* 14:213–18.

Calhoun, L.G., J.W. Selby and L.E. Selby. 1982. The psychological aftermath of suicide: An analysis of current evidence. *Clinical Psychology Review* 2: 409–20.

Calhoun, L.G., J.W., Selby and J. Steelman. 1988–89. Individual and social elements in acute grief: A collation of funeral directors' impressions of suicidal death. *Omega* 19:365–3.

Calhoun, L.G., J.W. Selby and M.E. Faulstich. 1982. The aftermath of childhood suicide: Influences on the perception of the parent. *Journal of Community Psychology* 10:250–54.

Dunkel-Schetter, C. 1984. Social support and cancer: Findings based on patient interviews and their implications. *Journal of Social Issues* 40:77–98.

Foglia, B.B. 1984. Survivor-victims of suicide: Review of the literature. In C.L. Hatton and S. M. Valente, eds., *Suicide: Assessment and intervention* (2nd ed.). Norwalk, CT: Appleton-Century-Crofts.

Ginsburg, G.P. 1971. Public conceptions and attitudes about suicide. *Journal of Health and Social Behavior* 12:200–207.

Glick, I.O., R.S. Weiss and C. M. Parkes. 1974. *The first year of bereavement.* New York: Wiley and Sons.

Gould, M.S. and D. Shaffer. 1986. The impact of suicide in television movies: Evidence of imitation. *New England Journal of Medicine* 315: 690–93.

Hatton, C.L. and S. M. Valente 1981. Bereavement group for parents who suffered a suicidal loss of a child. *Suicide and Life-Threatening Behavior* 11:141–50.

Hauser, M.J. 1987: Special aspects of grief after a suicide. In E.J. Dunne, J.L. McIntosh and K. Dunne-Maxim, eds., *Suicide and its aftermath.* New York: W.W. Norton.

Henley, S.H.A. 1984. Bereavement following suicide: A review of the literature. *Current Psychological Research & Reviews* 3:53–61.

Henslin, J.M. 1971. Problems and prospects in studying significant others of suicides. *Bulletin of Suicidology* 8:81–84.

Herzog, A. and H.L.P. Resnik. 1969. A clinical study of parental response to adolescent death by suicide with recommendations for approaching the survivors. *British Journal of Social Psychiatry* 3:144–52.

Kobasa, S.C. 1979. Stressful life events, personality, and health: An inquiry into hardiness. *Journal of Personality and Social Psychology* 37:1–11.

Kronitz, R.C. and K.E. Rudestam. 1979. *The application of family systems theory to adolescent suicide.* Symposium, International Congress for Suicide Prevention and Crisis Intervention, Ottawa, Ontario.

Pennebaker, J.W. and R.C. O'Heeron. 1984. Confiding in others and illness rate among spouses of suicide and accidental-death victims. *Journal of Abnormal Psychology* 93:473–76.

Pfeffer, C.R. 1981. The family system of suicidal children. *American Journal of Psychotherapy* 35:330–41.

Phillips, D. and L. Carstensen. 1986. Clustering of teenage suicides after television news stories about suicide. *New England Journal of Medicine* 315:685–89.

Revicki, D.A. and H.J. May. 1984. Occupational stress, social support and depression. *Health Psychology* 4:61–77.

Richman, J. 1986. *Family therapy for suicidal people.* New York: Springer.

Rogers, J., A. Sheldon, C. Barwick, K. Letofsky and W. Lancee. 1982. Help for families of suicide: Survivors Support Program. *Canadian Journal of Psychiatry* 27:444–49.

Rohrbaugh, M. and M. McGoldrick. 1985. *Family response to suicide.* Paper presented at the meeting of the Eastern Psychological Association, Boston, Massachusetts.

Rudestam, K.E. 1971. Stockholm and Los Angeles: A cross-cultural study of the communication of suicidal intent. *Journal of Consulting and Clinical Psychology* 36:82–90.

——1977. Physical and psychological responses to suicide in the family. *Journal of Consulting and Clinical Psychology* 45:162–70.

——1987. Public perceptions of suicide survivors: A critical review. In E.J. Dunne, J. McIntosh and K. Dunne-Maxim, eds, *The aftermath of suicide: Research and therapy.* New York: W.W. Norton.

Rudestam, K.E. and P. Agnelli. 1986. The effect of the content of suicide notes on grief reactions. *Journal of Clinical Psychology* 43:211–20.

Shepherd, D.M. and B.M. Barraclough. 1974. The aftermath of suicide. *British Medical Journal* 2:600–603.

Sheskin, A. and S.E. Wallace. 1976. Differing bereavements: Suicide, natural and accidental deaths. *Omega* 7:229–42.

Silver, R.L. and C.B. Wortman. 1980. Coping with undesirable life events. In J. Garber and M.E.P. Seligman, eds., *Human helplessness: Theory and applications.* New York: Academic Press.

Solomon, M.I. 1982–83. The bereaved and the stigma of suicide. *Omega* 13:377–87.

Tolsdorf, C. 1976. Social networks, support, and coping: An exploratory study. *Family Process* 15:407–415.

Vachon, M.L., A.R. Sheldon, W.J. Lancee, W.A. Lyall, J. Rogers and S.J. Freeman. 1982. Correlates of enduring distress patterns following bereavement: Social network, life situation and personality. *Psychological Medicine* 12:783–88.

Wallace, S. 1973. *After suicide.* New York: Wiley.

15

The Social Aftermath of a Suicide in the Family: Some Empirical Findings

Lawrence G. Calhoun and James W. Selby

Historically, suicide has been viewed in the West as a highly stigmatizing event. Suicide has been condemned by social custom and by religious teaching. Surprisingly, however, systematic empirical investigations of the social context that survivors (as in the obituary notice "is survived by . . .") encounter were rather limited until the middle 1970s. Surveys (for example Kalish, Reynolds and Farberow 1974) suggested that suicide was perceived as a highly negative cause of death and family members were expected to be embarrassed and shamed by it. But, studies in which cause of death was systematically varied were not available. There has recently been a significant amount of research attention devoted to the opinions and attitudes of the public toward suicide, and while much still remains to be known, some tentative answers are emerging. Studies have been conducted from different perspectives, focusing on different questions, with an increasing variety of populations. This chapter is focused on one specific subset of studies on the social aftermath of suicide. In this chapter we will describe some of the studies we have conducted to provide information on the ways in which others perceive the surviving family and some ways in which members of surviving families of a suicide perceive themselves. These studies have been designed to examine the social aftermath of suicide from different viewpoints and with different methodologies.

General Social Perception: Strangers

An initial study was designed systematically to examine whether or not general social impressions others have of the parents of a child who dies are different when suicidal deaths are compared to natural causes (Calhoun, Selby and Faulstich 1980). The participants for the study were 119 adult citizens of a large southeastern city. Ninety-two percent were between the ages of 18 and 55, and 54 percent were married.

Brief descriptions of a child's death by suicide or illness were prepared with the assistance of a staff member of a large urban paper, and were then set in

214

type. The story described the child as either a boy or a girl and as having died from a viral illness or suicide by hanging.

Potential subjects were approached at a large shopping mall and asked if they would be willing to participate in a study of reactions to newspaper stories about the death of a child. One hundred and twenty agreed to participate (but data for one person were uncodable) and 12 refused. Participants were asked to read a photocopy of the "newspaper story" and then provide ratings on twelve Likert-type scales that tapped a variety of reactions toward the child and his surviving family including the following: how psychologically disturbed each parent was before the death; how well the respondent would like each parent if she met them; blame attributed to each parent for the child's death; whether the story should have mentioned the cause of death; and questions about discomfort in interacting or expressing sympathy to the parents.

A multivariate analysis of variance with the 12 rating scales as dependent variables, and gender of child, gender of respondent, and type of death as the three independent variables indicated only a significant main effect for type of death. Univariate analyses of the impact of the cause of death indicated a general pattern of more negative social impressions of the parents of the child who committed suicide. Respondents expected to like the parents less, parents were blamed more, and participants were more likely to believe that the newspaper should not have printed the cause of death when the death was suicide.

In a second study (Calhoun, Selby and Faulstich 1982) we attempted to replicate and extend the findings from the previous study. The focus was on whether parents of the child suicide would be viewed negatively by a different sample of participants and whether the presence of environmental pressures on the child would act as a mitigator of parental blame for a child's death.

The participants in this investigation were 77 men and women approached in the same way as in the previous study (Calhoun et al. 1980). Forty-six percent were married, and 95 percent were between the ages of 17 and 55.

Stories were set in type and they described a boy or girl who had died either from a viral illness or from suicide. In addition, the child was described either as having failed a series of tests in school or as experiencing success in school. Our expectation was that for both types of death (or perhaps with somewhat greater likelihood for a suicidal death) the described presence of an environmental source of stress, such as failure on several tests, would lead to a less negative reaction to the child's parents.

The general pattern of results for cause of death was very similar to those we had previously obtained. Parents were seen as more psychologically disturbed before the death, as more responsible for the child's death, as more likely to have been aware of potential problems, and expected to be liked less when the child's death was suicidal. The statistical interaction between success/

failure in school and cause of death identified a pattern of responses that were somewhat unexpected, but congruent with the general view that the survivors of a suicidal death face a more negative social climate than the family of a child who dies of an illness. When the death was described as suicidal, mothers and fathers were rated as more likely to have been aware of potential problem in their child when she was described as failing in school; no such difference was obtained when death was due to an illness. In this second study, the results once again suggested that parents of the child suicide were viewed more negatively in a variety of ways; in addition, parents of a child who committed suicide and who had been experiencing school problems, were expected to have been able to tell that the child was headed for serious difficulty.

While the pattern of obtained results in these two studies suggested that parents of a child suicide would be likely to encounter somewhat more negative perceptions, there was no evidence that a similar process would operate when both the decreased and the survivor were adults. In still another study (Calhoun, Selby and Walton 1985–86) we used typeset obituary notices to examine reactions to the surviving spouse.

The "obituaries" described either a 45-year-old man or woman, who had died by a self-inflicted gunshot wound, leukemia, or in a two car motor-vehicle accident (these three causes of death occur at about the same rate for middle-aged persons in the United States). One hundred and twenty adult citizens participated (11 refused participation) having been approached in a variety of locations (e.g., convention center, local corporations). Participants were asked to read the "obituary" and respond to a series of Likert-type scales similar to those used in previous studies.

Compared to both accident and leukemia, the surviving spouse of a suicide was seen as more likely to have been to blame in some way for the death, more likely to be ashamed of the cause of death, and more likely to have been able to do something that might have prevented the death. Respondents also indicated that inquiries about the cause of death were less appropriate for suicide than either for deaths due to accident or leukemia. Again the general pattern of results was the same as in the previous two studies: the surviving spouse of a person briefly described in a "newspaper" account was viewed in a reliably less positive light when death was self-inflicted. These three studies, however, asked individuals to respond to persons who had only been described to them, i.e., to others who were strangers to them. Would similar patterns of results emerge when the respondents knew the target individuals in more personal ways?

SOCIAL PERCEPTION BASED ON PERSONAL KNOWLEDGE

A potentially important question is whether the differences in social perception obtained with ratings of strangers briefly described would also be present when individuals were asked about others whom they had known personally. For the two studies described in this section we employed not only different populations and target persons, but different data gathering methods as well.

Knowledge From Professional Experience

One group of individuals whose work brings them daily into contact with bereaved persons is funeral directors. Their work provides them with the opportunity to observe what happens to surviving families and the forms that interactions of others with the family take. One of our subsequent studies relied on the participation of 25 licensed funeral directors (Calhoun, Selby, and Steelman 1988–89). They were males between the ages of 21 and 61, and they reported an average of 18.7 years of work experience.

A fourteen item semistructured interview was utilized and directors were asked to answer based on their experiences with, and observations of, funerals and bereaved persons. The interviews covered several areas; those of particular interest for this discussion include reactions of the family and of others to the family of a suicide.

All 25 of the funeral directors indicated that they had encountered reactions to family members that were different when death was self-inflicted. In their responses, two main themes emerged. Family members were perceived as experiencing greater shock and more difficulty coping with the death, and suicidal deaths were described as generating more questions and guesses about the reasons for the death.

Twenty-one of the directors indicated that others react differently toward bereaved persons when the death is suicidal. A main theme in their answers was that others do not know how to behave in the presence of the bereaved family; they do not know what to do or say. Nine of the 25 indicated that another difference is that others feel greater compassion toward the family of a suicide. But, distressingly, all but one (24) of the 25 indicated that others experience significantly greater difficulty in trying to express sympathy to the family. Fifteen of those 24 cited lack of certainty others have about what to do or say to show their support of the family. An additional question concerned whether others experienced more social discomfort interacting with a family bereaved by suicide and 22 directors indicated others did. The theme of uncertainty as to how to behave was again the most prevalent one in the directors' responses.

A final question asked the participants whether they had noticed anything about the events surrounding the funeral, visitation of the family, or burial that was in some way different for suicidal deaths: 80 percent indicated there were differences. Of these, 9 indicated that there was more curiosity displayed by others when the death was suicidal. For example, curiosity about method of death, state of the body, and the like. One director indicated that suicidal deaths occasionally attracted curiosity seekers who did not know the family, but who came to the funeral home to try to see the body and to ask questions about the individual who had died.

The information provided by the funeral directors suggested that, from their perspective, suicidal deaths elicit behaviors that are different in a variety of ways from deaths from other causes. While others may feel greater compassion toward the family of persons who commit suicide, there is greater social discomfort, more curiosity, and significantly less confidence about how to act toward the bereaved family.

Knowledge of Others From Personal Experience

The information obtained in the study of the views of funeral directors suggested that suicide is a cause of death that leads to different reactions and perceptions in a variety of ways, most of which can be described as negative—a further confirmation of our previous work. Would persons who personally knew the family also describe similar reactions? An additional study was conducted with persons who had personal experience with and knowledge of others who had experienced bereavement (Calhoun, Selby, and Abernathy 1984).

 Potential participants—all of whom were undergraduate students at a large university in the southeastern United States—were recruited in the following way: Investigators visited several classrooms and requested the collaboration of individuals who in the last three years had known someone else who had experienced the death of a friend or relative. Those who had the necessary experience and who were willing to be interviewed provided their names and were subsequently contacted. The study sample consisted of 23 women and 12 men with a mean age of 20.5, 91 percent of whom had never been married. Most of them described persons who had experienced the death of a family member (71 percent). Cause of death was classifiable into three categories: suicide (11), accident (13), and natural causes (11).

A structured interview covering a variety of topics—including the survivor and perceptions of bereavement—was utilized. As part of the interview, participants were asked to provide ratings of their perceptions of the bereaved person and of his experience on a variety of dimensions.

Analysis of the impact of the cause of death (accidental, suicidal, or natural) on the 13 ratings of the funeral, bereavement, and consequences of death for the family revealed significant differences on only 3 of the 13. On the rating of difficulty in expressing sympathy to the surviving family at the funeral, participants describing suicidal deaths indicated others had consistently experienced more difficulty in expressing sympathy. Ratings of how uncomfortable they believed others to be indicated those describing suicidal deaths believed others to have had significantly greater discomfort talking to the surviving family at the funeral. An apparently contradictory finding was obtained on the item asking respondents to estimate the amount of difficulty they would have in coping with the death if they had been in the bereaved person's place. Suicidal deaths were rated significantly lower in expected difficulty than accidental deaths.

The results of this study suggested two general conclusions, with the note of caution required by the population studied (university students) and the methodology used (each individual was responding to a different death). First, there were fewer differences obtained in this study between deaths of different types as compared to those in which individuals responded to hypothetical others or to persons with whom they did not have a personal relationship. This suggests that knowing the bereaved family personally may mitigate some of the negative social consequences for the survivors that can be produced by suicidal deaths. Second, while such a mitigation of negative social perception may occur when the bereaved family is known personally, social awkwardness and discomfort when in the presence of the surviving family are still expected.

THE EXPERIENCE OF THE SURVIVING FAMILY

Of the many perspectives on the social situation faced by the family bereaved by a suicide, the point of view of the bereaved themselves may have the greatest intuitive validity and the highest level of relevance to the clinician trying to be of assistance to surviving family members. An additional study addressed the perspective of the bereaved (Range and Calhoun, in press).

Participants were 57 students enrolled in a large southern university. Most were single with a mean age of 21.4. They were recruited during regular class periods in which an "experimenter" visited the class and asked students who wished to volunteer to write their names and phone numbers on a piece of paper if they had experienced the loss of a loved one during the past year. Potential participants were also asked to indicate in general terms the cause of death. The resulting sample consisted of 17 persons whose loved one had died accidentally, 13 who died an anticipated natural death (e.g., long illness), 13 who died naturally but unexpectedly (e.g., cerebral aneurism), and 11 persons whose loved one committed suicide (there were also three persons who lost a loved one in homicides, but we will not discuss those here).

A semistructured interview was again the data collection method of choice. Items covered not only general information about the participant and the deceased, but also a variety of aspects of their experience with bereavement including how their friends treated them after the death, how they wanted people to treat them, if they had been asked to explain or give details about the death, how they presently felt about the death, and other aspects of their experience.

As with any attempts to identify statistical differences between groups on one dimension (cause of death) when groups differ on several dimensions results of our comparisons must be examined with caution. For example, the accidental deaths typically occurred on the highway, the deceased persons in the natural causes groups tended to be older, and there was some difference between groups as to whether the deceased was a friend or relative. Further, we conducted several univariate comparisons, thus increasing the potential problem of unreliability in statistical significance.

Our results did suggest that persons bereaved by suicide described their experience as different in a few ways. Persons who dealt with suicidal or accidental death of close others were much more likely to report having to explain the nature of the death (accident, 94 percent of the group, and suicide 88 percent) than when deaths were either from anticipated (31 percent) or unanticipated natural deaths (33 percent). It was in whether or not they told the precise truth to others about the nature of the death that very clearcut differences were evident for the group who dealt with a suicidal death. Forty-five percent of persons who dealt with a suicide, but none in any of the other groups, said that they had misrepresented the cause of death to some people. For example, one person indicated that the explanation he or she routinely gave was that the individual had died of a serious illness, rather than giving the real cause of death, which was suicide.

While there were no statistically reliable differences between groups on several other dimensions (e.g., what people did that was helpful, how people treated them directly, etc.), the pattern of results and its consistency with data from other sources suggests that the individual bereaved by a suicide of another whom he cares about may feel less direct social support from others and may also experience significant social discomfort when asked to elaborate on the nature of the death.

THE RULES OF BEREAVEMENT: ONE SOURCE OF SOCIAL DISCOMFORT

Others report they are likely to experience social discomfort in the presence of those bereaved by suicide. The responses of the bereaved themselves suggest that others, even if they feel more compassion, experience less success in communicating social support to the surviving family. Among the several possible reasons for the discomfort experienced or expected when interacting with bereaved persons is the social rules that guide (or fail to do so) behavior in that context. The viewpoint of our sample of funeral directors explicitly suggested that lack of clarity about what to say or do in the presence of the surviving family was more likely in suicidal deaths. We undertook two additional studies to investigate the degree to which the social rules are different for suicidal deaths (Calhoun, Selby and Abernathy 1986).

Social rules are the beliefs members of a group have about which behaviors should, should not, or may be performed in a particular situation. Are the rules that guide the behaviors of others in the presence of the surviving family different for suicide when compared to deaths from other causes?

In Study 1 of the rules for interacting with bereaved persons our subjects were undergraduate students, 120 men and 117 women. Participants were given written instructions to imagine that they were observing the interaction of a visitor at a funeral home with the surviving spouse of a middle-aged neighbor who had died in a two-car motor vehicle accident, of leukemia, or by a self-inflicted gunshot wound. Subjects were then asked to rate each of 37 possible rules on two scales, one of appropriateness of the behavior and another on whether persons should or should not do that in this particular context.

Twenty-eight of the 37 potential rules actually met minimal criteria to be considered rules, and these 28 were analyzed in separate analyses of variance. (Again the potential compounding of alpha error suggests caution in interpreting significant differences.) There were reliable differences due to cause of death on 10 of the 28 comparisons, with the greater number of specific differences being between suicide and leukemia. In every instance of reliable differences, ratings of interactions with persons bereaved by suicide were in the more inappropriate and the "should not do" direction. While there were considerably fewer reliable differences between suicidal and accidental deaths than between leukemia and suicide, the direction of the differences was the same—suicidal deaths were rated as presenting more social constraints for those interacting with the family.

In Study II of social rules we attempted to cross-validate the findings in our first study. Participants in Study II were 62 men and 64 women citizens of a medium-sized city in the southeast who ranged in age from slightly under 18 to over 65 years of age. Ten of the rules from the first study were used along with three additional items. Subjects were asked to respond to the same set of materials as in Study I, but they were asked to rate possible behaviors on only one scale, should/should not do. (Study I indicated that results obtained with each of the two scales were almost identical.) Potential subjects were approached in a large shopping mall, and of 170 approached, 126 agreed to participate.

Because one of the rules (laughs about how the person died) was unanimously given the lowest (should not do) rating by all subjects, it was not included in the multivariate analysis of variance (MANOVA). Among the reliable effects identified by the MANOVA was a main effect for cause of death. The pattern of results from Study II was quite consistent with that obtained with the student sample in Study I. Reliable univariate differences were observed on 4 of the 12 rules. Saying that the death was "for the best" was viewed as significantly more appropriate for leukemia than for either accident or suicide. Telling the surviving spouse one "knows the cause of death" was viewed as less appropriate for suicide than for an accidental death. Finally, asking about the cause of death or talking of people who died the same way, were rated as significantly less appropriate for suicidal deaths than for either accident or leukemia.

The pattern of results from these two studies of the social rules governing interactions with the friend or relative of a person who had died indicate that individuals who are in a position to provide social support are in a significantly more socially constrained situation (Price and Bouffard 1974) when death is suicidal. This seems to be particularly true when comparisons are made between death from natural causes and suicide. Suicide seems to present potential comforters with a social situation offering the maximum opportunity for social discomfort. There is a lack of clarity about what they should do, and yet there is greater clarity about what they should not do.

GENERAL PATTERNS IN THESE STUDIES

Our studies suggest, rather consistently, that persons who must face the difficult task of coping with the suicidal death of a loved one are likely to encounter a social environment that may add significant burdens to the coping process. General social perceptions that others, particularly strangers, have of the family will include significant negative elements. Some diffuse attribution of blame for the event seems likely and others often expect the surviving family to be embarrassed and ashamed. The surviving family may also experience social discomfort about the cause of death; survivors may prefer to misrepresent the cause of death to others, at least under some circumstances.

While the general attitudes and social perceptions may not be reliably different for suicidal deaths (compared to deaths from accident or natural causes) when the survivor and the perceiver have a personal relationship, even individuals in the immediate social network may experience more social discomfort when trying to support the surviving family of a suicide. The possibility of an altruistic paradox may exist for those who wish to comfort and stand by the surviving family. On the one hand, others may feel higher levels of sympathy and compassion for the survivors of a suicide in the family, but on the other hand the lack of prescriptive and the predominance of proscriptive social rules may lead others to experience significant levels of social distress and discomfort in the presence of the family. Because of this expected social discomfort, others may either avoid the family or behave in ways that are less likely to be perceived as helpful by the grieving family members. The general social context is less positive, social perceptions of the family tend to be more negative, the survivors themselves may experience greater social discomfort about the cause of death, and, while others may wish to be highly supportive, they may be socially immobilized by the significantly higher levels of social constraint about interacting with the surviving family of a suicide.

SOME DIRECTIONS FOR FUTURE WORK

More research seems always to be needed. In the present instance, however, additional study would seem to have the potential not only of answering some scholarly inquiries, but also of providing information that can be of practical use both to those who face the tragedy of loss through suicide and to those who may attempt to be of assistance to them.

Clearly needed is a direct investigation of the degree to which overt social behavior may be different when deaths are suicidal. While ethical considerations must clearly be met, procedures in which direct observations are made of the interaction of the family with other persons seems a desirable next step. For example, such observations might be unobtrusively and tactfully made at funeral homes, funerals, and burials. Available data suggest a variety of potential ways in which interactions may be different when the cause of death is suicide: the quality of interaction, the amount of interaction, the content and amount of verbal exchanges, behavioral identification of social rules (e.g., what do most people do, are there interactions that lead to negative social reactions), and so forth.

A second area that needs further investigation is the gathering of information directly from those who have experienced a suicide in the family. While there is a significant amount of information on the psychological experiences of those bereaved by suicide (Calhoun, Selby and Selby 1982), studies focused on the social and interpersonal experiences of the bereaved are desirable. While some information is becoming available (Dunn and Morrish-Vidners 1987–88) further work on the social experience of survivors is clearly necessary.

A third direction for future work on the social aftermath of suicide is the utilization of diverse methodologies so that all aspects of the social experience of the bereaved are examined. One general approach could be the use of comprehensive and "experimentally" elegant research methodologies, such as those that have already been employed to study such difficult situations as bereavement following an accidental death of a loved one (Lehman, Wortman and Williams 1987) and the psychological impact of a diagnosis of cancer (Taylor, Lichtman and Wood 1984). The use of sophisticated statistical strategies and the inclusion of many variables can provide unambigious tests of specific hypotheses.

On the other hand, however, it seems desirable also to employ naturalistic methodologies (Calhoun and Tedeschi, in press; Dunn and Morrish-Vidners 1987–88; Lincoln and Guba 1985) to investigate the experience and social worlds of survivors of a suicide in the family within the constraints of their own language and points of view. Such a naturalistic approach lends itself more readily to descriptions of the personal experiences of those who are encountering or who have encountered bereavement. It is unfortunate that the current editorial zeitgeist of most journals in psychology tends to be at best unsympathetic and at worst actively hostile toward research conducted within a less than positivistic frame of reference. Those who have personally faced the dreaded challenge of the suicidal death of a loved one may have much to teach us about the experience. Naturalistic approaches offer us a way of learning from those who have personally faced the tragedy of a loss to suicide.

REFERENCES

Calhoun, L.G., C.B. Abernathy and J.W. Selby. 1986. The rules of bereavement: Are suicidal deaths different? *Journal of Community Psychology* 14:213–18.

Calhoun, L.G., J.W. Selby and C. Abernathy. 1984. Suicidal death: Social reactions to bereaved survivors. *Journal of Psychology* 116:255–61.

Calhoun, L.G., J.W. Selby and M. Faulstich. 1980. Reactions to the parents of the child suicide: A study of social impressions. *Journal of Consulting and Clinical Psychology* 48:435–36.

——1982. The aftermath of childhood suicide: Influences on the perception of the parent. *Journal of Community Psychology* 10:250–54.

Calhoun, L.G., J.W. Selby and J. Steelman. 1988–89. Individual and social elements in acute grief: A collation of funeral directors' impressions of suicidal deaths. *Omega* 19:365–73.

Calhoun, L.G., J.W. Selby and L. E. Selby. 1982. The psychological aftermath of suicide: An analysis of current evidence. *Clinical Psychology Review* 2:409–20.

Calhoun, L.G., J.W. Selby and P. B. Walton. 1985–86. Suicidal death of a spouse: The social perception of the survivor. *Omega* 16:283–88.

Calhoun, L.G. and R.G. Tedeschi. Positive aspects of critical life problems: Recollections of grief. *Omega*.

Dunn, R.G., and D. Morrish-Vidners. 1987–88. The psychological and social experience of suicide survivors. *Omega* 18:175–215.

Kalish, R.H., D.K. Reynolds and N. L. Farberow. 1974. Community attitudes toward suicide. *Community Mental Health Journal* 10:301–308.

Lehman, D.R., C.B. Wortman and A. F. Williams. 1987. Long term effects of losing a spouse or child in a motor vehicle crash. *Journal of Personality and Social Psychology,* 52:218–31.

Lincoln, Y.S. and E.G. Guba. 1985. *Naturalistic inquiry.* Beverly Hills: SAGE Publications.

Price, R.H. and D.L. Bouffard. 1974. Behavioral appropriateness and rituational constraint as dimensions of social behavior. *Journal of Personality and Social Psychology* 30:579–86.

Range, L.M. and L.G. Calhoun. Community responses following different types of death: The perspective of the bereaved. *Omega*.

Taylor, S.E., R.R. Lichtman and J.V. Wood. 1984. Attributions, beliefs about control, and adjustment to breast cancer. *Journal of Personality and Social Psychology* 46:489–502.

16

Suicide, Durkheim, and Sociology

Steve Taylor

In looking at how sociology has been applied to any form of behavior we are immediately confronted by a pivotal problem, one that even sociologists themselves are not agreed upon; what is meant by society and how should it be studied? Sociology is, therefore, a theoretical discipline. Even those engaged in applied research cannot avoid this, for the very act of research entails making certain questionable assumptions about the nature of social reality and how it becomes intelligible to us (Johnson et al. 1986). Clearly, a detailed discussion of these issues is neither possible nor appropriate here but, in discussing the two main approaches in the sociology of suicide, I shall be less concerned with the findings of particular studies than with theoretical assumptions underlying them.

Most works in the sociology of suicide can be fit into one of two traditions. First, there is a "scientific" sociology, grounded in positivism, which seeks to explain suicidal behavior—in all or in part—in terms of various social variables. Second, there is a sociological approach that stresses the distinction between science and "social science," and uses various interpretive methodologies to explore how the meanings of suicidal actions are constructed and applied in given empirical situations. In this chapter I shall outline the major characteristics and limitations of each approach and then, reassessing Durkheim's classic and pioneering study, suggest some of the questions that sociological students of suicide should be asking themselves.

SOCIOLOGICAL EXPLANATION OF SUICIDAL BEHAVIOR

Durkheim was the first (and some would argue the only) sociologist to produce a systematic and comprehensive theory of suicide. As comprehensive summaries of Durkheim's work exist elsewhere (Douglas 1967; Taylor 1982), I shall concentrate here on how Durkheim arrived at his theoretical position on suicide and contrast it with the theories of later students who were, apparently, following the Durkheim tradition.

Durkheim's approach was based on a distinction between the explanation of individual cases of suicide and the explanation of a society's suicide rate. The apparent stability and consistent differences between suicide rates was a "social fact" that could only be explained sociologically. According to Durkheim, differences between suicide rates were a function of the extent to which individuals were constrained by the moral forces of collective social life. Society constrains individuals in two ways. First, it integrates them by binding them to the values and norms of social groups. Secondly, it regulates their potentially limitless desires by defining specific goals and means of attaining them. Durkheim's four types of suicide were developed from this fundamental conception of social and moral order. Egoistic and altruistic suicide arose from the respective under- and over-integration of the individual; while anomic and fatalistic suicide stemmed from under- and over-regulation.

Durkheim used correlations between suicide rates and various rates of external association to demonstrate the existence of his key causal concepts. For example, the statistics showed that Catholics were relatively more "protected" from suicide than Protestants; people who were married with children were less inclined to suicide than the unmarried or childless; and a society's suicide rate declined in times of war or political upheaval. Durkheim was not suggesting that differences in religion, family life, and political activity were in themselves causes of differences in suicide rates. Rather, he was using the relationships between suicide and religious, domestic, and political life to reveal a common underlying cause of suicide—the extent to which individuals were integrated into the social groups around them. While over-integration can also produce (altruistic) suicide, in modern "individualized" western society, the more individuals are integrated into society the more they are protected from suicide.

Similarly, Durkheim used the positive relations between suicide and periods of economic fluctuation to illustrate the existence of anomic suicide. In periods of rapid economic change, increasing numbers of people find themselves in changed situations where the norms and values that had previously regulated their conduct become less relevant to their changed situation. Individuals are then in a situation of moral deregulation, or anomie, and consequently are more vulnerable to suicide.

Although Durkheim's work had a major influence on subsequent sociological work on suicide, it is important to bear in mind the limits of this influence. Later generations of empiricist sociologists, while approving of Durkheim's pioneering work in defining the suicide rate as an object of enquiry and correlating suicide with a range of social variables, were more than sceptical of his attempt to explain them in terms of invisible moral forces of egoism, altruism, anomie, and fatalism. The majority of these later students adopted a positivist view of science. Positivism holds that science, and therefore good social science, proceeds by careful observation and description of factual phenomena and the relations between them. Only then can hypotheses and theories be constructed that are then tested by reference to the relevant established facts. There is, then, a rigid distinction between "observational" and "theoretical" categories. According to positivists, scientific explanation is characterized by a focus on "factual," i.e. observable, phenomena and by the attempt to exclude value and moral judgements.

From this point of view, Durkheim's notion of invisible but real collective moral forces "acting upon" individuals and inclining them toward, or from, suicide was metaphysical and "unscientific," and Durkheim's general ambition for a science of morality an impossibility. Consequently, later sociological research into suicide rates, while bearing a superficial resemblance to Durkheim's work and often claiming to be developing or testing his ideas, has been confined to the relationships between suicide and observable, or concrete, social phenomena. As Cresswell (1972) observed: "Later writers had considerable justification, in my view, in ignoring his philosophical realism."

As a result of this shift in orientation there has been relatively little theoretical development in the sociology of suicide since Durkheim. A great deal of work has restricted itself to fact gathering and testing. This work does not seek to explain the suicide rate as such, but examines particular suicide rates (and other statistical sources) for social, psychological, and environmental factors that appear to be consistently related to suicide. Although there is a little explicit theory, underlying this work is the implicit theory that explanations of suicide will begin to emerge when more "facts" about suicide are established. Other studies attempt to document, and sometimes explain, the suicide rate of particular populations; for example, status groups (Davis and Short 1978; Newman et al., 1973) or cultural groups (Hendin 1964; Iga 1986).

Even sociological theories that have attempted to construct more general theories of differences in suicide rates may be distinguished from Durkheim's approach in the sense that order is sought at the nominal and phenomenal level. Durkheim's notion of an internal moral constraint has been replaced by various notions of external constraint. For example, Halbwachs (1933) argued that most of Durkheim's correlations could more simply be explained in terms of the differences between urban and rural life. Urban life was more transitory and impersonal, and left increasing numbers of individuals isolated and more vulnerable to suicide in times of crisis. Gibbs and Martin (1964) claimed (quite rightly) that Durkheim's notion of social integration was too loosely defined to allow proper empirical testing. They proposed, instead, a concept of observable and measurable status integration. Individuals typically occupy a number of statuses; the less these statuses overlap in a population the more vulnerable, on average, are its members to suicide. Henry and Short (1954) attempted to explain increases in suicide in times of economic change, and also why suicide is relatively more common in high status groups (and homicide more common in low status groups). They proposed a concept of external restraint. The less individuals are restrained by the presence of others around them, especially by people above them, the more likely they are to direct feelings of frustration and aggression inward against themselves and the more vulnerable they are to suicide.

In summary, most sociologists seeking to explain suicide have adopted Durkheim's methodology, but coupled it to a positivistic view that sees suicidal behavior caused by external social factors. In general, sociologists have found suicide positively linked to a range of social and institutional factors often associated with the social development of modern society. For example, suicide has been positively linked to industrialization (Miley and Micklin 1972), urbanization and isolation (Halbwachs 1933; Sainsbury 1955; Cavan 1965), status change (Gibbs and Porterfield 1960; Marshall and Hodge 1981), lack of status integration (Gibbs and Martin 1964; Bagley 1973), lack of external restraint (Henry and Short 1954; Gold 1958; Maris 1969), and decline in religious commitment (Stack 1983; Breault 1986). Of course, just as sociologists have no monopoly over the study of suicide rates, not all sociologists working in this perspective study them. More recently, sociologists have become more interested in a range of nonfatal suicidal actions. For example, Platt (1984) has revealed links between parasuicide and unemployment.

Underpinning sociological work on suicide are polemical as well as theoretical issues. Suicide is typically thought of as an essentially isolated and individual act. Some sociologists feel that the more they can show that even such an apparently individual act as suicide is linked to social factors, the greater will be the apparent relevance of society to individual actions. Other sociologists, however, have been very critical of this work. The following section examines the basis of this critique and the proposed alternative.

SOCIOLOGICAL INTERPRETATION OF SUICIDAL MEANINGS

In the sociology of suicide the main alternative to positivism comes from interpretive studies. Although there are many different schools within interpretive sociology, certain common assumptions can be identified. Interpretive sociology claims there are significant differences between the study of the natural world and the social world. People engage in conscious, intentional activity and, through language, attach meanings to their actions. What is known as society is the product of the meaningful interaction of individuals.

The application of this perspective to suicide involves treating as problematic what is taken for granted in the positivist perspective. Rather than merely examining the distribution of suicidal behavior and factors associated with it, interpretive sociologists argue that the first task is to establish what different cultures mean by suicide, and how suicidal meanings are applied to phenomena in given situations. A major implication of this is that suicide rates are not necessarily unambiguous social facts (in the Durkheimian or positivist sense) but are the end result of social processes of negotiation, judgement, and decision making.

Interpretive work in this area raises something more fundamental than traditional concern with the accuracy of suicide rates, discussed by writers such as Morgan (1979), Barraclough (1987), and Jobes and Josselson (1987). For these students, suicide is likened to a natural phenomenon whose true statistical distribution is, or is not, being reflected by the official figures. However, for the interpretivist the problem is not that "real" suicides are being "missed," but that suicide is itself a product of social definition. The ideas and beliefs that different cultures and subcultures hold about suicide and self-injury determine what is seen, and hence classified, as suicide. From this perspective the statistics may well be accurate, in the sense that they reflect what various bureaucracies define and recognize as suicide, but they are not necessarily valid for the kind of research undertaken by sociologists and others because the meanings associated with suicide vary between cultures and within cultures.

These ideas were first applied to official suicide statistics by Douglas (1967) when he questioned the very idea of a real suicide rate. Atkinson (1978) developed some of Douglas' ideas with research into the work of coroners and their officers. He showed how certain types of death (for example, poisoning or hanging), other significant evidence from the scene of death, and certain evidence from the life history of the deceased (for example, depression, social problems, isolation) act as suicidal cues which, taken together, enable officials to build up a suicidal biography. Atkinson shows that a death will only be recorded as a suicide when the officials are able to find evidence consistent with general cultural assumptions in western societies about why people kill themselves and how they go about it. Atkinson suggests that sociologists and others using official suicide rates who find them consistently correlated to social and psychological factors, such as social isolation and depression, may not be discovering the causes of suicide (or indicators of the causes) but rather, the criteria officials use to label some deaths as suicides.

The implications of this line of critical analysis go well beyond the viability (or otherwise) of official suicide statistics. Whether the researcher uses official data generated by coroners, medical examiners, or hospital records, or collects her own raw data through interviews or surveys, essentially the same distorting processes are at work. By collecting data in terms of concepts—for example suicide or attempted suicide—that necessarily make theoretical assumptions about phenomena; by asking some questions and not others; by seeing evidence as relevant or irrelevant, officials in data production or researchers in data collection cannot avoid imposing values on the data (Pawson 1988). Thus the direct access to the observable world and the separation of facts and values that is assumed in positivist studies is simply not possible in practice. For example, the notion of true rates of suicide, or attempted suicide and suicidal thought (Smith and Crawford 1986) assumes either that suicidal phenomena exist in some way independently of human thought about suicide (which is a logical absurdity), or that there is in given societies a consensus about what constitutes suicide and how it is recognized and categorized, (which is simply empirically false) (Taylor 1982).

Interpretive sociologists, if they attempt to explain suicidal behavior at all, begin by looking at the meanings that suicidal individuals construct for their actions. They argue that, as far as possible, these meanings should be understood in terms of the immediate social contexts from which they emerge. The preference is for data from case records, interviews, and personal documents that enable researchers to try to construct the inside story of suicidal experiences.

Douglas (1967) made the most comprehensive attempt to create an interpretive alternative to the positivist sociological approach to suicide. He argued that the sociologist's first task should be analysis of the situated or concrete meanings of particular suicidal acts. The next task is to look for dimensions or patterns of meaning. Douglas called these the social meanings of suicide and suggested that some of the most common meanings included revenge, escape, repentance, and the "cry for help." The third stage, although Douglas does not really develop this himself, would be to link the social meanings of suicide to wider cultural values and institutional practices. More recently, Baechler (1979), following Douglas' approach, has suggested that suicidal behavior, rather than being simply an end, is a means or strategy by which people seek to achieve particular ends. Explanation of suicide must therefore be built upon the suicidal strategies that people employ in given situations.

As well as providing some valuable descriptions of the phenomenology of suicidal experiences, the interpretive approach to suicide, has raised some significant questions about the apparently "hard" and quantifiable data employed in most studies of suicide. However, the interpretive approach does not really offer a consistent solution to the problems it raises. Douglas, for example, rejects the official suicide statistics, but calls for careful observation and description of real world suicidal phenomena, through case histories, documentary sources, etc. There is a contradiction in this position. The statistics are rejected because they are the end products of negotiations and judgments based on the values of those who compile them. But precisely the same arguments could be applied to the case histories on which Douglas builds his own analysis of the social meanings of suicide. Alternatively, if an accurate description of suicidal phenomena is possible, then it is possible, in principle, to have accurate statistics, which brings Douglas very close to the positivist tradition he is allegedly criticizing. In the final analysis it appears that Douglas and others working in this perspective, commit the fundamental positivist error of assuming that there can be some kind of direct access to the observable world (Hindess 1973; Taylor 1982).

A LIMITATION OF SOCIOLOGICAL APPROACHES

While the positivist and interpretive approaches described in the previous sections have included valuable studies, it must be concluded that any sociological explanation of suicidal behavior remains limited, and there has been little theoretical development since Durkheim. Those working in the field sometimes see this as the result of empirical and technical issues to be solved by more data and better research methods. Without disputing the need for these, the logic of the present discussion is that sociology's limitations in this area also have much to do with the epistemological assumptions of the dominant positivist and interpretive approaches.

While positivism condemns us to seek order from the observation of factual phenomena, the interpretive critique takes us to a position where either no explanation of suicide is possible (Garfunkel 1967; Sacks 1972; Atkinson 1978) or, as in the work of Douglas and Baechler for example, we are returned to the positivist myth of a directly observable world where accurate description is possible. This would be a particularly bleak outlook for the sociology of suicide, or anything else, if these were the only alternatives. However, despite their differences, positivism and interpretivism share things in common that distinguish them from other theoretical stances (Johnson et al. 1986). First, they both accept a positivist view of science, the debate being whether it is, or is not, applicable to the study of society. Second, in their different ways, both accept an empiricist view of knowledge; that is, they both see knowledge arising from the observer's or the subject's experience of the world. Third, both approaches assume that explanation can be induced from data so that data orders theory.

In this context it is useful to contrast these assumptions with those made by Durkheim. Usually Durkheim is placed firmly in the positivist camp. I have demonstrated elsewhere that this is an error (Taylor 1982; 1987). Certainly, Durkheim wanted sociology to be scientific, which distinguishes him from the interpretivists, but he had a very different view of science from the nominalism of the positivists. Durkheim adopted a realist view, which sees science as the attempt to explain observable phenomena through the discovery of underlying and unobservable generative mechanisms and causal processes (Harre 1970; Bhaskar 1978). Detailed discussion of this issue is outside the scope of this chapter. However, it is significant that, because of the apparent failure of positivism to produce "scientific" sociology, there is renewed interest in the realist view of science and social science in sociological theory (Keat and Urry 1975; Sayer 1984; Pawson 1988). This has led to a much more enlightened and

informed interpretation of Durkheim's work. My argument here is that sociological (and other) students of suicide may have much to learn from reassessing
Durkheim's theory of suicide and the key issues arising from it.

I am not advocating wholesale adoption of Durkheim's theory and method.
His work, *Suicide,* has been rightly criticized for, among other things, its dependence on official suicide rates and claim that they "proved" the theory (Douglas
1967), its loose and unoperational definition of key causal concepts (Gibbs and
Martin 1964), and for ignoring the microsocial contexts of suicidal actions and
using a mistaken concept of suicide (Taylor 1982). I am suggesting that sociologists of suicide look again at Durkheim's general social theory and at the specific
questions he raised for a sociology of suicide. I shall call these the Durkheimian
Questions and suggest that the sociology of suicide is much the poorer for our
failure to address them.

THE DURKHEIMIAN QUESTIONS

By definition, a sociological approach to suicide is committed to showing, in
one way or another, that individual suicidal actions are related to the influences
of wider society. This contention raises issues and dilemmas pursued vigorously
by Durkheim, but generally ignored in the later sociology of suicide. I shall
deal here with what I take to be three of the most important questions. First,
what is the relationship between individual suicidal action and society (relational
problem)? Second, how do we understand and explain how society influences
suicide (epistemological problem)? Third, what are the sources of these social
influences on suicide (ontological problem)?

Although Durkheim is popularly caricatured as a crude social determinist
who "dissolved" the individual into the group, little could be further from the
truth. For Durkheim, the individual was both an organism and a social being.
The relationship between the individual and society was, therefore, problematic
and potentially volatile. While society necessarily leaves its mark on people, it
can never "take them over" in the manner assumed in some sociological theory.
In each individual there is a double center of gravity (homo duplex), a social
being and an individual being that has its roots in the organism. As Mestrovic
and Glassner (1983) have explained, integration or psychological well-being
came from harmony or balance between these antagonistic poles of human
existence. Excessive domination of the individual over the social produces egoistic and anomic suicide, while domination of the social over the individual
produces altruistic or fatalistic suicide. Despite the shortcomings of Durkheim's
account (for example, he lacked a concept of the unconscious) there is the
realization that a key problem in sociology is exploring the extent to which the
"social" being superimposes itself on the "natural" being in individual persons. In later studies this issue is missing. Positivism tends to lose the individual,

reducing it to an object driven toward suicide by various factors. While the interpretive approach focuses on individual subjectivity, the relationship of the construction of suicidal meanings to wider social influences remains something of a mystery.

The second issue concerns how we understand the influence of society on suicide. Durkheim argued that as the nature of social reality is not given to us by our experience as members of society, it is not enough merely to describe relationships between suicide and other observable phenomena. All we are doing is observing the various effects or manifestations of society, which cannot lead us to explanations of it. Durkheim's theory of suicide was thus an attempt to reveal the hidden, underlying causes of differences in suicide rates, which he attributed to currents of egoism, anomie, etc. The problem for the sociologist adopting this rationalist approach (Johnson et al. 1986) comes in relating theoretical categories developed independently (i.e., deductively) from the data to empirical phenomena. It was certainly a problem that, despite valiant efforts, Durkheim never resolved satisfactorily in *Suicide* (Taylor 1984). However, it is a problem that most sociologists of suicide have not even begun to confront. They have assumed that explanation can be constructed (i.e., inductively) from the data. This empiricist conception of knowledge and theory construction has been subject to such devastating critiques at the level of social theory that sociologists of suicide—and suicidologists generally—cannot remain deaf to it forever, (Harre 1970; Willer and Willer 1973; Pawson 1988).

Durkheim saw differences in suicide rates as products of different forms of collective consciousness, or collective representations. This brings us to the third Durkheimian dilemma. What are the origins of these causal forces? Durkheim was clear that they were more than reflections of the material world and thus did not, as we have seen, try to explain suicide in terms of social or environmental factors. Alternatively, he did not see them as reducible to thought. Durkheim, unlike the interpretivists, argued that suicidal phenomena had a reality over and above people's experiences of them and the meanings they are given in day-to-day situations.

Durkheim's work confronts the problem of trying to explain a material world where real things happen, but which we can only make sense of through the conceptual categories and belief structures that shape our thought. For Durkheim, the forces of social life were reducible neither to matter nor mind, but had to transcend both. While Durkheim never achieved this synthesis (except in his rhetoric) he was, again, asking the right questions. How are we to achieve an objective analysis of meaningful, moral phenomena? Later studies have resolved this issue by ignoring it. They provide analyses where suicide is either the product of material factors (industrialization, urbanization for example) or the result of different meaning structures and systems of categorization. In other words, sociologists have retreated to one or other of the horns of the philosophical dilemma that Durkheim tried to synthesize. That hardly represents progress on our part.

Suicide is a profound book. Behind Durkheim's pioneering statistical work and his ingenious theory of suicide lie fundamental dilemmas about the nature of society, how it becomes intelligible to us and how its influence might relate to individual suicidal actions. By focussing on Durkheim's methodology at the expense of his theory and the assumptions underlying it, sociologists have largely ignored these issues. The sociology of suicide, in my view, is much the poorer for it.

CONCLUSION

Reviewing the literature on the sociology of suicide is generally disappointing. Of course, there are many excellent works; for example, Halbwachs' study (1930); Cavan's (1965) attempt to link statistical data and individual cases in terms of social disorganization; Douglas' (1967) sophisticated and original analysis of the social meanings of suicide; and Iga's study of Japanese culture and suicide. There is, however, a general pattern of rather meaningless correlations, recycling of old ideas under new labels, uncritical acceptance of data, and technical errors—for example, the notion that tests of significance designed for random populations may be usefully applied to empirical populations. Most disappointing is the general lack of originality and creativity in attempts to explain the social dimensions of suicide. It is a sad comment that the best and only comprehensive sociological theory of suicide dates back to 1897. I have suggested here that the lack of sociological explanation of suicide comes, in part, from the empiricist assumptions underlying both dominant approaches. This view assumes theory emerges from the data. In contrast, in the Durkheimian or rationalist approach, theory orders data.

The implication of this discussion is that sociological students of suicide—and sociologists generally—should give much more attention both to explicit theory construction and to the general relationship between theory and data. I am not suggesting that it is simply a question of choosing the ''right'' theoretical approach, nor that we should engage in more armchair theorizing at the expense of empirical research. I am suggesting that, as research necessarily entails making theoretical assumptions, a greater awareness of the issues involved would give researchers more understanding of key questions to be asked, the nature of their own data, and the directions that future research could and should take. In this context, as I have tried to show, Emile Durkheim left the sociology of suicide a rich legacy. It is a pity that we have not used it more effectively.

REFERENCES

Atkinson, J. 1978. *Discovering suicide.* London: Macmillan.

Baechler, J. 1979. *Suicides.* London: Blackwell.

Bagley, C. 1973. Authoritarianism, status integration and suicide. *Sociology* 6:395–404.

Barraclough, B. 1987. *Suicide: Clinical and epidemiological studies.* London: Croom Helm.

Bhaskar, R. 1978. *A realist theory of science.* Sussex: Harvester.

Breault, K. 1986. Suicide in america: A test of Durkheim's theory of religious and family integration. *American Journal of Sociology* 92(3):628–56.

Cavan, R. 1965. *Suicide.* New York: Russell and Russell.

Davis, R. and J. Short. 1978. Dimensions of black suicide: A theoretical model. *Suicide and Life Threatening Behaviour* 8:161–7.

Douglas, J. 1967. *The social meanings of suicide.* New Jersey: Princeton University Press.

Durkheim, E. 1952. *Suicide: A study in sociology.* London: Routledge and Kegan Paul.

Garfunkel, H. 1967. Practical sociological reasoning. Some features in the work of the Los Angeles suicide prevention centre. In E. Shneidman, ed., *Essays in self destruction.* New York: Science House, Inc.

Gibbs, J. and W. Martin. 1964. *Status integration and suicide.* Corvallis, OR: Oregon University Press.

Gibbs, J. and A. Porterfield. 1960. Occupational prestige and social mobility of suicides in New Zealand. *American Journal of Sociology* 66:147–52.

Gold, M. 1958. Suicide, homicide and the socialisation of aggression. *American Journal of Sociology* 63:651–61.

Halbwachs, M. 1930. *Les causes of suicide.* Paris: Alcan.

Harre, R. 1970. *The principles of scientific thinking.* London: Macmillan.

Hendin, H. 1964. *Suicide and Scandinavia.* New York: Grune and Stratton.

Henry, A.F. and J.F. Short. 1954. *Suicide and Homicide.* New York: Free Press.

Hindess, B. 1973. *The uses of official statistics in sociology.* London: Macmillan.

Johnson, T., C. Dandecker, and C. Ashworth. 1986. *The structure of social theory.* London: Macmillan.

Jobes, D. and A. Josselson. 1987. Improving the validity and reliability of medical–legal certification of suicide. *Suicide and Life Threatening Behaviour.* 17(4):310–25.

Keat, R. and J. Urry. 1975. *Social theory as science.* London: Routledge and Kegan Paul.

Maris, R. 1969. *Social forces in urban suicide.* Illinois: Dorsey Press.

Mestrovic, S. and B. Glassner. 1983. A Durkheimian hypothesis on stress. *Social Science and Medicine* 17:315–27.

Miley, J. and M. Micklin. 1978. Structural change and the Durkheimian legacy: A macrosocial analysis of suicide rates. *American Journal of Sociology* 78(3):657–73.

Morgan, H. 1979. *Death wishes.* London: Wiley.

Newman, J., K. Whittemore and H. Newman. 1973. Women in the labor force and suicide. *Social Problems* 21:220–29.

Pawson, R. 1988. *Measure for measure: A manifesto for empirical sociology.* London: Routledge and Kegan Paul.

Platt, S. 1984. Unemployment and suicidal behavior: A review of the literature. *Social Science and Medicine* 19:93–115.

Sacks, H. 1972. An initial investigation of the usability of conversational data for doing sociology. In D., Sudnow, ed., *Studies in social interaction.* New York: The Free Press.

Sainsbury, P. 1955. *Suicide in London.* London: Chapman and Hall.

Sayer, A. 1984. *Method in social science: A realist approach.* London: Hutchinson.

Smith, K. and S. Crawford. 1986. Suicidal behavior among "normal" high school students. *Suicide and Life Threatening Behavior* 16:313–23.

Stack, S. 1983. The effect of religious commitment on suicide: A cross national analysis. *Journal of Health and Social Behavior* 24:362–75.

Taylor, S. 1982. *Durkheim and the study of suicide.* London: Macmillan.

Taylor, S. 1984. A matter of mind over mythology. *Times Higher Education Supplement* 18.5

Taylor, S. and C. Ashworth. 1987. Durkheim and social realism. In G. Scambler, ed., *Sociological theory and medical sociology.* London: Tavistock.

Willer, D. and J. Willer. 1973. *Systematic empiricism: A critique of a pseudo-science.* Englewood Cliffs NJ: Prentice Hall.